SAHAJANAND ON AGRICULTURAL LABOUR AND THE RURAL POOR

SAHAJANAND ON AGRICULTURAL LABOUR AND THE RURAL POOR

An edited translation of *Khet Mazdoor*
with the original Hindi text and
an Introduction, Notes, and Glossary by

WALTER HAUSER

MANOHAR
2005

First published 1994
First paperback edition 2005

ISBN 81-7304-600-X

Published by
Ajay Kumar Jain for
Manohar Publishers & Distributors
4753/23 Ansari Road, Daryaganj
New Delhi 110 002

Distributed in South Asia by
Foundation Books
4381/4, Ansari Road
Daryaganj, New Delhi 110 002
and its branches at Mumbai, Hyderabad,
Bangalore, Chennai, Kolkata

Printed at
Lordson Publishers Pvt. Ltd.
Delhi 110 007

Contents

Preface to the Paperback Edition ix

Preface to the First Edition xvii

Introduction xxi

PT. I Edited Translation of Khet Mazdoor

Author's Introduction 1

Chapter I
Agricultural Labour: Then and Now 10

Chapter II
Labourer or Kisan? 44

Chapter III
Their Problems 72

Chapter IV
Their Solution 90

Chapter V
How to Achieve These Solutions? 111

PT. II Original Hindi Text of Khet Mazdoor **125**

Glossary 209

Index 235

Dedicated to the memory of Swami Sahajanand
and his commitment to a life of justice and decency
for the agricultural labourers and
the rural poor of India.

Dedicated to the memory of Swami Sahajanand
and his endeavours to a life of justice and decency
for the agricultural labourers and
the rural poor of India

Preface to the Paperback Edition

Swami Sahajanand wrote the *Khet Mazdoor* tract appearing here in 1941. He was in his time, spanning the decades from 1920 to his death in 1950, one of the remarkable thinkers and doers of India's Freedom Movement. Sahajanand was in every sense the reformer and the quintessential spokesman for the poor and the socially marginalized of rural India. He not only spoke for the poor but he gave them a voice in the public arena of freedom. It was a unique double role made possible by the symbiotic engagement Sahajanand had achieved with the peasants and agricultural labourers of the rural countryside. It was ultimately they, the people of rural India, who gave force and political meaning to activists like Sahajanand and, of course, many, many others. What was unique about Sahajanand is that his activism was based not on perception or imagination but on the lived experience of a lifetime in the fields and villages of India, especially in the Gangetic North Indian countryside of eastern U.P. and Bihar, which was his primary base.

It is those experiences among the rural poor and the meanings he drew from them, which Sahajanand represents in the pages of this small tract. The descriptions are as rich and powerful in their graphic definitions as they were in 1941 when Sahajanand was writing in the Hazaribagh Central Jail. And I would suggest that they are as relevant in 2004 to our understanding of life on the social and economic margin as they were in 1941, or as they were in 1994 when this tract was first published. Sahajanand had a deep sensibility about who we are as human beings and what it means to be poor, whether, as in this case, peasant or agricultural labourer. So he asks rhetorically, "but who cares for the poor?" It is this theme that absolutely consumes Sahajanand in the five short chapters of the *Khet Mazdoor* tract. His descriptions and his proposals for change bear a close reading by activists and students of rural India today, just as they did when he was writing, now more than 60 years ago.

If this was a political tract in its time, it remains so today, just as it is a historical document of compelling richness and value. I would suggest that both qualities of the tract are enhanced by the inclusion of the unedited Devanagari text of Sahajanand, together with the edited English translation. And for those who are approaching this essay for the first time, the editorial endnotes are meant to define the political, intellectual, and ideological context within which Sahajanand was writing. The endnotes also provide bibliographic references in order to amplify sources Sahajanand mentions in his text, and to introduce other more recent scholarship, thereby to reinforce Sahajanand's argument. And the glossary is meant to lift from Sahajanand's pages the vivid qualities of the local, vernacular experience of what it means to be poor and to be exploited. The terms in this glossary are not those taken from the definitions given in the law of landlord and tenant, or those conceived in the mind's eye of colonial administrators; they are rather terms and meanings drawn from the lived experience of the rural poor in the fields and villages of Gangetic Bihar, and conveyed by Sahajanand in this remarkable, and remarkably graphic tract.

In writing a fresh preface for this paperback edition of *Khet Mazdoor*, I am reminded of Sahajanand's American contemporary Carl Sandburg, who wrote with the same deep sensitivity of a Sahajanand about the circumstances and strength of the poor, or The People, as he called them. I quote here from Sandburg's 1936 poem *The People, Yes*, as I have often before, to make my point about Sahajanand and Sandburg, who, though oceans apart, were committed spokesmen for The People. Sandburg writes as follows:

> The people will live on. The learning and blundering people will live on.
> They will be tricked and sold and sold again and go back to the nourishing earth for rootholds.
> The people, so peculiar in renewal and comeback.
> You can't laugh off their capacity to take it.
> The mammoth rests between his cyclonic dramas. Yes.
> There are dreams stronger than death. And finally,
> Who shall speak for The People? Who has the answers?
> Where is the sure interpreter? Who knows what to say?

We can say with confidence that Sahajanand spoke for the peasants and agricultural labourers of India and that he understood and interpreted their social and economic circumstances with an uncanny sensibility born of affection and experience. He was, to use Sandburg's apt phrase, the sure interpreter. He knew what to say in 1941 and sixty-four years later at the beginning of the twenty-first century, his words and ideas still have a deep and abiding meaning. Nowhere in all that he wrote and said did he speak with a more compelling voice about the social, economic, and cultural exploitation of man by man than he does in the five chapters of the *Khet Mazdoor* tract. Having mentioned Sandburg and his observations on life in America of the Great Depression era, it is perhaps appropriate to note that though we live in a different time and a vastly different economy, 35 million Americans nevertheless live in poverty in 2004. It is a phenomenon reported in the powerful book by David K. Shipler, a former *New York Times* reporter, *The Working Poor: Invisible in America* (New York: Alfred A. Knopf, 2004). It is as compelling a story of America in 2004 as Sahajanand's *Khet Mazdoor* was of India in the decade of the 1930s.

If there is anything new to be said about Sahajanand's argument since he made it in 1941 or since the 1994 publication of *Sahajanand on Agricultural Labour and the Rural Poor*, it is that in the world of information technology, and the forces of the market notwithstanding, human society in the year 2004 is significantly sustained, as it always has been, by those among us who earn their livelihood by the sweat of their brow. Whether these workers are defined as farmers, peasants, agricultural labourers, factory workers, or those employed in the many service industries of the world's economies, the argument still holds whether in India or America. It is these workers who provide the food and fibre and services that make life what it is in the 2004, very much as they did in 1941. The condition of their lives is what Sandburg, Sahajanand and Shipler were writing about in 1936, 1941 and 2004 and it is those universal meanings that tie these thinkers, authors and activists into the common humanity that makes us who we are in the year 2004. And it is that common humanity that demands of all of us in India, the United States, or wherever on the planet our experiences may situate us, to seek the justice and decency that will make of the human condition what Sahajanand sought throughout his career and specifically for the agricultural labourers and rural poor of India in 1941. That was Sahajanand's message then as it is now.

Which is precisely of course why this small tract is being reissued in 2005. The logic that sustained its argument in 1941 is a logic that makes it relevant to the here and now both as politics and as a vehicle for social science scholarship. The rural economy of India is vastly different now than it was then but the larger human issues of which Sahajanand wrote are no less compelling in their meaning and import in the contemporary present than when the Swami put pen to paper. So writing a preface for a tract that was published ten years before is made far easier by Sahajanand's prescient sensibilities about what it all meant, and what in many respects, it still means today. Another advantage of introducing a new edition of an earlier publication, are the benefits one gains from the insights of prominent reviewers. The *Khet Mazdoor* tract happily attracted many such reviews, or more appropriately in a number of instances, review essays and I am pleased now to turn briefly to four of these reviews and reviewers to sustain my point about the contemporary relevance of Sahajanand's 1941 tract.

The most thoughtful and detailed review of the issues raised by Sahajanand in 1941 appears in the *Bulletin of Concerned Asian Scholars* 28:3-4 (1996) by the hand of Gail Omvedt, a scholar-activist in the true sense of the word. Omvedt, who is also one of the most sensitive observers of the causes and meaning of rural poverty in India and worldwide, writes with a particularly sure hand about Sahajanand's representation: "Working in an era of nationalist upsurge and of struggle for hegemony over the peasant movement among socialists, communists, and left nationalists, Swami Sahajanand became engaged in debates and clashes over the causes of rural poverty, the nature of class divisions among the peasantry, and the role of the peasantry in revolutionary change – issues that remain controversial into the 1990s. He wrote and campaigned in Hindi, without formal education in English. Yet as this collection of his writings from jail demonstrates, the views of this 'organic intellectual' of one of the largest mass movements of the world, are relevant today". Having captured the vernacular, intellectual, and ideological qualities of Sahajanand's politics in these few lines, Omvedt goes on to explain why these issues remain relevant, namely that despite widespread industrialization [which is of course also true in India], "the largest section of exploited toilers in the world still live and work on the land. The rural arm of the third world has the greatest poverty in the world today, with an estimated one billion poor (633 million of them in Asia), according to the International Fund for Agricultural Development."

In terms of the specifics of the poverty debate as argued in *Khet Mazdoor*, Omvedt explains that Sahajanand holds to the 'exploited peasantry' paradigm, which sees the rural poor impoverished due to forces external to agriculture, as opposed to the 'peasants as exploiters' view, "which sees the rural poor as exploited primarily by the rural rich". Following this logic, Sahajanand then argues for "unity in exploitation and in the struggle of agricultural labourers and the peasantry as a whole", especially, it turns out, for the collaborative unity of poor peasants and agricultural labourers. Omvedt goes on to provide a trenchant discussion of the debates and engagements Sahajanand had with the Congress, the Communists, and so too on the issue of class divisions on the land. While Sahajanand leaned heavily on Lenin, he nevertheless identified these class divisions in specifically Indian cultural terms, and essentially denied their antagonistic nature. In the end, for Sahajanand, the core issue in resolving rural poverty was reform, modernization, and enhanced production.

In a brief but important section on caste and gender, Omvedt reveals what must have been a dramatic meeting between Sahajanand and B.R. Ambedkar in Bombay following a massive demonstration of Konkan tenants. This was in 1938 and though there were many points of agreement on fundamental issues between these two major players in the politics of the time, it is precisely on a point of politics that their encounter collapsed. Ambedkar could not and did not accept the fact that Sahajanand still had faith in the Congress leadership, although by 1938 that connection was very fragile indeed. The Bombay meeting was no doubt more than an interesting sidelight in the careers of these two remarkable men.

It is Sahajanand's central concern for melding the social and economic interests of poor peasants and agricultural labourers into a unified peasant movement, which Omvedt examines in detail and that also attracted the widest interest among other reviewers. A case in point is the extended essay by the historian Amit Kumar Gupta in the *Economic and Political Weekly* (11 February 1995). He discusses the issue in the context of the wider Kisan Sabha movement which Sahajanand led, while wondering why landless agricultural labourers were no better organized before 1941 or after, than was the case, especially given Sahajanand's central argument in the *Khet Mazdoor* tract.

It is of course a legitimate question and is specifically addressed by the final two scholars whose review essays I cite as points of departure in seeking a more subtle understanding of Sahajanand's theoretical formulations. The historian Peter Reeves, writing in the Australian journal *South Asia* 19:1 (1996) wonders rhetorically why the *Khet Mazdoor* tract, written in 1941 was not published at the time, or any time before Sahajanand's death in 1950. Reeves observes on the strained ties of the Kisan Sabha with the Congress and the real fear of the Congress in any potential alliance between the Kisan Sabha and rural labour. He also comments on the tensions within the Kisan Sabha as between peasants as tenants on the one hand and landless agricultural labourers, that is *khet mazdoors*, on the other. Reeves then goes on to argue: "Using these pointers it is possible to detect signs in *Khet Mazdoor* that it was intended primarily as a piece of internal organizational polemic and that it was this which made its publication inappropriate, either at the time or later. This suggestion is prompted by the line of 'strategic' discourse embedded in the text of *Khet Mazdoor* which suggests that this draft text was as much an exercise in arguing – within the Kisan Sabha, with the leadership of the Sabha – for a positive attitude to the *mazdoor*, as well as a positive position on the question of the *kisan-mazdoor* alliance, as it was about presenting an analysis of the contemporary rural situation for its own sake." This is a fascinating line of reasoning which becomes especially pointed in view of the observations made by Arun Kamal in his *Biblio:* essay.

Kamal, writing in the May-June 1995 issue of *Biblio*: notes that "just before his death [in June 1950] the Swami had assigned the job of organizing *khet mazdoors* to Khadagdhari Mishra, alias Tumaria Baba at the state Kisan Sabha conference at Rajgir in May, 1950". Kamal, who is the reviewer obviously most familiar with the times, issues, and people involved in these events, then writes that "the foundation conference of the All India Khet Mazdoor Union was held under the presidentship of the same Tumaria Baba". What transpired at that conference and after is obviously beyond the purposes of this introductory preface. But the issues raised by Gupta and Reeves are obviously relevant to what was happening in the 1940s and 1950s and to our understanding of what Sahajanand was thinking and writing in 1941, and Kamal's insights add a further dimension to the political calculus of peasant and *khet mazdoor* in the writing and life of Sahajanand Saraswati. Apparently Sahajanand was indeed moving systematically in the direction of organizing agricultural labourers when death intervened.

I am particularly pleased to conclude these review reflections with the observations of Arun Kamal, who, apart from his familiarity with the politics of the 1940s, comes from the world of Hindi literature and makes what I consider to be particularly sensitive comments on the value of a bilingual publication of the kind we have before us. He writes: "Although *Khet Mazdoor* was written 1941, it still remains fresh and valid. Nowhere does the passage of time diminish its original appeal. It endures because it is rooted in the experiences of life and is written in a racy, vigorous Hindi idiom. One of the few books to appear in a bilingual edition, the volume leads the reader into the complexities of translation." He continues: "It is a pity that our social sciences have not yet made much use of the discursive material available in Indian languages, particularly in Hindi. This book provides scholars unfamiliar with Hindi texts a rare opportunity of reading the original with the help of an attendant translation. This is perhaps the first attempt of its kind that places a Hindi prose-text side by side with its English rendering, allowing the reader a fuller appreciation of the subject."

Kamal, himself a poet and short-story writer, makes a number of fundamental points in this brief assessment, namely that the lived experience of peasants and certainly of most political activists, was a vernacular experience both at the social level and in the arena of politics. That was certainly the case with Sahajanand, 98 per cent of whose politics, printed speeches and published scholarship was conveyed precisely in the vernacular Hindi which appears in the *Khet Mazdoor* tract now appearing in this paperback edition. There is simply no alternative to conveying Sahajanand's ideas in the language in which they were originally expressed, however valuable the translation might be to expanding the readership of those ideas. Kamal then makes a final important point, which has to do with the issue of translating across cultures as well as languages. He writes: "This small tract offers a new perspective on the entire agrarian problem. Though Western concepts and terminology have frequently been used [by Sahajanand], the overall perspective remains essentially Indian. The Swami's knowledge in economics and politics is brought to bear upon his first hand experiences in the field." In other words, the conceptual system, the lived experience, and the language in which they are conveyed are all Indian. Hence, the fundamental importance of representing the experience and the concepts in the vernacular language of their author. However global the planet we live on in 2004, the issues of communicating across the cultures which define our humanity have much to do with expressing our ideas in our respective languages. Arun Kamal suggests rightly that a bilingual text like the one before us is one way of bridging those cultural and intellectual divides. If this small volume has been a positive move in that direction, it will have been well worth the effort.

The 1994 edition of *Khet Mazdoor* included relevant bibliographic references mainly to sustain but also to elaborate the meanings of Sahajanand's 1941 tract. For all the obvious reasons there continues to be an active interest in the subject and accordingly, a growing literature. I will mention here only a half dozen recent titles that bear directly on the issues Sahajanand raised in 1941 and that may serve as points of departure in this very large field of inquiry. I will list these alphabetically, including a number of titles which were mentioned in the 1994 edition as forthcoming:

Pranab K. Bardhan, *Poverty, Agrarian Structure, and Political Economy in India: Selected Essays* (New Delhi: Oxford University Press, 2003).

Amit Kumar Gupta, *The Agrarian Drama: The Leftists and the Rural Poor in India, 1934-1951* (New Delhi: Manohar, 1996).

Walter Hauser, "Swami Sahajanand and the Politics of Social Reform, 1907-1950," *Indian Historical Review* 28:1-2 (July 1991 and January 1992), pp. 59-75, [Issued in April 1996].

Walter Hauser, "Violence, Agrarian Radicalism and Electoral Politics: Reflections on the Indian People's Front," *The Journal of Peasant Studies* 21:1 (October 1993), pp. 85-126.

David Ludden, *An Agrarian History of South Asia* (Cambridge: Cambridge University Press, 1999).

"Rural Labor Relations in India," a Special Issue of *The Journal of Peasant Studies* 26:2/3 (January-April 1999).

Palagummi Sainath, *Everybody Loves a Good Drought: Stories from India's Poorest Districts* (New Delhi: Penguin Books, 1996).

Finally, on a personal note, I must thank Ramchandra Sharma of Ghazipur for his continuing support of my efforts to understand the life and career of Swami Sahajanand. As the son of Sahajanand's brother, Sharma is the Swami's real nephew and continues to issue reprints of Sahajanand's early social and political tracts. While earlier efforts to publish the collected works of the Swami have not been successful, independent and separate efforts of Sharma and the Sitaram Ashram of the Swami, among others, continue to produce reprints of some of the vast corpus of Sahajanand's writing.

I should also note that all of the acknowledgements appearing in the original 1994 edition of *Khet Mazdoor* stand, with my gratitude to all those named for having made it all possible. In addition I must now mention the names of Kailash Chandra Jha, Philip McEldowney, and Florence Hauser, each of whom in their special ways has helped to bring this paperback edition to the light of day. And to that short list I need to add the name of Ramesh Jain of Manohar Publishers, whose idea it was in the first place. Of course, the responsibility for what is presented in this introductory preface, and what it all means, is entirely mine.

Charlottesville, Virginia Walter Hauser
November 2004

Preface to the First Edition

This small volume is comprised of two parts. Part I is the edited translation of Swami Sahajanand Saraswati's political tract *Khet Mazdoor*, and Part II contains the original unedited Hindi text of that manuscript as it was written in 1941. I have explained in the Editor's Introduction my efforts to adhere as closely as possible in the translation to Sahajanand's style and meanings, while at the same time achieving a smooth and easily readable English text. This has meant maintaining many of Sahajanand's metaphorical usages but cutting others and tightening the text in other ways, especially to avoid some of the repetition Sahajanand often used to reinforce his point. It is precisely to make nis as complete a text as possible and to permit comparisons between the edited translation and the original that Sahajanand's Hindi text is included in this volume.

In a further effort to achieve a fully accessible document, brief introductory notes have been provided at the beginning of each of the five short chapters. More extended Editorial Notes follow each chapter. These notes are meant to provide the intellectual and political context within which Sahajanand was discussing the social and political economy of rural India in the 1930s and 40s, especially as it affected agricultural labour and the rural poor. The notes are also the place where Sahajanand's many references are provided as complete a set of bibliographic definitions as possible. Additional relevant titles are also presented in the Editorial Notes.

All transliteration conventions are explained in the initial Editor's Notes and in the introductory comments to the glossary. The glossary is a specific effort to introduce us to the richly descriptive language Sahajanand employed in making his argument. It is a language which clearly emerges from the lived experience of a man who had devoted many years in the social environment that is rural India.

Any author or editor incurs many debts in putting together a manuscript of this or any other kind. My greatest debt is to Swami Sahajanand himself and to the khet mazdoors, the agricultural labourers and the poor peasants with whom he was concerned in this phase of his career, and in this small tract. It is for this obvious reason that this volume is dedicated to Sahajanand's memory and his commitment to achieving a measure of justice and decency for those living on the social and economic margin in the villages of India. I am also indebted to everyone at the Shri Sitaram Ashram for the kindness and cooperation I have been shown from my first visit there in the late 1950s to my most recent visit in early April 1993.

In a small volume of this kind it is impossible to mention all the names of the leaders, activists, and cadres who have come to inform my understanding of Swami Sahajanand and his role in the peasant politics of the 1930s and 40s. They involve literally hundreds of political figures either with or opposed to the Swami and his movements, and from all political parties, including of course the Congress, but most notably the Congress Socialist Party, the Communist Party of India, and the Kisan Sabha itself. In an effort to represent this array of activists I will mention only one name, that of Panchanand Sharma of Indupur Village in the Barahiya Tal of Monghyr District who was one of the last of the local activists from the 1930s and who died in 1991, shortly after our last meeting in Indupur. I learned much from Panchanand as I did from everyone, about what it meant to be a peasant, a khet mazdoor, and an activist. It was a learning process that came from long conversations in his small hutment in Indupur and as we walked many miles to the villages of the Tal, where that movement in the late thirties became so significant a social and political force in the activism of the day.

The remaining names are those of persons who have been directly involved in the preparation of this manuscript and without whose prompt and generous assistance these pages would not have seen print. Some I refer to in the Editorial Notes, with specific reference to assistance provided in areas with which I was unfamiliar. These include Romila Thapar, Madhusudan Mishra, David White, Shashi Kant Jha, and Sumit Guha. Dharma Kumar read the full manuscript and raised important questions, apart from providing me free access to her fine personal library, a very great convenience indeed. Ravinder Kumar and his staff at the Nehru Memorial Museum and Library made the superb facilities of that institution available to Rosemary Hauser and myself with a degree of professionalism and kindness that we deeply appreciate. Similarly, S.K. Goyal and his staff at the Institute for Studies in Industrial Development in New Delhi, especially K.S. Chalapati Rao and the computer wizards at the ISID, provided both invaluable data bases and technical facilities far beyond the understanding of this computer novice. Jadunandan Prasad and Myron Weiner whose names I mention in the Editor's Introduction, K.P. Sharma, Daniel Conable, Ramesh Jain, Pamila Nanda and Makhan Lal Saha all helped make this book possible.

The two people who were most directly involved are my friend of many years K.C. Jha, whose unique role in this effort I explain in the Editor's Introduction, and Rosemary Hauser, who was researcher, proof reader, word processor and much else in the recent months we have been at this effort, and for years before. And finally, Abha Jha whose Madhubani cooking is an art form at least equal to the paintings that come from that fascinating part of North Bihar, provided sustenance in more ways than one throughout this effort.

To each of these friends, so generously prepared to share both their time and their understanding of Indian society and culture, I am deeply grateful. The responsibility for what appears in these pages, and its interpretation is inevitably of course, mine alone.

New Delhi
May 1993

Walter Hauser

Introduction

In mid-April 1940 Swami Sahajanand was arrested and imprisoned at the Hazaribagh Central Jail in Bihar. He had served as chairman of the Reception Committee of the Anti-Compromise Conference at Ramgarh in March, where in association with Subhas Chandra Bose and others he called for immediate direct action against the British. It was a call he repeated shortly at the Fifth Session of the All India Kisan Sabha at Palasa which he served at the time as General Secretary, and again in early April during the agitations of the National Anti-Compromise Week. Almost immediately thereafter he was arrested and incarcerated at Hazaribagh. He was released in March 1942, a year before the expiration of his three year term as a political prisoner.

These were not only years of transition in the political life of the nation but in the career of Sahajanand himself as a social and political activist. They were also two of the most productive years in Sahajanand's career in terms of the prodigious amount of writing he completed in those twenty-three months. The history of his jailing and release is another story, but apart from the numerous pamphlets, political tracts, and Kisan Sabha speeches, most of which were published either in Hindi or English, and all of which were reported on by the intelligence arm of the colonial state, most of Sahajanand's political writing and personal reflections were produced during the time he was in jail. He had an earlier career of social activism in the teens and 1920s, which also resulted in a substantial record of publication, but that too is another story to which I will return momentarily.

With rare exception the vast corpus of Sahajanand's writing, whether social and political advocacy, or personal reflection on his public career, was published almost immediately, especially in the advocacy phase of that career in the teens, twenties, and thirties when he was most active. Others of his writings were published after his release from prison, and yet others after his death in 1950. The *Khet Mazdoor* tract, similar in length to many of the pamphlets he had published as a Kisan Sabha activist before his imprisonment and after, was among those few manuscripts which were not published either during his lifetime or after. Why this manuscript was not published would be an assessment amounting now to no more than conjecture. What we do know is that as a historical text it provides us access to the thought and mind of one of the more remarkable thinkers and doers of his time. Certainly, few would dispute that as a peasant leader he was among the two or three most eminent activists in the nation. The *Khet Mazdoor* text opens a window on to that activism at a crucial stage of Sahajanand's career.

It was my rare good fortune to have seen the original copybook manuscript of *Khet Mazdoor* while a post-graduate student doing dissertation research in eastern U.P., Bihar and West Bengal. I worked intermittently at Sahajanand's Shri Sitaram Ashram at Bihta in Patna District during 1958 and 1959, while conducting research primarily in the Bihar State Archives, but also in the U.P. and West Bengal archives and the National Archives of India. At the same time I was conducting a wide range of interviews with many of the figures active in the politics of the thirties. It was my greater good fortune to have had a camera adequate to the task of micro-filming that manuscript copybook, recalling that this was at a time before sophisticated micro-filming equipment was available. In any event, as a student, buying dozens of 36 exposure rolls of standard black and white film in Patna and making what were in effect photo copies by the light of the sun on the ashram veranda was about the extent of my financial and technical capabilities. It is that filmed copy of *Khet Mazdoor* which was briefly cited in my 1961 University of Chicago dissertation, and it is from that film copy that the edited translation and the original Hindi text presented here have come.

The public and academic image of Sahajanand, insofar as it has emerged in the last decade or two, has largely been that of a caste politician reflecting the early stages of his career, and then in the 1930s, active as the leading figure in the Bihar Provincial Kisan Sabha, and in the later thirties the All India Kisan Sabha. During this latter phase it is presumed that he was essentially representing the interests of well-to-do, or at best middle peasants, to use the common parlance. There is of course enough truth in these images to carry much weight, depending on who is making the argument. But these are perceptions which dramatically undervalue the mind and activism of an exceedingly complex man, whose most common characteristic was one of being intellectually, socially, and politically always on the move in the direction of change, not simply for the sake of change but in the interest of justice and equity wherever injustice and exploitation, whatever its form, might be found. The change he sought was transformational, as is evident from his entire career and certainly from his *Khet Mazdoor* essay.

Sahajanand was born in the Ghazipur District of eastern U.P. in 1889, and took the vows of renunciation in 1907 to become a Dandi Sannyasi of the Dasnami order. The religious life of meditation and study engaged him until 1913 and 1914, when he moved from asceticism to a life of social activism, involving himself initially in representing the status interests of Bhumihar Brahmans. The ritual credentials of Bhumihars as Brahmans were drawn into question by other Brahmans inasmuch as they engaged in cultivation, thought at best to be an un-Brahmanical activity. By the early twenties, Sahajanand's interests shifted to Gandhian politics of the freedom movement, and then in the late twenties and early thirties to what we may refer to as the politics of peasant activism. In these transitions he was not only entering new arenas of activism, but in that very process engaging in ideological and political conflict with his former allies. For example, the leading figures in the Bhumihar Brahman Mahasabha with whom Sahajanand was associated in the teens and twenties, were also among the largest land controllers of Bihar and hence his most vigorous antagonists in his peasant activism phase. And by the same token, his admiration for Gandhi shifted in the middle and late thirties to sharp opposition over the issue of peasant rights within the context of the struggle for political freedom from the British.

It is in fact correctly assumed that Sahajanand in the 1930s was involved in an activism of peasant tenants, many of whom had tenancy rights in whose defence the Kisan Sabha and Sahajanand were engaged. What is however not fully understood is that among those peasants were not only upper caste Rajput, Bhumihar, and Kayastha tenants, but also tenants from middle agricultural castes, Yadavas, Kurmis, and Koeris among others, and indeed from lower middle castes and Untouchable castes as well. In fact, into the late thirties, Sahajanand was systematically moving in the direction of an activism representing the marginal poor whether peasants or landless agricultural labourers or some permutation of the two, regardless of caste.

The poignant question he poses in Chapter I of *Khet Mazdoor*, "But who cares for the poor?" may be taken as a metaphor for the transformed Sahajanand and the transformation in the agrarian society of India he was seeking.[1] It is a question he had posed in much of his other and earlier writing and consumed much of his political thinking and action in the last years of his life. It is this question which is at the core of the *Khet Mazdoor* text. Sahajanand makes the point with a degree of social, economic, and cultural candor rarely encountered in political discourse, whether in 1941 or in 1993. His argument is also made with a degree of forcefulness, and at times prescient foresight to make this a text not only of historical interest in the man and his movement, but as relevant to the political economy of rural India in 1993 as it was in 1941.

The graphic language and the sensitivity to the lives of the rural poor which it conveys, speaks of a man who experienced those lives first hand. His is not simply a political statement, although it is certainly that, but the personal testament of someone who understood what less-than-minimum wages meant, who understood the nature of debt and the bondage it often forced on the poor, and perhaps most profoundly, who understood the maltreatment an agrarian society and culture forced on the poorest of the land because of their social status and economic position as agricultural labourers. While Sahajanand refers to these conditions in painfully vivid terms, he does so with a determination that there is a lively awakening in the consciousness of the rural poor to who they are and what can and must be done to effect change. Whether that be by negotiation and compromise or by militant struggle, change must and will come, to use Sahajanand's turn of phrase.

These are some of the many issues raised in this brief tract, namely those of wages, land hunger, indebtedness, and the maltreatment of those on the social and economic margins of society. The effort in the edited English translation has been to retain as much of the directness and vividness of language and the style in which it was written as possible, while at the same time making a fluid, readable English text which conveys the meanings Sahajanand sought to convey when he was writing in Hindi in 1941. The Editorial Notes following each chapter are meant to provide as effective an intellectual context as is possible when working across two languages and fifty-two years of time. In an effort to achieve as complete a textual document as possible, Sahajanand's original Hindi text of *Khet Mazdoor*, with no editorial intervention on my part, is provided in Part II of this small volume.

This is a document which introduces us to Sahajanand at an advanced stage of his career. The best treatment of that career is his own *Mera Jivan Sangharsh* [My Life Struggle], with useful interpretations in the Introduction of the re-issue of Sahajanand's *Gita-Hriday* [The Heart of the Gita] by Dandi Swami Vimalanand Saraswati, and in the Introduction to the partial re-issue of Sahajanand's *Kranti Aur Samyukta Morcha* Revolution and the United Front] by "Chandra Bhushan". My essay in the *Indian Historical Review*, "Swami Sahajanand and the Politics of Social Reform, 1907-50," examines Sahajanand's career in the context of the ascetic functioning in the social arena, and is concerned primarily with the Swami's early career.[2] It is a career, at whatever point we intersect it, which must be understood in terms of the logic of its time. We cannot legitimately impose our 1993 perceptions, whether social, economic, ecological, ideological, or political on Sahajanand's 1941 view of the world in which he lived and functioned as a peasant activist.

Because I appreciate that there is a wide interest in Sahajanand and the role of peasants in the history of twentieth century India, I will conclude with a brief reference to sources. I preface these remarks with the suggestion that this interest in Sahajanand and the role of peasants in their own and the nation's history was not always as lively as it has been in recent years. I mention in the preface and acknowledgements the name of Professor Myron Weiner who first called my attention to the possibility that there might be Kisan Sabha materials at Sahajanand's ashram in Bihta. When I first reached there in late 1957 for a brief visit, following the Fifteenth Session of the All India Kisan Sabha at Bongaon, in West Bengal the materials were in something of a shambles. I had also been told by Bankim Mukherji in Calcutta, who himself held some AIKS papers, that there were materials in Bihta but he knew little about them. I have mentioned my subsequent work and filming at the Bihta ashram. My efforts in 1958-59 to have that small but rich collection appropriately housed in an Indian library or archive, were regrettably, largely unsuccessful and then only after the creation of the Nehru Memorial Museum and Library. Through the efforts of Dr. K. Suresh Singh, IAS, and my student James R. Hagen, and with the cooperation of the then Deputy Director, V.C. Joshi, we were able in 1974 to have much of the Bihta material moved to the NMML and micro-filmed, xeroxed, or otherwise preserved. The NMML now holds by far the finest collection of Kisan Sabha materials. See my Editor's Note No. 11, Chapter II of this volume for details on the Nehru holdings.

A small part of the Bihta materials came to the Manuscripts Division of the University of Virginia in 1965, when I found some of the collection water-damaged from the Ganga-Son flood of that year and volunteered to have the worst-damaged material preserved professionally at Virginia. I understand there are Sahajanand and Kisan Sabha materials in Calcutta, as there also must be in some party archives and other collections. And some materials presumably remain at Bihta. For example, see the note by Dr. Surendra Gopal and Dr. Hetukar Jha, hoth of Patna University on their use of that material, "An Important Document for the Study of the History of Peasant Movement in the Andhra Pradesh During the Second World War," *Marxist Miscellany* No. 10 (December 1977), pp. 81-87.

Finally, I must make clear that the rough, literal translation of *Khet Mazdoor* from Hindi to English was done in 1959 with, and largely by Dr. Jadunandan Prasad, and that the subsequent refinements with and largely by my friend K.C. Jha, who is effectively co-editor of this volume. At the same timé, I must make completely clear that the responsibility for all translation, editing, and interpretation is entirely mine.

Notes to Introduction

1. See my Editorial Note 15, of Chapter I on this issue.
2. Sahajanand's memoirs, *Mera Jivan Sangharsh* (Bihta, Patna; Shri Sitaram Ashram, 1952), were reissued by the People's Publishing House, New Delhi (1985). Sahajanand's original *Gita-Hriday* was published in Allahabad: Kitab Mahal, 1948. The second edition by Swami Vimalanand at the Shri Swami Sahajanand Smarak Nyas, Buxar (1988). The original *Kranti Aur Samyukta Morcha* was published by Shramjeevi Pustakmala, Patna (1943), and the partial second edtion by the CPI(M-L) – connected Sahajanand Shodh Sansthan, Varanasi (1987). An effective journalistic summary is provided by Arun Sinha in his *Against The Few: Struggles of India's Rural Poor* (London: Zed Books, Ltd., 1991), Esp. pp. 47-62. Useful information may also be found in some of the essays appearing in V.C.P. Chaudhury, ed., *Swami Sahajanand Saraswati: Onkar se Hunkar Tak* [Sahajanand: From Religious Contemplaiton to Militant Activism] (Patna: Rahul Press, 1990). My essay, appears in the *Indian Historical Review*, Vol. 18. Nos. 1-2 (July 1991-January 1992).

Khet Mazdoor
Swami Sahajanand Saraswati

"The agrarian programme must be centered around the Soviets of Agricultural Labourers' Deputies."

(*Lenin, "April Theses"*)

AUTHOR'S INTRODUCTION

[Keeping in mind that Khet Mazdoor is a political tract of its time, Sahajanand's central theme in this brief introduction is that kisans and agricultural labourers are all peasants and must pursue their political agenda of justice and freedom in a single, unified peasant movement. He also asserts the central importance of agricultural labourers in the social and political world of agrarian India, and provides a capsule history of peasant activism in the 1930s. Ed.]

The full range of questions relating to "agricultural labourers" (*khet-mazdooron, kheti ke mazdooron*), by which I mean herdsmen, ploughmen, and others who directly work the land, is central to the more general problem of the exploited and oppressed masses of the people.[1] These questions must therefore be a matter of serious concern when we consider the broader social issue of human exploitation. That the problems of agricultural labourers should be provided with just and proper solutions is thus absolutely essential. Accordingly, those who claim to be supporters of the working masses and are committed to resolving their problems must in the same way devote themselves to identifying the causes of distress among the khet mazdoors. If they really wish to do something to benefit the peasants, and set free the labourers, then the seriousness of their intentions will be measured by the degree to which they commit themselves to honest efforts on behalf of these agricultural labourers.[2] If peasants are closely associated with cultivation and its related problems, agricultural labourers have an even more direct and intimate link with the productive processes of agriculture. They are the root, the very foundation, literally the hands and feet of cultivation. So whenever questions of agriculture and the peasantry are raised, the problems of agricultural labour must inevitably be at the forefront of any such discussion. In these circumstances it is completely dishonest to presume that the problems of agriculture have been resolved until and unless the problems facing agricultural labour have been fully addressed and resolved as well.

But the situation today is rather peculiar.[3] Whereas on the one hand there are bands of enthusiasts deeply committed to the interests of the really poor and determined to remove their sufferings, there are on the other hand the exploiters and the rulers, or to put it another way, the blood suckers of the labourers, who with their henchmen are deeply disturbed by these new developments. Hence they too take up the grievances of the agricultural labourers - not to redress them or in any way to benefit the khet mazdoors, but rather to force those who are exploited and oppressed into conflict with one another. The object of these efforts is to weaken any prospect of a united front [of kisans and khet mazdoors] so that their struggles will wither away in this factional strife. The oppressed and the suffering masses have only one strength and that is the power of their collective action. Consequently if their unity is weakened their whole struggle will collapse.

In fact, the growing strength of the Kisan Sabha and the very intensity of the movement have brought the zamindars and those who surround them to their wits' end. Their hearts and minds have been seized with a sense of fear and panic which cannot be described. The result has been that they have attempted in every way to crush the kisan movement. Whether legally or illegally, they do not miss any opportunity in this effort. The repression of the kisans and the kisan activists which has taken place in recent years in the name of law and order, especially in Bihar but in other provinces as well, is simply amazing. The range and number of cases instituted against the kisans is an entirely new phenomenon in the history of the Kisan Sabha. The indiscriminate assaults and looting, the goondaism and *lathi raj* [literally, the rule of violence, force, and intimidation by use of the *lathi*, or big stick] which have been committed by and on behalf of the zamindars, is also new. At times it has seemed as if there were no government. There was no one to care for the oppressed except the workers of the Kisan Sabha.[4]

While the zamindars were perpetrating these kinds of violence on the Kisan Sabha and its workers, they were at the same time providing the financial means and other direct support to create an organized movement among the agricultural labourers. This was a widespread phenomenon in Bihar, but it was also found in some other rovinces, namely in those places where the kisan movement was strong. Apart from the zamindars, others having a desire for cheap leadership, fame, and money, also indulged in such activities. They are in fact confirmed opportunists. The result has been a mushroom growth of false leaders among the agricultural labourers. Meetings began to be held at many places where big resolutions were passed. Along with some justified demands, impossible demands were also made of the kisans, with the threat that if these demands were not met, ploughing of fields for example, would not be done. Actually at some places agricultural work was brought to a halt.[5]

Along with this one other thing happened. In Bihar when huge kisan demonstrations were organized in Patna and in thousands of other places, in imitation these self-styled leaders also began to organize such demonstrations of agricultural labourers. In Patna one such demonstration was somehow organized. At Motihari when the Bihar Provincial Kisan Conference was being held, another demonstration of agricultural labourers was staged. Some persons who call themselves Gandhi-ites [*Gandhiwadi*] had their hands in this effort. Or to put it another way, all those persons and groups who for one reason or another were opposed to the Kisan Sabha and its movement and could not tolerate it, have had their hands in this kind of agricultural labour movement. Even those who were not directly involved in these efforts, nevertheless continued to provide their moral support. When I saw a pamphlet printed in English which contained a report on the movement, my surprise knew no bounds. As far as I could determine, the so-called report had been printed not in Hindi or in any other Indian language, but only in English. As if the agricultural labourers knew no other language than this; they could manage their work in the fields with English alone!

The report clearly revealed that this movement had nothing to do with the real issues of benefitting agricultural labourers. Rather it had been organized to mislead the world outside the village. It was simply a new means for propaganda and publicity. This was why the report was printed in English, so that the outside world might read it. Not only this, at the time of the Haripura session of the Congress, held in 1938, it was widely reported that a meeting of the All-India Khet Mazdoor Sammelan would be held. It was also announced that Sardar Vallabhbhai Patel would be its president. But for whatever reason such a conference was neither held nor did Sardar Vallabhbhai become its president. But this makes it clear who was behind the agricultural labourers' movement and what their motives might be. There is no one who does not know that Sardar Vallabhbhai is perhaps the greatest enemy of the Kisan Sabha.[6]

It is also a fact that these false movements have been utilised by their leaders to benefit themselves in council and assembly elections.[7] Hence they become most active just before and after the elections. Afterwards there is no trace of these movements or their leaders. I have personally felt that those very leaders who in their daily actions have ruined and dishonoured the agricultural labourers, have caused them starvation and rendered them homeless, they are often the persons who instigate these contrived movements and meetings. In fact, they do nothing for the khet mazdoors. On the contrary, they do just the opposite. And why should they lag behind in showing outward sympathy as a matter of mere formality; they have nothing to lose.

This does not mean that those who are in this movement are cent percent - all of them of this type, and that not even one, two or four join this work honestly. No doubt such people also participate in these efforts on behalf of the agricultural labourers. But they are few in number. They are of the belief that by doing this work they can render real service to the agricultural labourers. But it is here that they blunder. The belief of doing good which drives them does not materialise because the prime movers of these movements do not in their hearts desire that the agricultural labourers should get real relief. They seek only their own ends. Then how will the poor be benefitted? They will be benefitted in the long run because despite the determined efforts of these false leaders to the contrary, this movement will gradually cause the oppressed to awaken. And when they begin to understand the reality of what is happening and who is at the root of their sorrows and sufferings, their dishonour, disgrace, hunger and disease, and when they also understand how to eradicate them, then their goals are certain to be realized. No one can prevent this. Accordingly, from this perspective everyone who wishes to serve the interests of the exploited and oppressed should heartily welcome this movement, however misdirected its purpose. It must help in some small way in awakening the khet mazdoors and in the end nothing can happen without such an awakening.

When this awakening happens these self-styled friends will come to their senses and then repentance over their cruel deeds will be their only option. But it will be too late. By that time the movement of the agricultural labourers cannot be stopped. Even now these false organizers are alive to this danger. That is why they seek to keep control of the movement by any means so that it should not gain momentum.

But their efforts will fail. It is beyond their power or anyone else's to initiate the movement of the tyrannised and the oppressed and then in the end to keep it under their control. It matters little that these movements are begun with great cleverness and ingenuity by their organizers. In fact, such movements often originate in this way. Indeed, it is these very organizers who, feeling apprehensive at the changes they have inadvertently initiated now seek to wipe out the movement. But such movements cannot die until they fully liberate the exploited and the oppressed.[8] It is a different matter if due to particular circumstances the movement finds it necessary to go underground for brief periods of time.

It is also a fact that many peasants active in the Kisan Sabha and its movement seek only to derive personal benefit from the Kisan Sabha without changing their harsh treatment of the agricultural labourers who work in their fields. Perhaps they believe that the Kisan Sabha is an organization of a particular class or group in the same way as the zamindars and their landlord association. But they should know that this Kisan Sabha instead of belonging to any particular class or group, belongs to all those who are exploited and suppressed and who are fully dependent on agriculture for their livelihood. Hence the more they are oppressed and depressed whether by the tyranny of the zamindars or the kisans, or anyone else, the closer they are to the Kisan Sabha and the Kisan Sabha to them. All exploitation is the same and the Kisan Sabha can never tolerate it no matter from which quarter it may come. Hence the Kisan Sabha must direct its energies first and foremost to the agricultural labourers, because finally, they are the worst sufferers.[9]

These are some of the key issues as I have observed them. Of course, there are other important issues which also need to be examined and understood. But in thinking about agriculture, none is more important nor more complex than that of agricultural labourers. Whether to regard them as kisans or labourers is itself a very large question and only after having resolved it can we march forward effectively and with determination. This is the purpose of the following lines and chapters, to seek such solutions by thorough examination and clear analysis of the issues involved.

Swami Sahajanand Saraswati
Central Jail, Hazaribagh
Mahashivaratri
24.2.41

Editor's Notes to the Introduction

1. As indicated in the introduction to the glossary, the effort in presenting Sahajanand's 1941 text in this edited translation is to convey as closely as possible the argument and meanings Sahajanand intended when he was writing. We will accordingly adhere to Sahajanand's definitions and usages much as he himself did in the original. It is his sharp and often graphic characterizations which make this a text of unambiguous clarity as Sahajanand describes the world of agricultural labourers from his unique perspective, and argues their cause.

Sahajanand frequently uses English definitions in parentheses to clarify and reinforce meanings, as in this first sentence of his introduction. In this translation these definitions will be shown in quotations marks with his original Hindi following in parentheses. Occasionally, rather than the English, Sahajanand will use a reverse transliteration, giving the English term in the Devanagri. When he does this for emphasis by placing the term in parentheses, I will do the same. When Sahajanand uses a Devanagri transliteration in the normal flow of the text, which he does rarely, it will be so indicated on first use with quotation marks and identified accordingly in the notes. When I provide a Hindi term or other notations for purposes of editorial clarity, these will appear in brackets. All Hindi terms which are frequently used in the text will be italicized only on first use, and common terms like kisan and khet mazdoor will be used interchangeably with their English equivalents. Additional definitions will be found in the glossary following the Hindi text.

2. As already indicated, the terms kisan and khet mazdoor will be used interchangeably with the English equivalents peasant and agricultural labourer in this translation. While Sahajanand provides clear and explicit definitions throughout and draws specific distinctions between categories of factory labourers and agricultural labourers and different categories of peasants, nevertheless he sometimes uses the term mazdoor to cover both factory and agricultural labourers and the term kisan in a general sense in referring to both peasants and agricultural labourers

as well. He does this as a matter of literary style and as will become clear, with specific political intent.

3. Sahajanand wrote the preface of *Khet Mazdoor* in February 1941, and the bulk of the manuscript during a two week period in July and August of that year at a time when he was in the Hazaribagh Central Jail. While sharply critical of the Raj as imperial Government in broadly general terms and especially in the later chapters over its failure to invest in the infrastructure of agriculture, Sahajanand reserves his primary critical wrath for the zamindars who create the climate of exploitation of which both peasants and khet mazdoor are victim, and for those peasants who themselves exploit the agricultural labourers in their employ.

4. The 1930s were a time of intense and often militant confrontation between the peasants and the zamindars and Sahajanand rightly defines the role of kisan activists in this process and the anxieties an organized movement of peasants caused in the upper reaches of land control. It was an anxiety reinforced not only by the effects of the depression from which zamindars obviously also suffered, but by a series of bad crop years at the beginning of the decade, and most notably by the real and potential threats to their rights in the land which the kisan movement and the legislation it inspired represented. It was a reminder of the anxieties which the revenue settlement procedures earlier in the century had generated and a harbinger of the more dramatic changes which were in the offing in the decades immediately ahead.

5. Sahajanand here raises the central paradox in relations between peasants and agricultural labourers. The question is the degree to which the economic interests of peasants with whatever tenancy rights they may hold on the one hand, and the social and economic interests of agricultural labourers who work in their fields for wages and with no rights in the land on the other, the degree to which those interests are compatible or mutually antagonistic. It is an issue that increasingly came to preoccupy Sahajanand and this short tract clearly reflects his continuing determination to grapple with the social and political ambiguities it posed for him as an intellectual and ideological question and for the khet mazdoors as a matter of life and death. His experiences in the fields of conflict over many years moved him to assume

as his own this life and death cause of the khet mazdoors, but always within the framework of a broader movement of all kisans, certainly including by his definition the poor and middle kisans. Therein lies the ambiguity and it is this tension which is apparent on every page of this document. Sahajanand's experiences and his determination to represent the cause of agricultural labourers were reinforced by his encounter with activists from the political left from the middle thirties onwards, and with Marx and the Russian revolutionary experience while in prison and at the very time he was writing this tract.

6. With a characteristic degree of bluntness, Sahajanand identifies in these two paragraphs his political opponents and those of the Kisan Sabha, namely the "Gandhi-ites" generally and Vallabhbhai Patel, specifically. It is a political disposition that went back to the early 1930s, when following a decade of deep commitment to Gandhi and his leadership of the freedom movement, Sahajanand began to question not only the Gandhian idea of trusteeship as it related to the zamindars, but specifically the association of Gandhi and some of his supporters in Bihar with zamindar interests, most specifically at the time of the 1934 earthquake with the Maharaja of Darbhanga, the largest landholder in Bihar and one of the largest in India. Sahajanand's differences with Gandhi and the Congress, and Congressmen generally, took the form of sharp conflict with Rajendra Prasad in Bihar and with Prasad, Patel and others in the dominant Gandhian wing of the Congress at the all-India level. In these India-wide confrontations, Sahajanand was allied with and supported by Indulal Yagnik from Gujarat and N.G. Ranga from Andhra. After its establishment in 1936 these were the three major figures in the All India Kisan Sabha.

7. The elections which brought into office responsible ministries and legislative assemblies in the provinces were held early in 1937, following on the Government of India Act of 1935. The election campaign thus spilled over from late 1936 into 1937. The Congress formed governments in eight of the eleven provinces of British India, including Bihar.

8. It is this process of a self-consciously awakened peasantry, defined in this text to include the khet mazdoors, and actively participating in the movement for the inevitable achievement of its just rights and freedom, that characterizes the central thrust of this tract and Sahajanand's career.

9. Here and in the concluding paragraph of his preface, Sahajanand issues a warning to peasants who think of the Kisan Sabha as a class organization of the well-to-do. That perception and the maltreatment of agricultural labourers by these or any other peasants is not acceptable in the unified movement of peasants and agricultural labourers Sahajanand envisions as the ultimate goal.

CHAPTER I

Agricultural Labour: Then and Now

[Whereas in his introduction Sahajanand laid out the broad themes of the argument he makes in this tract, in this first chapter he traces the history of agriculture in sweeping social and cultural terms as a basis for identifying the existence of agricultural labour in India. A central element in the emergence of a cultivating category of khet mazdoors are the concepts swayamkrita *and* aswayamkrita, *i.e., to do one's own cultivation, by one's own hands, or to have it done by others. Sahajanand then goes on to trace the growth of agricultural labour in the 19th and 20th centuries following closely the nationalist and Marxist logic on this issue especially as formulated by Rajni Palme Dutt. He concludes with a theme to which he returns again and again, namely that the distress of the khet mazdoor is not defined by caste, community or religion, but rather that it affects everyone. It is not limited only to Untouchables and lower castes. Ed.]*

Today in all parts of the world, we are witness to movements for justice and change among the downtrodden and exploited masses of the people. Not only are they raising fundamental issues of their condition but resolving them with firm determination, and doing so in their own way. Then how strange that the problems of labourers in agriculture which have caused them to be ground down and literally consumed to death should not be raised in the same way. When thousands, indeed lakhs of activists, young and old, men and women have joined battle to solve once and for all the problems of bread and clothes for the kisans and the factory workers, then how can the inter-linked question of those engaged in agricultural labour remain unresolved?[1] We must respond to this riddle by examining it in its true colours and in the full light of day. And if we do not take up this work or ignore it, we do so at our peril. If we fail in our efforts, the false leaders, the enemies of the khet mazdoors, finally they will bring the issue to the fore. In these circumstances these questions will pursue us relentlessly. We cannot be rid of them; time itself will force change upon us.

And why should this not be so? Not only have those who work in the fields been tortured and repressed, but with factory workers and kisans they occupy an equally prominent place in contemporary society. These reasons alone would be sufficient to force their problems upon us. But more importantly, their numbers are vast, indeed far greater than those of factory workers themselves. Furthermore, and of particular significance, the number of agricultural labourers is in a state of constant growth, like the entrails of the devil. Peasants with small holdings are being forced off the land by so-called zamindars whose numbers are increasing dramatically and in this process the number of agricultural labourers, that is, landless peasants is also increasing dramatically. It is clear that lands are fast passing out of the hands of the peasants. These lands either pass into the hands of zamindars who mercilessly rack-rent the peasants and live extravagantly in far off cities, or these lands revert to usurers and moneylenders who settle them with those tenants who pay the highest rent. And most often these rental agreements are temporary or short-lived, so that the land may be resumed and settled again with others who can pay still higher rents or benefit the moneylender in other ways. A further consequence is that the peasants remain in a constant state of fear before these landed moneylenders, shopkeepers, and zamindars. They dare not utter a word against them. It is this process which will be considered more closely in what follows.

As a matter of fact when human beings first turned to settled agriculture and as the area under cultivation expanded, a very high proportion of the population was engaged in cultivation. But there was a vast difference between the conditions obtaining then and those obtaining now. In ancient days with improvements in agriculture and its dramatic expansion the proportionate number of workers in the fields began to decline and people gradually took to other occupations. Now, however, that pattern has been reversed and the numbers of those engaged in agriculture has again begun to grow. As people are being forced from the land and from non-agricultural occupations as well, the tide is clearly flowing in the wrong direction. The full consequences of this development cannot be anticipated. This gradual dispossession from any means of livelihood of those who give their sweat and blood to feed not only themselves but literally everyone, is exceedingly dangerous. It is a grave situation which we must consider with our hearts and minds and do so firmly and with courage, otherwise it is sure to sweep us away. Simple and uninformed solutions have no place in these circumstances. Unless one is in full command of the facts and complexities of this history, solutions will not only escape us but potentially worsen the situation. What is needed is a thorough and candid inquiry. So let us begin.

Everyone knows that when populations began to increase on the earth questions of human livelihood became more and more complex. Consequently a determined search began for other means of survival than feeding on wild creatures, grasses and fruits. In this process the idea of settled agriculture developed, that by sowing barley and wheat seeds production could be increased ten and twenty fold. This concept ushered in a great revolution in the means of human subsistence. There were wide stretches of fertile land available for plowing and sowing. All that was required was to cut and clear the forest. As a result cultivation came to be undertaken on a vast scale. Almost everyone was engaged in this work. There were neither restrictions on the availability of land nor zamindars or government to exact rents or cesses as is the case today. It was a time when virtually everyone was engaged in agriculture and sustained themselves chiefly upon it. Words like *vishah*, *vishampati*, and similar terms found in the Vedas and the Mahabharata are suggestive of this history.

No doubt later the words *vish* or *Vaishya* came to signify a particular caste or social category to whom the task of cultivation was specifically entrusted while the remainder of the population took to other occupations and professions. This occurred with the development of *varna* and *ashrama* divisions in society defining specific occupations or castes and stages of life. The sum and substance is that when different groups or sections of society were so constituted and entrusted with separate responsibilities, a varna called Vaishya was then specifically employed in agricultural operations. Now this is no longer the case. No one can say who is a Vaishya or not because everyone carries on cultivation. Formerly it was not that other varnas did not carry on cultivation. Even Brahmans carried on some cultivation, a fact clearly shown in the Vedas. Manu, in the beginning of the fourth chapter of his *smriti* has written that agriculture is considered to be a nectar or ambrosia (*amritam karsanam matam*) by which indeed, one also can live (*tenaivapi jivyate*), suggesting that even Brahmans did cultivation.[2] Other authors of the smritis have also made the same point. Even then, however, it has been accepted that agriculture was the chief occupation of the Vaishyas and that it was their responsibility to produce food grains for everyone.

But in the beginning the terms Vaishya or vish signified the *praja*, or subjects, i.e.,the people generally. In fact the meaning of the word praja is the same as that of the term *janata*, namely, the people, masses or multitude [*jansamooh*]. The meaning of the term *vishampati* is *prajapati* or *raja*, i.e., king. It seems that because at that time sowing was done by many persons together, the term vish came into common usage for the first time. People did this work because of its newness but primarily because it avoided the need to go to remote places in search of food, which could now be produced near the homes of the cultivators themselves. It was thus natural for everyone to take to cultivation. In this way the terms vish or Vaishya came to refer to all the people, the masses, the subjects or the public generally.

This was the first condition of those working in the fields, or to put it another way, of field labourers, i.e., agricultural labourers or khet mazdoors. Of course in these circumstances today's questions relating to agricultural labourers could not have come up. The Mahabharata reveals that "there were no social distinctions or divisions in the creation of the universe by Brahma. Everyone was equal and the subsequent creation of different varnas was the result of people doing different work, i.e., undertaking different occupations." (*Na vishesosti varnanam sarvam brahmam idam jagat. Brahmana purvam sristamhi karmabhir varnnatam gatam*). (Moksha-dharma 188/90).[3] This suggests that in the beginning everyone was engaged in the same kind of work.

But over time and with the increase in population, new occupations were required. For example, there were both internal conflicts as well as attacks by enemies from the outside which required armed reaction. Beyond this and with the growth of knowledge, special social divisions came into being to accommodate these new occupational changes.[4] Even in warfare neither agricultural operations nor intellectual activity could cease. Hence, while the duty of fighting was entrusted to a special group or varna, so too intellectual activity and agriculture were entrusted to the Brahmans and Vaishya class respectively. In this way the words vish or Vaishya instead of being used in the more general sense of subjects or the public at large, came instead to refer to a particular group, varna, or division of human society.

Of course, a fourth group was also formed which came to be called a "reserve" group (*sanrakshit dal*).[5] These were the *Shudras*. Their primary responsibility was physical work, which is why they came to assist the other three varnas whenever and wherever necessary and in all possible ways. But it was not that they did not engage in any work of the mind. Different kinds of craftsmen and *mistries*, or those with specialized mechanical skills were generally found among the Shudras. In the smritis also craftsmen have been referred to as Shudras. So while the Shudras carried on the work of a "reserve force" (*rakshit sena*) to service the other varnas, on the other hand they also performed all those tasks connected with the arts, crafts, and skilled labour required by the society, so much so that even the task of cooking was regarded as belonging to the Shudras. This is clearly stated. Hence even Brahmans working as cooks have been regarded as Shudras as is evident from the following extract from the Sanskrit *sloka*: . . . *pachakashchaiva sadete shudravad dvijah* [literally, . . . as well as cooking. [When a] twice-born man [does any of] these six [occupations, he is] like a Shudra.] So how could Shudras have become skilled craftsmen without the mental ability to do so? And if this had not been taken to be the meaning of the word Shudra, then why should the Rishi Raikva have addressed the *Kshatriya* King Janasruti repeatedly as a Shudra as is seen in the Chandogya Upanishad (4.2.3-5): *are! tva sudram ajaharemah sudram*? [Literally, You, Shudra, we have brought the Shudra!][6] Whatever meaning has been given to the work of this sage by the linguists, it is clear that the word Shudra did not have so restricted a meaning then as is unfortunately the case today.

The case was similar for the Vaishyas before the varna system had been formulated. No doubt after the formation of the varna system, the term Vaishya, instead of being used in the sense of subject [*praja*] or the people at large [*janata*], came to refer to a specific section of society. It was also at this time that the Shudra class was formed. One other thing came to pass when the right to cultivate, instead of being held in general, came to be restricted. It was at this time that the practice of getting the physical work of cultivation done by others had its origin. It has already been explained that when the ordinary right to cultivate came to be restricted to the Vaishyas, other varnas were nevertheless not excluded from engaging in agriculture. Especially Brahmans had this right to produce grain for their own use. References to the *Manusmriti* on this issue have already been cited and other smritis have emphasized this point as well. I have examined the issue in detail in my book *Brahmarshi Vansh Vistar* [The Expansion of the Brahman Family].[7]

Even though permitted to cultivate, it was the practice with the Brahmans that as far as possible instead of cultivating with their own hands they should get this work done by others. However, it was laid down that when they were unable to get the work done or when labourers were not available or could not be satisfied for whatever reasons including agreement on wages, then Brahmans could personally carry on cultivation with their own hands. These two types of cultivation were referred to as *aswayamkrita* and *swayamkrita*, respectively. The latter term means that cultivation is done by one's self, i.e., with one's own hands and the former means that it gets done by others. These prescriptions have also been referred to in many other ancient texts.

Whatever might have been its meaning at the very beginning, the practice of utilizing agricultural labourers in the ways in which we do today dates from the times I have been discussing here. In countries outside India references to "serfs" or slaves working in the fields in ancient days are of a similar nature. In practice there might have been substantial differences between these systems and the Indian system, but in theory, both systems were similar. After all there were also differences between "serfs" working in the fields and slaves, who had existed before and continued even during the period of serfdom in scattered places. But these slaves were disappearing and their place was being taken by serfs or agricultural labourers. Whereas the very body and soul of the slaves belonged to their masters, the relationship with the "serf" or agricultural labourers was a different one. For example, in some cases they worked not only in the fields of the *malik*, or owner, but in the fields given them by their owners as well. The master could not get anything and everything done whenever he liked. Sometimes it happened that instead of working in the fields of their master they used to give him a fixed portion of their produce in the form of tribute. Consequently, as compared to the slaves they had a degree of partial freedom at least in outward form. In the same way it was natural that differences should exist among these agricultural labourers and their conditions from country to country. Karl Marx, the messiah of the exploited and the oppressed has provided a detailed description of this phenomenon in his book *Wage-Labour and Capital*:

> The slave did not sell his labour-power to the slave-owner, any more than the ox sells his labouring force to the farmer. The slave, together with his labour-power, was sold to his owner once and for all. He is a commodity that can pass from the hand of one owner to that of another. He himself is a commodity, but his labour-power is not his commodity. The serf sells only a portion of his labour-power. It is not he who receives wages from the owner of the land; it is rather the owner of the land who receives a tribute from him. The serf belongs to the soil, and to the lord of the soil he brings its fruit.[8]

In this description the partial freedom of the agricultural labourers is clearly shown. Whereas the full responsibility for the sustenance of the slave lay with his master, agricultural labourers on the contrary in effect fed their masters. The master or malik had no other responsibilities for the well-being of his labourers.

Thus we find that this was the second stage of the condition of those working in the fields, i.e., the agricultural labourers. Whereas on the one hand there was a relative decline in the numbers of those living by working in the fields, and some members of the society took to other occupations, on the other hand there came into being those persons who worked in the fields of others for which they either got small plots to cultivate or subsistence wages.[9] Though there is no term in modern usage to identify those who work on their own land as labourers, still in comparison to the conditions obtaining at earlier stages of agriculural development, we call them agricultural labourers or workers. And this is entirely appropriate. Even before, they were truly workers or "labourers" (*shramjeevi*), some of them clearly in the sense in which the term is used today.

<21.7.41> After a very long time these workers of the fields came to the third stage in their development.[10] Before this the numbers of those depending on agriculture was gradually decreasing. Now the circumstances were such that this trend was reversed dangerously in the direction of a steady growth. This was in a very real sense

a major turning point in Indian agriculture and in the history of agricultural labour. The brief description given above makes clear that in the first two stages the agricultural population was showing a decline. This decline may be viewed either in "absolute" terms or in terms of a "comparative" decline. The decrease in the number of those working in the fields was of the second type. The population was gradually increasing. Hence the number of those who during thousands of years gave up agriculture and took to other occupations was certainly small relative to the population as a whole. But nevertheless, if these circumstances prevailed over millennia, then the actual numbers of cultivators in the meantime would have grown dramatically. After all in dividing a small or large population into similar parts, the part having the greater number must be larger but when compared to the whole it will be comparatively, or relatively small. But it is true that not everyone crowded into agriculture. Consequently at that time there was no difficulty in maintaining a livelihood on the land.

But with the third stage of agricultural development, circumstances changed. On the one hand all cultivable lands were gradually brought under cultivation. As the population of those groups, varnas, and communities engaged in agriculture grew, they began to experience a shortage of cultivable land. Only those potentially cultivable lands remained fallow which could not be cultivated without the application of modern technology or huge capital investments. When all the land was thus occupied, no "virgin soil" remained.[11] The only way to acquire new land was to seize it from others, which is in fact what happened. There was a mad rush for amassing private property. The result was that whereas some came to have more lands than they required, many had either no lands or very little land. As a result, out of sheer helplessness they either became ploughmen, labourers, or took lands from these large holders on the most demanding conditions and highest rent. In this way there was a substantial increase in the number of agricultural labourers in the modern sense of the term and this number has continued to grow.[12]

A most important concomitant development was that whereas previously new industries and occupations were opening, now that process stopped and even those in existence from before were closing down. Anyone who has read the history of the rise and growth of modern industry over the last four or five hundred years can easily understand this fact. In England and other countries handloom and powerloom workers and those engaged in other occupations had to quit this work forcibly and take either to cultivation or join roving bands of thieves, dacoits and beggars. Everyone knows how in India the thumbs of the weavers were cut off and their occupations and those of others ruined.[13] Even today oil pressers, flour grinders, sugar refiners and thousands of others have been reduced to penury in the face of machines and factory competition. This new type of dislocation has been steadily increasing and it is a process assuming ever new forms. It has become the burning issue of the day. At first machine owners take possession of industries run by human hands. Then big industrialists drive out small factory owners. In the end a small group of big businessmen open thousands of large factories and render everyone else unemployed. In this way "monopoly" has achieved or is achieving economic dominance.[14]

We must consider what those who have been deprived of their traditional occupations and professions will do. They cannot satisfy themselves and their children by eating stones nor can they subsist on thin air. After all how many will find employment? These new factories cannot employ everyone. It is also a fact that those who are uneducated or otherwise not well- qualified cannot get employment. And the poor have no means to gain an education. But who cares for them?[15] The conditions today are such that either highly trained specialists or women and children are most in demand. Machines have rendered it possible that work which could previously not be done without having men of sound physique can now be carried on by boys, girls and mostly women and children who are very poorly paid. The result is that men find less employment. But the earnings of women and children alone are simply not sufficient to maintain a family's subsistence. In such conditions where are these men to go or what are they to do? <22.7.41> This is a question which is all-consuming in the present circumstances. There is no apparent way out. Consequently out of sheer helplessness the unemployed take to agriculture. But fields for ploughing are also not available. They too have become very dear and this dearness is increasing day by day. But this much is certain, if one is willing or able to pay whatever amount is demanded, land is available . But the avenue to other occupations or employment seems locked forever. Hence the dilemma, not unlike that of the crow sitting on the mast of a ship in the midst of a vast and endless ocean. The crow has no option but to remain sitting on that mast, helplessly and against all odds, though he is almost certain to die. And where to go should he choose to leave that mast? Similar is the situation for those who take to agriculture out of sheer desperation, however costly and burdensome their choice might be.

In these circumstances, these so-called gentlemen, the large landholders, exact the highest cost, the highest rent or revenue possible. I know such cruel and blood-sucking zamindars who grab three-fourths of the produce of the land and leave one-fourth to the peasant. The tragedy is that the peasant must defray all expenses incurred in cultivation out of that one-fourth share of produce, which is simply impossible. Everyone agrees that under normal circumstances the cost of production consumes at minimum one-third of the total produce, yet the peasant receives only a one-fourth share. Under such conditions what can the peasants save for their families? In fact, they do not get even the equivalent of their wages. And consequently they fall daily into the clutches of money-lenders and usurers; the peasant in effect becomes the "slave" of the money-lender. As a matter of fact they are peasants in name only. They toil in the fields like oxen, even more so. In these conditions and inasmuch as they do not get even their full wages they are in fact, worse off than agricultural labourers. And it is not that they are few in number. Such peasants number in crores and their numbers are increasing out of all proportion to the rural population as a whole, as will be demonstrated in what follows.

One other thing happens. When the family members of the cultivating peasants grow in number and at the same time the joint-family breaks up, this has a serious effect on the process of cultivation itself. Fields which were formerly large now become very small because of continued fragmentation. They become narrow strip fields, much like water courses. While the family grows in size its fields become smaller and smaller. No one knows to what limits this fragmentation will go.[16] As a result, the holdings of at least 80 percent of the peasants are so small that they cannot provide sustenance for their families sufficient to fill even one-half or one-fourth of their bellies, and that too only with coarse grain. These kinds of "uneconomic holdings" rack the peasants with utter ruin, much as a disease. And still no cure is being sought to ward off or prevent this disease. These 80 percent or in some places even 90 percent of peasants are often so poor and wretched that one feels ashamed in calling them labourers, inasmuch as labourers get more or less a fixed wage. But here not even that is true.

This is such an evident fact that absolutely no one doubts it. Nevertheless, the blood-sucking butchers who control the land ask why then do the peasants take to agriculture when they cannot get even their wages? Why do they not give it up? No man undertakes any work without the prospect of earning some profit. Then are these peasants mad to do so? Through such questions these gentlemen wish to imply that the peasant families working on these tiny holdings are in fact able to earn an adequate livelihood. They do not speak with a clear heart. This is rather a brazen attempt to show that the impossible is possible. These people think themselves to be clever. But like the clever scribe who lost his children in the depths of the river, they too are guilty of grave miscalculations in their cleverness. When the very bones of the peasants will turn to dust, then perhaps they may come to their senses. Do they not know that neither earth nor sand can satisfy the hunger of man or beast and sustain life? In some provinces visited by terrible famine, corpses of men and animals in the hundreds, even thousands have been found, who, driven by hunger, had literally eaten sand and soil in their agony. I have already referred to the story of the crow on the mast of the ship. With no other recourse, the peasant in similar circumstances, the poor peasant, turns to a bankrupt agriculture thinking only to keep the wolf away from his door, with little concern for future consequences. He is like the "drowning man grasping at a straw." Peasants in these desperate circumstances do not make profit or loss calculations, nor are they capable of doing so. They feel that at least they have the means to labour, and think of the wages their labour may bring. But they do not know that a conspiracy has already been hatched to rob them of their wages. They are dealing with persons who would seek benefit even by selling the shrouds of the dead. It is an issue to which we will return.

How the land of the peasants is being grabbed and how the number of agricultural labourers, including these so-called peasants, is increasing like the entrails of the devil, this process needs further clarification. Only then will the naked truth be fully revealed. If one goes through the census reports and other documents of government in which these issues are examined in elaborate detail, and compares them with other non- official figures, the rapidity with which the numbers of agricultural labourers is increasing will become readily apparent. The same is true for the number of zamindars engaged only in rent collection. The *Census of 1911* estimates the number of zamindars or landlords luxuriating on rent extraction alone to be 28 lakhs [2,800,000] for the country as a whole. By 1921 their number had risen to 37 lakhs

[3,700,000] and in 1931 it had reached 41 lakhs [4,100,000]. That is to say in twenty years there had been an increase in the number of rent-receiving zamindars of [approximately] 50 percent, which is an entirely remarkable figure over such a short period of time. Over the same period the number of peasants cultivating their own lands dropped from seven crores and 46 lakhs [74,600,000] in 1921 to six crores and 55 lakhs [65,500,000] in 1931. That is to say in one decade 91 lakhs [9,100,000] of peasants were deprived of their lands. This means that more than nine lakhs [910,000] of peasants were deprived of their lands every year.[17] These figures clearly show that if this state of affairs were to continue then in about 70 years' time all the peasants would become landless. And 14-15 years have already passed.[18]

Now we can see that as the number of parasitic rack-renting zamindars increases and the peasants are thereby deprived of their lands, similarly the number of agricultural labourers, that is those peasants with no lands of their own, will also increase. Hence they will either take lands from those who have land in the form of *shikmi*, *batai*, or some other tenancy arrangement, paying a high rent and then carrying on cultivation, or they will work on the fields of others at a very low wage, earning enough only to fill their bellies by a half or a quarter while living in rags. Under these conditions they will remain agricultural labourers and nothing more. This issue will be dealt with more exhaustively in the next chapter. Here we need to know only that even according to government figures the number of agricultural labourers is increasing so rapidly that it has today reached beyond all limits. This is by any consideration a shocking fact. R. Palme Dutt in his book *India Today*, published in 1940, has written about this issue at page 218 in the following way:[19]

> In 1842 Sir Thomas Munro, as census commissioner, reported that there were no landless peasants in India (undoubtedly an incorrect picture, but indicating that the numbers were not considered to require statistical measurement). In 1882 the census estimated 7 1/2 millions "landless [day] labourers" in agriculture. The 1921 census returned a total of 21.7 millions, or one-fifth of those engaged in agriculture. The 1931 census returned a total of 33.5 millions, or one-third of those engaged in agriculture. Since then it has been estimated (as in the debates in the Bengal legislative assembly on the amendment

> to the tenancy act in 1938; the Madras figures given above also indicate the same) that the real present proportion is nearer one-half.[20]

At different places this number has been estimated at five crores [50,000,000], which means that the number of peasant families engaged in agriculture is roughly 10 crores [100,000,000]. These figures indicate only the number of families or at most those working members and not their whole numerical strength. For example, the figure does not include the old, the infants, and other dependants of the family. Only the earning members have been included, otherwise, inasmuch as peasants constitute 80 percent of the population, the total number of persons associated with agriculture would be something between 28 and 32 crores [280,000,000 to 320,000,000].[21] By this calculation, the number of agricultural labourers together with their children must be somewhere between 10 and 14 to 15 crores [100,000,000 to 150,000,000]. The number can on no account be less than 10 crores [100,000,000] inasmuch as their children and others must also earn. Only the infants and the really old are excluded in these figures.

In the Madras province referred to by Palme Dutt, the number of rent receivers in 1901 was only 20 per thousand, a number which rose to 50 per thousand, i.e., by a factor of two and a half in thirty years. Over the same time period the number of landless agricultural labourers increased from 345 to 429 per thousand, that is from one-third it became nearly one-half. <23.7.41> In the same way if we compare the condition in Bengal in 1921 with that of 1931 we find equally vast changes. Whereas in 1921 the number of landlords realizing rent was only 3,90,562 [390,562], in 1931 their number rose to 6,33,834 [633,834] that is to say it increased by 61 percent. On the contrary, the number of peasant families working in their own fields decreased from 92,74,924 to 60,79,717 [9,274,924 to 6,079,717], that is to say it decreased by 50 percent [actually 34.45 percent]. In the meantime, the number of agricultural labourers rose from 18,05,502 to 27,18,939 [1,805,502 to 2,718,939] which means that it increased by 34 percent [actually 50.6 percent].[22] Similarly, if we turn to Punjab the same story is repeated there. The United Provinces as well as the Central Provinces and Berar appear to show a similar pattern. In the Punjab the number of "rent-receivers" increased from 6,26,000 to 10,08,000 [626,000 to 1,008,000] between the years 1911 and 1921. The rate of increase was 62 percent. In the Central Provinces and the United

Provinces the increase within the same period was 52 percent and 46 percent respectively. This state of affairs is undoubtedly very dangerous. It is pointless to dwell on this issue in greater detail. These figures speak for themselves.

How the people of India are coming to depend increasingly on agriculture is evident from the fact that whereas in 1891, 61.1 percent of the population depended on agriculture, this figure increased to 66.5 percent in 1901, to 72.2 percent in 1911 and 73 percent in 1921. Of course there has been some confusion in the 1921 census in the numbers of those subsisting on agriculture. The statistics of the three censuses preceding it being 61.1, 66.5 and 72.2 indicates that the 1921 percentage should be in the range of 78 percent.[23] Still the pattern of increase has been recognized. In the same light if we take into consideration the following twenty years, it must be agreed that agriculture is the only source of subsistence for 80 to 85 percent of the population today. On the other hand due to the gradual disappearance of old industries and handicrafts, the numbers of those subsisting on these non-agricultural occupations is gradually decreasing, even though new kinds of machines, mills, and industries have recently been introduced on a wide scale. This clearly means that it has not been possible for these new types of factories to provide employment for all those who with the destruction of handicrafts, have no other means of livelihood. Therefore those who argue that when people are deprived of one means of livelihood they can find employment of a different type in new industries are wrong and do not understand the real implications of capitalism. And we find that in this country whereas in 1911 the number of those subsisting on industrial occupations was 5.5 percent, in 1921 this figure came down to 4.9 percent and in 1931 it decreased to 4.3 percent.[24]

We have calculated before that if people are being deprived of their lands at the rate the figures suggest, then in more or less 70 years all lands will be owned by those who do not cultivate them personally. Consequently cultivators will become completely landless and after obtaining lands on conditions imposed by the arbitrary will of the landlords, will either cultivate, starve, earn wages, or steal and rob. But we should also not forget that this is an age of "large scale farming" based on scientific methods. So while on the one hand peasants may be deprived of their lands even earlier than the estimated 70 years, and it is feared that it may take less than half that time, on the other hand in the new circumstances they will be unable to get those lands again on *shikmi* terms as was possible before. They will be reduced to the kind of agricultural labour found in the tea gardens of Assam and in the coffee or rubber plantations and who together number nearly 10 lakhs [1,000,000] and are generally referred to as coolies. But not everyone will be able to find such employment. The rest will either starve or work as labourers on large farms as is the case in America and other countries. There a handful of multi-millionaires own big mills and large farms, while countless numbers are their slaves and pass their days on the crumbs offered them as wages.[25]

It is clear from the foregoing description that the problem of agricultural labourers, of those working in the fields is an intricate one. Their numbers multiply in many ways. And the remarkable thing is that only yesterday they were peasants with land sufficient to meet their basic needs. But suddenly, today, deprived of these lands, they are in want. While yesterday they were engaged as productive cultivators, today there is no one who cares for them. People of every caste, community, and religion are experiencing this same dramatic transformation. Those who assume that agricultural labourers are only Harijans or lower castes are wrong. Out of helplessness everyone is being forced into this condition.

Editor's Notes to Chapter I

1. In Indian usage a lakh is 100,000, written as 1,00,000 and a crore is one hundred lakhs, or 10,000,000, wrtten as 1,00,00,00C. In this translation we will maintain Sahajanand's original usages with appropriate explanations where necessary.

2. Inasmuch as we will not be using diacritical marks either for Hindi or Sanskrit terms in this translation, in the case of Sahajanand's occasional Sanskrit references the closest approximate transliteration will be employed. I should like to thank Professor Romila Thaper, Dr. Madhusudan Mishra of the Rashtriya Sanskrit Sansthan in Delhi, and Dr. David White, my colleague at the University of Virginia for providing translations and interpretations of the Sanskrit phrases in this chapter and text.

3. The translation appearing here is Sahajanand's. David White's translation of this passage is as follows: "in the beginning there was only Brahma the creator; there was no differentiation among varnas. It was because of people undertaking different occupations that the varna system evolved." White does not find the implied phrase, "everyone was equal," which Sahajanand introduces obviously to reinforce his developing logic, but the assumption that because there were no differentiations, there was thus a sense of equality can certainly be made. Sahajanand's identification of this text as from Moksha-dharma 188/90 can be found in the Critical Edition at 12.181.10.

4. While Sahajanand was deeply immersed in the classical literature of Hinduism, including obviously also that on varna, he was apparently equally familiar with the contemporary English language work on caste. His discussion here on the growing complexity of the early social experience and the emergence of jati in functional and occupational terms, bears an almost uncanny resemblance to the logic on the subject argued by E.A.H. Blunt writing in 1931. Blunt was the Superintendent of Census Operations for the United Provinces in 1911. For example, quoting from the 1969 Indian edition of Blunt: "As civilization progresses, the needs of the community grow more numerous and more complex, and the occupations which supply those needs have to adapt themselves to changing conditions. The more primitive

die out, fresh trades and industries spring up to supply new demands, and differentiation or specialization of processes takes place everywhere. In the past, when the tendency towards heredity of function was still strong, such changes of occupation frequently, perhaps generally, led to changes in the constitution of the castes concerned." (See E.A.H. Blunt, *The Caste System of Northern India, With Special Reference to the United Provinces of Agra and Oudh* (Delhi: S. Chand and Company, 1969), pp. 235-236.)

5. Frequently in this text, Sahajanand uses English terms to reinforce or clarify the meanings he intends to convey. In this edition these will appear as Sahajanand gave them in the original, either in parentheses or inverted commas, i.e., quotation marks. On those few occasions where Sahajanand provides a Devanagri transliteration rather than the English, the same convention will be followed. Notes and definitions which have been added as explanation or for editorial clarification will appear in brackets.

6. Dr. White suggests that Sahajanand may be taking some liberties here in Hindi-izing the Sanskrit, but our concern, as Sahajanand himself makes clear, is with the social and political interpretations he places on his classical sources, just as he does later with the historical record and his contemporary sources. The other consideration of course is that with all of his Sanskrit references, Sahajanand may well have been working from memory while in the Hazaribagh jail. In the Chandogya Upanishad 4. 2. 5 of the Radhakrishanan Edition, the phrase appears as *ahaharemah sudra.*

7. *Brahmarshi Vansh Vistar* (Kashi: Swami Purnanand Saraswati, 1924). This title was the second and expanded edition of Sahajanand's earlier *Bhumihar Brahman Parichay* [Introduction to the Bhumihar Brahmans] (Kashi: Raj Narayan Shukul and Shyam Narayan Sharma, 1917). In the meantime the 1924 title has been reissued a number of times, most recently in the late 1980s. For a brief comment on this earlier phase of Sahajanand's career see my essay "Swami Sahajanand and the Politics of Social Reform, 1907-1950," in the *Indian Historical Review* 18:1-2 (July 1991- January 1992).

8. Whether Sahajanand had available to him in prison or before that at his ashram in Bihta copies of the many sources he cites in this tract, or whether as in the case of his extensive use of Rajni Palme Dutt's *India Today*, he utilized the citations of other authors, is not clear. The assumption is that he did both, for we know that he read

widely and was intimately familiar with official reports bearing on agriculture, indeed we know also that he provided evidence before a number of official and unofficial commissions of inquiry touching on agricultural and social conditions in the rural countryside.

Because Sahajanand most often did not provide specific references to his sources beyond what he mentions in the text, and because the Marx literature is so voluminous, it is difficult to identify with any degree of accuracy precisely which edition of a particular work Sahajanand was using or referring to. Accordingly, in the interest of providing as much bibliographic access to Sahajanand's sources as possible under the circumstances, we will list here that title which falls closest to the time of Sahajanand's writing, and which by virtue of its distribution network, might have been available in India in the 1930s and early 1940s. *Wage-Labour and Capital. Value, Price and Profit* (New York: International Publishers, 1935). This edition appeared in the publisher's Marxist Library as Volume 37 of the Works of Marxism-Leninism. A publisher's note indicates that the book is "here published in the original version as delivered by Marx in English [to workingmen] and edited by his daughter, Eleanor Marx Aveling." A Moscow edition, "translated by C.P. Dutt," was issued in the same year by the Co-operative Publishing Society of Foreign Workers in the U.S.S.R. There were at least five earlier editions published in the United States and in England. Karl Marx was born in 1818 and died in 1883.

That the Marx literature was being widely read in India at this time is of course well known. The full history of this fascinating encounter has yet to be written although as new scholarship emerges and as memoirs of Indian Socialists and Communists of the time become available, more of its contours are beginning to emerge. See for example some of the rich transcriptions in the Oral History Project of the Nehru Memorial Museum and Library in New Delhi and for other titles see also Editorial Note 19 following.

9. It is important to note that in this discussion of the social bases of agriculture, viewed at the broad macro-level of economic, cultural, and varna experience, Sahajanand is very explicit in describing the presence on the land of agricultural labourers who worked in the fields of others. He defines this history both in terms of his sense of its development and reinforces

it by appeal to the classical texts of Hinduism, a procedure he follows frequently to justify and explain his changing perceptions of the agrarian condition of the India he knew in the first half of the 20th century. I make the point here to distinguish Sahajanand's developing argument from that of the nationalist and Marxist scholarship which he adopts to a very substantial degree for the history of agricultural labour in the 19th and 20th centuries, a point to which we will return later in this chapter and the next. Suffice it to say here that one of the most explicit and influential statements of the nationalist, Marxist position is that of Surendra J. Patel, *Agricultural Labourers in Modern India and Pakistan* (Bombay, 1952), where he describes pre-colonial Indian society as a place where "there was no room for the existence of an independent and distinct class of agricultural labourers whose main source of livelihood was work on the land of others for which they received compensation in kind or cash;" or, "Under the traditional village communities, all the members were either cultivating owners or engaged in domestic industries and village administration; there was neither any room, nor any need for the existence for a separate class of agricultural labourers." (Patel, pp. 9 and 62.) While Sahajanand, writing in 1941 and no longer living in 1952 could obviously not have read Patel, he was, however, deeply influenced by Rajni Palme Dutt who was himself a powerful influence on Patel, and both Dutt and Patel, especially Patel, have been very much at the centre of the deindustrialization debate, cited in that continuing intellectual and political engagement as less than sound scholarship on the one hand and as near-classics on the other. See my Note 13 of this chapter for a brief comment on the debate and its literature.

10. Dates indicating the day, month and year appearing in the margins of Sahajanand's original copybook manuscript of *Khet Mazdoor* are retained in this translated edition at the same point of the text. Assuming these are the dates Sahajanand began or ended a day's writing, at least of this text, it is evident that he produced about ten pages of hand-written copy a day over the fourteen days it took him to complete the 144 page original of *Khet Mazdoor*. Inasmuch as Sahajanand dated his introduction remarks in February 1941, we can only presume that in the intervening five months he was preoccupied with

related reading and other writing, of which he did a prodigious amount in the two years he was in prison. Sahajanand's original Hindi text appears as Part II of this volume.

Sahajanand was in the Hazaribagh Central Jail at the time. He was imprisoned for a three year term in April 1940, following his involvement in organizing, with Subhas Chandra Bose, the All India Anti-Compromise Conference at Ramgarh in March of that year, his role as General Secretary of the Fifth Session of the All India Kisan Sabha at Palasa, and in mobilizing the National Anti-Compromise Week in early April. In each instance he took a strident anti-war position, which would change only following the entry of the Soviet Union into the war in June 1941, and the Kisan Sabha policy statements supporting the Communist Party of India's "People's War" stand. Those statements were issued by the All India Kisan Committee in October 1941, and by the Central Kisan Council in February 1942. Sahajanand was released from prison in March 1942, a year before the expiry of his three year sentence. For a brief account of this history see the last chapter of my forthcoming book, *Sahajanand and The Politics of Peasant Activism in Twentieth Century India*.

11. The land use data generated by John Richards and his associates is particularly revealing on this issue. For Bihar, James R. Hagen calculates that by 1890 four of the five districts of South Bihar, now termed Central Bihar, namely, Patna, Gaya, Shahabad, and Monghyr had "reached the optimal natural limit or 'margin' of cultivation," and Bhagalpur reached that geographic limit in 1900. Of the six districts in the North Bihar plain, Muzaffarpur, Darbhanga, and Saharsa reached the optimal geographic limit of cultivation by 1890, Purnea in 1920, and Saran and Champaran in 1950. The important point here is that at the time Sahajanand was writing and throughout the critical decade of peasant activism in the 1930s, nine of the eleven districts of Gangetic Bihar, including all those in which that activism was most intense, had in fact reached the limit of cultivation to which Sahajanand is here referring. Indeed, in most of these Gangetic districts, that limit had essentially been reached by 1890. The pressures on the land and its agriculture in very real human terms, were precisely those Sahajanand feared and describes in the balance of this document. For the Bihar figures see the important essay by J.F. Richards, James R. Hagen and Edward S. Haynes, "Changing

Land Use in Bihar, Punjab and Haryana, 1850-1970," in *Modern Asian Studies* 19:3 (July 1985), esp. p. 705 to 709, and Appendix I. For a more detailed consideration of the critical relationships between demographic trends and the extension of arable land in Bihar, see James R. Hagen, "Indigenous Society, The Political Economy, and Colonial Education in Patna District: a History of Social Change from 1811 to 1951 in Gangetic North India," (PhD Dissertation, University of Virginia, 1981), pp. 288-317, available in the NMML in New Delhi.

12. In this and the next several paragraphs, Sahajanand is not date-specific and in effect seems to be collapsing the 18th, 19th, and 20th century experiences of his perception into a kind of historic present thereby to argue his point about the numbers and conditions of agricultural labourers.

13. The story of the 18th century weavers of Bengal and their thumbs has had a general currency in the polemics of empire and colonialism, sufficient to have become a kind of metaphor for the effects of British rule on the Indian economy and Indian society generally. It is of course an exceedingly complex issue, but essentially the questions posed by the weaver story are, who did what to whom for what reasons and who benefitted and who lost in the process. For our purposes the polemic itself, whether political, ideological, or academic, is of no immediate interest, except to cite its history and some of its leading protagonists, thereby to provide the context within which Sahajanand's larger argument is made, although I would suggest that even this is not necessary to the conclusions Sahajanand reaches about the depressed conditions of the khet mazdoors and the rural poor. But because the issue is so intriguing and because the story has so recently been given its widest popular currency in the 200 years and more since its origin, we will nevertheless proceed, however briefly.

In his widely-acclaimed Mahabharata-like novel, *The Great Indian Novel* (New Delhi: Penguin Books, 1992), Shashi Tharoor has woven a wonderfully rich montage of Indian history and culture with enough fact to make it believable and enough fiction to make fascinating reading. Appropriately, he prefaces the novel with a quote from the prominent German literateur Gunter Grass to the effect that "in India, some stories should be kept alive by literature. . . Literature must refresh memory." And so the story of the Bengal weavers has been memorialized in the last decade of the 20th century, to wit, "foreign observers then could only bring themselves to write about the glories of the Empire. Not of the Indian weavers whose thumbs the British had cut off in order to protect the machines of Lanchashire; not of the Indian peasants whose lands had been signed over to zamindars who would guarantee the colonists the social peace they needed to run the country; and not of the destitution and hunger to which these policies reduced Indians. . . The British killed the Indian artisan, they created the Indian 'landless labourer', they exported our full employment and they invented our poverty." (pp. 94-95.)

The story of the weavers had its origins in a book by William Bolts, *Considerations on Indian Affairs* (London, 1772), where the author recounted the pressures under which the weavers were placed by agents of the East India Company, essentially to produce more goods at lower cost and on monopoly terms for the Company. Bolts, himself a Company agent of German background, who had fallen out of favour with the Company and been cashiered before returning to London (presumably for imbibing too freely in the private trade), is quoted accurately and at length by Romesh Dutt, one of the most prominent of the late 19th and early 20th century nationalist writers, on the weavers and winders of silk having "been treated also with such injustice, that instances have been known of their cutting off their thumbs to prevent their being forced to wind silk." (Dutt, *The Economic History of India Under Early British Rule* (London, Seventh Edition, 1950), p. 27, citing Bolts, pp. 191-194. Dutt's book was originally published in 1901.) The point here is that the weavers and winders were alleged to be cutting off their own thumbs because they were under inordinate pressure from the Company to produce more, better quality, and cheaper goods for a Company that was itself in dire financial straits and needed to provide London with more trade goods, not less. In other words, the Company was seeking to enhance production, not limit it inasmuch as their interests and those of Lancashire were in fact at the time in direct competitive conflict. The story is obviously much more elaborate, but these are its essential outlines.

Bolts, who had a cause to defend, his own, makes the allegations in his 1772 book, which then becomes one of many volleys in the polemic which shortly resulted in the Regulating Act of 1773. The polemic continues through the 19th century, including references by Marx in Vol. I of *Das Kapital* in 1867, and the nationalist writings of the late 19th century and early 20th centuries of which the work of Dutt is certainly among the more important contributions.

Apparently at some point in the late 19th century the 1772 story is worked into current nationalist accounts, now with the variation that it was the British who had cut off the weavers' thumbs to prevent them from producing textile goods and thus competing with Lancashire. Whatever may have been the case in terms of 19th century imperial policy and practice vis-a-vis Lancashire textiles and Indian textiles and its consequences for Indian weavers, it is clear that in the tragic and confused years of the 1760s, 70s, and 80s, with the Company Directors literally clammering for Indian exports, Company agents in India would not have been cutting off anyone's thumbs, least of all those of the weavers on whom they were so heavily dependent.

It is also clear that British imperial policies in the 19th century were not designed to serve Indian interests, and it is the nature of those policies and the extent and degree to which they affected the Indian economy, and specifically the weavers, which is at the heart of much of the deindustrialization debate of contemporary vintage.

Dutt certainly remains an important title on the nationalist side of the debate and C.J. Hamilton, *The Trade Relations Between England and India (1600-1896)* (1919), and reissued in Delhi in 1975 by Idarah-I Adabiyat-I Dilli, is one of the early and important British responses to Dutt. There has been much scholarship and emotion invested in the issue since, examples of which include the work of Daniel Thorner, "De-industrialization in India, 1881-1931," in Alice and Daniel Thorner, *Land and Labour in India* (Bombay: Asia Publishing House, 1962); Morris David Morris in the *Indian Economic and Social History Review* 5:1 (1968), pp. 1-16 and 5:4 (1968), pp. 319-388, and more recently his long essay, "The Growth of Large-Scale Industry to 1947," in *The Cambridge Economic History of India*, Vol. 2: *c. 1757-1970*, edited by Dharma Kumar and Tapan Raychaudhuri (Cambridge: Cambridge University Press, 1982), pp. 553-676.

For the counter view, see Amiya Kumar Bagchi's work, including his "De-industrialization in India in the Nineteenth Century: Some Theoretical Implications," *Journal of Development Studies* 12:2 (January 1976), pp. 135-164; "De-industrialization in Gangetic Bihar, 1809-1901," in *Essays in Honour of Professor Susobhan Chandra Sarkar*, edited by Barun De (New Delhi: People's Publishing House, 1976), pp. 499-522; and his *Private Investment in India, 1900-1939* (Cambridge, Cambridge University Press, 1972), for 20th century developments. An extended critique of the first two Bagchi essays is found in Marika Vicziany, "The Deindustrialization of India in the Nineteenth Century: A Methodological Critique of Amiya Kumar Bagchi," *IESHR* 16:2 (April-June 1979), pp. 105-146, which is followed by Bagchi's biting reply, pp. 147-161. The issue is also examined in a number of other essays in the *CEHI*, Vol. 2, already cited. See especially for example, Dharma Kumar, "Regional Economy in South India, 1757-1857," pp. 352-277. For Dharma Kumar's most recent thinking on the issue of weavers and the question of their shift to agriculture, see her new introduction to the reissue of her 1965 Cambridge book, *Land and Caste in South India: Agricultural Labour in the Madras Presidency During the Nineteenth Century* (New Delhi: Manohar, 1992), esp. pp. xxxvii-xxxix. Irfan Habib touches on many of these issues in his sharp critique of the *CEHI*, Vol. 2, in "Studying a Colonial Economy---Without Perceiving Colonialism," *Modern Asian Studies* 19:3 (1985), pp. 355-381; to which Dharma Kumar replies briefly but pointedly in the same issue, "The Dangers of Manichaeism," pp. 383-386. There is also a wide range of new work appearing in the pages of *IESHR*, *MAS*, and in monographic form. Specifically on Bengal, Hameeda Hossain, "The Alienation of Weavers: Impact of the Conflict Between the Revenue and Commercial Interests of the East India Company, 1750-1800," in *IESHR* 16:3 (1979), pp. 323-345, and her book, *The Company Weavers of Bengal, 1750-1813* (Delhi: Oxford University Press, 1988); as well as Ranjan Kumar Gupta, "The Economic Life of a Bengal District, 1793-1857," PhD Thesis, Calcutta University, 1976. Apart from Dharma Kumar's work, the handloom issue is examined for regions outside Bengal by Konrad Specker in his "Madras Handlooms in the Nineteenth Century," *IESHR* 26:2 (1989), pp. 131-166; for Central India by Sumit Guha in "The Handloom Industry of Central India: 1825-1950," *IESHR* 26:3 (1989), pp. 297-318; and Peter Harnetty, in "'Deindustrialization' Revisited: the Handloom Weavers of the Central Provinces of India, c. 1800-1947," *MAS* 25:3 (1991), pp. 455-510. N.K. Sinha, *The Economic History of Bengal*, Vol.I (Calcutta, 1956), of course, also remains an important source.

Finally, inasmuch as Sahajanand was writing in 1941 based on his own 20th century experience as a peasant activist and follows the deindustrialization logic closely in explaining the rise in the numbers of agricultural labourers, it is perhaps relevant to note Habib's citing both Bagchi and D.R. Gadgil on the revival of the handloom industry in India in the 20th century (a phenomenon apparently continuing into the 1990s), which would suggest that the steep decline of artisanal weaving crafts and their conversion to agricultural labour might not be so significant a factor in the 20th century as Sahajanand argues. It is an issue to which we will return in another context in the pages following. (See Habib, *MAS*, p. 364, and more specifically, Bagchi, *Public Investment*, pp. 220-228, and D.R. Gadgil, *The Industrial Evolution of India in Recent Times, 1860-1939* 5th edition (Delhi, 1971), p. 180.)

I am grateful to Dr. Sumit Guha of St. Stephen's College of the University of Delhi for his congenial responses to my many queries about the intellectual and economic history of 18th and 19th century India on which I have relied heavily in drafting this note. He has been generous with his time and his library and I appreciate both, though whatever interpretations I have drawn from the factual account are entirely my own.

14. This conditional description of something having happened or being in the process of happening is a favourite stylistic device of Sahajanand's which he uses throughout this manuscript for emphasis, as he does frequent repetition and overstatement. In the interest of a fluid translation I have limited these usages while retaining them often enough to convey the sense, style, and quality of Sahajanand's original Hindi text. I have however retained all the metaphor and graphic description and richness of language in so far as it can be conveyed across the barrier of translation.

15. This phrase, "But who cares for the poor?" appears frequently in much that Sahajanand is writing at this point of his career.

He was obviously deeply seized by the poverty and human desperation he saw around him at the social and economic margins of rural life and it was this sensibility that increasingly moved him in the directions represented so explicitly in this tract.

16. Sahajanand's 1941 anxiety about fragmentation has of course been amply borne out by the experience of fifty intervening years since his writing. There are a number of indicators to be noted, first the nature of the operational holding used for statistical definition by the Government of India, as "all land which is used wholly or partly for agricultural production and is operated as one technical unit by one person alone or with others *without regard to the title, legal form, size or location.*" (Italics added.) Both the 1976-77 and 1980-81 *Report on the Agricultural Census* of the Ministry of Agriculture of the Government of India comment on the "preponderance of the marginal holdings which accounted for more than half the number of operational holdings in the country. In fact, while the total number of holdings in the country increased from 71 million in 1970-71 to 81.6 million in 1976-77, i.e., an increase of 15 per cent [in Bihar the percentage of increase in number of holdings was 31 percent], during the same period the number of marginal holdings increased from 36.2 million to 44.5 million showing thereby an increase of 23 per cent." (*Report for 1976-77*, New Delhi, 1983, pp. i and 10.) The 1980-81 *Report* reinforces the point: "The distribution of holdings, however, continued to be very skewed with small and marginal holdings accounting for about three-fourths of the total number of holdings. . . representing only 26 per cent of the operated area." (New Delhi, 1987, p. i.) Marginal holdings are those below one hectare, small holdings are those between one and two hectares, with a hectare equal to 2.5 acres.

The dramatic meaning of these figures is demonstrated even more explicitly in the land fragmentation data for 1961-62 adduced by Alan Heston and Dharma Kumar based on the 17th Round National Sample Survey. They report that for operational holdings of between one and two acres, the average number of fragments for all of India is 4.4, with an average parcel size of .37 of an acre. In the two most populous states, U.P. and Bihar, the number of fragments were respectively 6.2 and 5.9, and the parcel size .26 and .28 parts of an acre each. Both sets of figures were the most extreme for the country as a whole. And these figures are now dated by thirty years. The assumption is that the actual cultivators on these miniature plots of land are the marginal poor Sahajanand was writing about in 1941. For a detailed discussion of the meaning of fragmentation see Heston and Kumar, "The Persistence of Land Fragmentation in Peasant Agriculture: An Analysis of South Asian Cases," in *Explorations in Economic History* 20 (1983), pp. 199-220.

17. Sahajanand is concerned in these pages with explaining that the numbers of agricultural labourers were increasing "like the entrails of the devil," to use his graphic language. His more central point in the tract as a whole, however, is to describe the conditions under which marginal peasants and agricultural labourers live in India, and it is the unique window his insights provide into the world of the rural poor in the 1930s, and remarkably in the 1990s that is the value of this tract as a social, political, and a historical document. The methods of collecting data and the scholarship in interpreting these data have been perfected in the years since Sahajanand wrote, so we need to exercise special care in not imposing our retrospective vision on his 1941 perceptions of the data, especially inasmuch as he was relying heavily on others for the statistical base to sustain his argument. Yet these qualifications should not prevent us from suggesting the broader context which time and new data and new scholarship and the political and economic changes which fifty years have produced, permit us to do.

Virtually all authors, whatever their ideological or interpretive disposition on the Indian economy, agree that census figures, indeed all statistical data, pose serious problems especially in attempting long term projections and in making comparisons over time and between disparate sets of data. These are issues that have to do with changes in classification from one census or statistical set to the next, in the definitions of enumerated categories, and potential flaws in the enumeration process itself. Commenting on the problems of dealing with the 1921 and 1931 census figures, Palme Dutt for example, observes that "Changes in the system of classification also prevent comparison with previous census returns." He then explains the possible adjustments that are necessary "to make even a rough comparison. Even this comparison is vitiated by further changes in the system of classification, through the removal of all those whose agricultural occupations is treated as subsidiary to other occupations, and in particular, through the removal of 7 million women, female relatives of agriculturists assisting in the work of the farm, to the category of 'domestic service,' thus giving an illusory apparent effect of a decline in the relative proportion of the population engaged in agriculture." (*India Today*, pp. 222-223 of the 1949 Indian edition.)

Although Dharma Kumar's primary concern in her 1965 book was in establishing the existence of substantial numbers of agricultural labourers prior to British dominance and prior to the availability of data of any kind on the issue, Kumar nevertheless observes on the problems posed by the classification and definition issue in the 20th century. "In 1961 there were 31 1/2 million agricultural workers in India, that is to say around one-fourth of the agricultural working force. (*Census of India*, 1961.) Some of these labourers may own some land themselves, but these minute holdings cannot afford even bare subsistence for a family, and the major part of the labourer's income is derived from working on land owned by others. In this sense these labourers are 'landless'. The exact definition of the term 'agricultural labourer' has been much debated in recent years, and what is more, has varied from one official enquiry to another, with the result that estimates of agricultural labourers in the same year, 1951, range from 18 per cent of the total agricultural population (*Census of 1951*) to 38 per cent (*First Agricultural Labour inquiry*). But for our purpose these differences of definition are not important. It is clear enough that there has been a large group of landless labourers throughout the twentieth century, and that they are among the poorest and most depressed sections of Indian society; what is not clear is how long this group has existed and how it came into being." (p. 3, 1965 edition.)

The comparability issue is raised in some detail by J. Krishnamurty, commenting specifically on the work of Surendra J. Patel, *Agricultural Labourers in Modern India and Pakistan* (Bombay, 1952). Krishnamurthy maintains that Patel's conclusion that the proportion of agricultural labourers to the agricultural population increased from a meagre one-seventh to more than one-third, "was reached on the basis of a serious misunderstanding of [the] census data. More recent evidence also suggests that

Patel's conclusions need drastic revision. . . First, the estimates for 1871-72 related to adult males, for 1881 to males, and for 1891-1931 to persons (i.e., males plus females). . . Using 1871-72 and 1881 data for males may exaggerate the increase in agricultural labour. . . The absence of a specific category 'agricultural labourers' in 1871-72 may also have led to a number of persons reporting themselves as cultivators who would otherwise have been deemed agricultural labourers. Patel's figures for 1891 (like his figures for 1881) are not taken from the census volumes but from *Financial and Commercial Statistics of British India* (Calcutta, 1899) and this has apparently led him into error. The figures obtained from the census volumes would suggest a much higher proportion of agricultural labour in 1891 (22.9 per cent instead of 13.0 per cent reported by Patel)."

Turning to more recent evidence for post-Independence India and extrapolating earlier data for the Indian Union as it was constituted after 1947, Krishnamurty concludes that "for the period 1901-1961 [available data] suggest that through this period about 25 per cent of the male agricultural working force were agricultural labourers. For both sexes (i.e., persons) a proportion of about 30 per cent appears to have been the norm. So the data for 1871-1931---largely following Patel's own methods---and our [data] for the Indian Union, 1901-1961, suggest no upward trend in the share of agricultural labour in the agricultural working force." Krishnamurty thus finds no signs of "structural transformation" in the distribution of the working force, and concludes that "Simple models of the decline of manufacturing employment and the mass conversion of cultivators and artisans into agricultural labourers cannot be sustained for the period after 1870, on the basis of available census evidence." (J. Krishnamurty, "The Growth of Agricultural Labour in India---A Note," *IESHR* 9:3 (September 1972), pp. 327-332.)

In a more recent essay and citing evidence from Bihar, Dr. B. Chaudhuri of the University of Calcutta essentially sustains Krishnamurty's logic. He writes: "The early censuses, particularly those of 1872, 1881 and 1891, seem to have greatly underestimated the number of agricultural labourers, one of the chief reasons, apart from the want of a precise definition of 'agricultural labourer', being that the enumerators were misled by answers from the 'agriculturalists', who 'left to themselves used terms indicative of their status in the land tenure system, rather than of their occupation', with the result that even the smallest holders deriving the largest part of their income from wage labour were not recorded as agricultural labourers." Turning specifically to the jump in numbers of agricultural labourers between 1921 and 1931, cited as critical by both Palme Dutt and Sahajanand, Chaudhuri explains that apart from more sophisticated methods of enumeration, "Developments preceding the depression seem to have had a greater role in the increased number of agricultural labourers during the decade 1921 to 1931. The influenza epidemic of 1918-19 sharply reduced the working population and necessitated the employment of a larger quantity of labour, while the post-war rise in agricultural prices, by enriching the big holders, at least a section of them, enabled them to pay for it." (See Chaudhuri's essay, "Agrarian Relations in Eastern India," in *CEHI*, Vol. 2, esp. pp. 168-169.)

Following this range of evidence, there is more than a little apprehension in citing figures for 1971 and 1981 on percentages of agricultural labourers in the cultivating population as a whole, especially inasmuch as the classifications for those census years have again been changed. Nevertheless, with these qualifications in mind, 1971 shows a figure of 36.5 per cent, and 1981, marginally less at 36.27. (See Table 12.5 under Basic Economic Data in *India 1991*, Research and Reference Division, Ministry of Information and Broadcasting, Government of India, 1992.) Figures for 1991 are not available at this writing.

The importance of these data is less to suggest that Sahajanand's 70 year projections or 35 year projections were skewed, but to point out that a figure of 25, 30, or 35 percent which is widely accepted, is a large number of agricultural labourers, and as Sahajanand rightly argues, certainly represents a minimum figure for those on the social and economic margin of poverty in rural India, in 1941 or in 1993. Sahajanand was concerned about the quality of life of this important segment of India's population, and its political representation. Both issues were important in 1941 and are the subject of almost daily reports in the public press in 1993.

18. Sahajanand's suggestion that fourteen to fifteen years of his projection, based on 1931 figures, had "already passed," appears to be an interlineated afterthought. Clearly only ten years had

passed when he was writing in 1941, and the fourteen to fifteen year figure may well be one of a number of minor modifications and additions in Sahajanand's hand which suggest that he was making such emendations as late as 1945 or 1946.

19. Sahajanand's references to Rajni Palme Dutt's influential *India Today*, are to the original 1940 edition, published in London by Victor Gollancz, Ltd. Dutt writes in the preface to the revised and enlarged Indian edition (Bombay: People's Publishing House, 1947), that the original 1940 edition was banned in India, and "the entire stock in England was destroyed in the blitz." But if banned, the book was nevertheless available in India and in the Hazaribagh Central Jail, inasmuch as Sahajanand relies on it for much of his specific data, many of his references, and for much of his logic and argument on the transformation of the colonial economy and the consequent growth in the numbers and percentages of landless labourers. That fact is a reflection of the very substantial influence Dutt had in England, Moscow, and India as an ideologue, a powerful intellectual, a leading European Marxist, founder of the Communist Party of Great Britain, political operative and reporter on Indian affairs both in London and Moscow. (On the connections between Dutt, the CPGB, the Comintern, and the CPI, see Madhu Limaye, *Socialist Communist Interaction in India* (Delhi: Ajanta Publications, 1991), esp. pp. 1-71; and for the most recent and serious scholarship on the subject see the two volumes by Shashi Joshi and Bhagwan Josh, *Struggle for Hegemony in India,1920-47: The Colonial State, The Left and the National Movement* (New Delhi: Sage Publications, 1992). This network obviously extended into India in many direct and intangible ways in influencing young Socialists, Marxists, and Communists, and it was precisely this group with whom Sahajanand came into daily, intimate contact following his 1940 arrest and his incarceration at the Hazaribagh Jail. And it was in that environment that Sahajanand read Dutt, Marx, and much of the Marxist canon, and wrote *Khet Mazdoor*, among other titles. Whether others of Dutt's many publications were available to Sahajanand we do not know, but we can assume that at least some were, given the history of his *India Today*. Among Dutt's other publications that might have been known and read in India are the following: *Modern India* (Bombay, 1926); *Socialism and the Living Wage* (London, 1927); *Lenin* (London, 1933); *Fascism and Social*

Revolution (London, 1934); *World Politics, 1918-1936* (London, 1936); and *The Political and Social Doctrine of Communism* (London, 1938). While some of these were pamphlet titles, others were full length books, from the pen of this prolific activist.

Page references to Dutt and all other sources in this translation will adhere to those originally used by Sahajanand. Rajni Palme Dutt's *India Today* was reissued in a second revised Indian edition in 1949, and has appeared in subsequent editions and reprints at least half a dozen times, most recently in January 1992 by Manisha Granthalaya (P) Ltd. in Calcutta. It should be noted that paginations in these several reprints and editions vary considerably from the original and from one edition and another.

20. Dutt's point in this quote and which Sahajanand follows, is to establish that in pre-colonial India or soon thereafter, i.e., in the late 18th and early 19th centuries, there were relatively few agricultural labourers and that as a result of imperial policy those numbers escalated both in absolute terms and as a percentage of cultivators, in a persistent process of taxation, debt, sale, eviction, and immiseration by which peasants inevitably became agricultural labourers. It is this view, propounded in its most detailed form by Dr. Surendra J. Patel, *Agricultural Labourers in Modern India and Pakistan*, to which I have referred in Note 9 above. The most elaborate counter-argument is that of the economic historian, Dharma Kumar in her *Land and Caste in South India: Agricultural Labour in the Madras Presidency During the Nineteenth Century* (Cambridge, 1965). The book has been reissued in its original form by Manohar in New Delhi (1992), with an extended retrospective introduction, where the author proposes minor modifications but essentially affirms her earlier findings based on a wide range of new scholarship in the field. Those findings suggested that in 1800 as a pre-colonial base date, agricultural labour was known, did exist, and functioned in economic, social, and cultural terms in cultivating the land of others.

In her original conclusion Professor Kumar draws into question not only the logic of Palme Dutt and Surendra J. Patel, one of the earliest proponents of the peasant immiseration to agricultural labour argument, but questions the nature of the data and the manner in which it is used. Referring to the same Dutt quote cited here by Sahajanand (and used in part by Patel in 1952 (p. 9), Kumar writes: "It does not strengthen one's confidence in this view to recall that there was no all-India census until 1871, that there was no Madras census in 1842, that Sir Thomas Munro was never Census Commissioner, and that in 1842 he was dead. Moreover, the assertion that now the 'proportion [of agricultural labourers] is nearer one-half is tendentious. It is based on the census data of 1931, which merely showed that agricultural labourers were 32 per cent of the agricultural population. To this Mr. Dutt has added the entire figure for 'unspecified labour' to arrive at a percentage of about 37-38." (Kumar, 1992, fn. 1, p. 189.)

21. The 1931 population of India was 338,119,000 so Sahajanand's lower figure here is a reasonably accurate percentage.

22. These percentage figures were transposed in Palme Dutt's original text (as they continue to be in subsequent editions and reprints), and Sahajanand used them as given by Dutt. Palme Dutt, however, does note that "the detail figures [between 1921 and 1931] are not comparable, owing to the change in classification, resulting in an illusory apparent decline of the total agricultural population by 2 million." Dutt holds that this "proves only the more overwhelmingly, the actually greater reality of the increase in the proportions of non-cultivating rent receivers and of landless labourers." (See *India Today*, p. 224, second revised Indian edition, 1949.) This issue is examined in some detail in Note 17 above. Sahajanand does not explain the classification discrepancy in his Hindi text.

23. Dr. B. Chaudhuri discusses the 1921 figures in terms that may be relevant to Sahajanand's observation here; they are cited above in Note 17. Dr. J. Krishnamurty shows the proportion of the workforce in agriculture for 1931 as 70.6 percent and in 1951 as 73.3 percent. (See his essay, "The Occupational Structure," in the *CEHI*, Vol. 2, p. 535.) Workforce figures were not enumerated in the 1941 census. The Government of India figures for 1971 and 1981 are 69.7 percent and 66.5 percent, respectively, keeping in mind that classifications have changed in these censuses. (See Table 12.5 in the section on Basic Economic Data, *India 1991*, Research and Reference Division, Ministry of Information and Broadcasting, 1992.

24. Krishnamurty's figures for manufacturing only and not including mining, quarrying, and construction, for the same date series Sahajanand cites are 9.1 percent, 9.0 percent, and 8.4 percent. For 1951 his figure is 9.1 percent, and Government of India figures for manufacturing only for 1971 and 1981, respectively are 9.5 percent and 11.3 percent. (See Krishnamurty in *CEHI*, Vol. 2, p. 535; and *India 1991*, Research and Reference Division, Ministry of Information and Broadcasting, 1992, Table 12.5, p. 359.)

25. Several points need to be kept in mind in considering Sahajanand's observations here about the agriculture economies of "America and other countries," which in fact he cites in Chapter IV in rather more positive terms in comparing their productive capabilities with those of India. Sahajanand had travelled widely in India, but there is no evidence that he had been outside of South Asia and in the 1920s and 30s, communication was rather more limited than it is today. Accordingly, Sahajanand was almost entirely dependent for information on the world beyond India on what he read, and we have already suggested that Rajni Palme Dutt was a particularly significant influence on Sahajanand's thinking at this time.

The other consideration of course is that in the depression years of the 1930s most world agriculture, including that of Europe and the United States, was in a state of deep crisis. The grim social and economic realities of that crisis in America have been recounted by John Steinbeck in his memorable novel, *The Grapes of Wrath*. Indeed, it was precisely some of the conservation and infrastructural changes in American agriculture, introduced in response to that 1930s crisis, which were the beginning of the productive revolution that continues in the United States to this day. It is these kinds of infrastructural investments Sahajanand proposes in the last two chapters of this tract as one way of bringing Indian agricultural production up to its full potential.

CHAPTER II
Labourer or Kisan?

[In Chapter I Sahajanand was concerned with describing the emergence of a category of rural labourers, khet mazdoors, in Indian agriculture. In Chapter II he distinguishes these agricultural labourers from factory labourers while at the same time arguing that they cannot be distinguished from poor peasants. There is, he says, no demarcation line between the two. In making his argument, he appeals to the Russian experience, especially as defined by Lenin, a wide range of official British Indian documentation, again drawing heavily on Palme Dutt, and most importantly his own sense of the lives of the rural poor. Sahajanand's political agenda is candidly stated in the final paragraph. It has to do with the movement of the khet mazdoors, which must "be organized like that of the kisans and only together with the kisans." Ed.]

Although we are in a general sense familiar with the conditions of agricultural labourers, there remains one fundamental issue yet to be considered. That is to examine the precise meanings of the term labourer as it applies in India. Without doing so we can neither fully appreciate the lives of those who labour in the fields nor propose solutions which might relieve their miseries. Hence before proceeding it is necessary to deal with this issue.[1]

The term "agricultural labourers" (*khet mazdoor* or *kheti ke mazdoor*) initially suggests that these are labourers in the same sense as factory workers or miners. Hence it is thought that measures meant for liberating these workers will also benefit agricultural labourers. This is a natural reaction. In fact some new labour leaders are applying this very idea in practice. But rather than benefitting the khet mazdoors, they have in fact added to their problems and to those of the kisans. Of course some have taken this course unwittingly because they misunderstand the meanings of the term labourer. But mostly it is those who are self-seekers who have assumed these leadership roles, and failed. Who knows whether they have achieved their personal objectives. This much we do know, that after some time they have fallen into silence and disappeared from public view.

<24.7.41> The trouble arises from the peculiar sense in which people have used the words labourer or mazdoor. In their place the [Hindi] words *shramjeevi* and *mehnatkash* are much more explicit in their meanings.[2] They clearly refer to those who engage in actual physical labour, who earn their living by working with their hands and feet. In English the words "worker and labourer" are used in this sense, namely those who work or labour. This is precisely the meaning of the words *mehnatkash* or *shramik*. All of these words suggest that labourers are not like the leisured rich who depend solely upon the earnings of others like zamindars, money-lenders, and capitalists. It is the case, of course, that labourers live by the sweat of their brow and support others as well. If the word labourer is used in this sense, as it ought to be, then there will be no possibility of confusion in the meaning of the term agricultural labourer.

But there is confusion because in English another word, "wage-worker" is used to mean labourer. The word "wage-labourer" is used in the same sense. The etymological meaning of these two words is "one who does physical work (*mehnat*) for wages or salary." Often the words servant and dependant [*bhritya*] are used in the same sense, although the real meaning of the word *bhritya* is one who is fully provided for and receives no other compensation. All those who depend on the earnings of one working person are called *bhritya*, i.e., dependants. Manu in the sloka *bhrityanamuparodhena* in the eleventh chapter of his smriti has used the word *bhritya* in this very sense.[3] Of course by treating the word labourer in the sense of "wage worker," people have come to regard those who work in the fields only for wages, as agricultural labourers. At the outset of the agricultural experience everyone who ploughed and toiled in the fields, as many still do today, was in a general sense an agricultural labourer, whereas today the term is used only to refer to those who plough and toil in the fields of others for wage payment in cash or kind. Such an interpretation leaves us open to many errors. The English terms "agricultural labourer" or "agricultural proletariat" imply this sense of working in the fields of and for others.

The fact is that the term "wage labourer" cannot accurately express the sense in which the word labourer [*mazdoor*] is used today. The term shows only that a man works in another's field or factory, etc., so that he may receive a fixed wage either in cash or kind. It does not show in any way whether the worker himself owns any land, a place to live, or whether he has access to other resources, or not. Today we find a large number of such workers who are called *babus* and are also referred to as lower middle class. For example, office clerks fall into this category. They have their own houses and may have some land and other property as well. However, those persons who own nothing and who without working will starve, they too are "wage workers." Herein lies the confusion.

But today the word labourer is generally used to describe those who have neither land nor a dwelling place, have absolutely no property of any kind and subsist by working in the fields or factories of others. They live in the houses of others and can be turned out by the house and factory owners at any moment; such people are called "free-labourers." They have ceased to have any relationships or links to any material or proprietary things which might impose on them any personal ties or responsibilities. The only property left to the free-labourer is his labour power; everything else has disappeared. Of course, he may have a wife, children, a father and others who depend entirely on his earnings. But beyond his labour power, the capitalist system generally does not concede even these dependent relationships. In theory it might be accepted that he must be paid wages sufficient not only to maintain his own strength, but to produce able-bodied children and hence labourers for the future. But in practice he is paid wages so low that it is difficult to sustain even himself.

In this age of machines and factories the labourer is regarded as a kind of "commodity," that is, his "labour-power" (*shramshakti*) is a "commodity." Just as with the price of cloth in the marketplace, his value too is subject to similar fluctuations. In the time of slavery, owners assumed full responsibility for their slave's well-being. If the slaves were sold, those who bought them then assumed this responsibility. I have referred to this phenomenon in the previous chapter. But the condition of the present day "wage-labourer" (*mazdoor*) is in many ways unique. Factory owners have no concern for him as a person. If they require one labourer, ten will come running.

Then why should they care for these labourers in any individual sense? As in the marketplace, when the price of goods falls sharply because of competitive rivalry among sellers, so too is the case with labourers and their labour power. Because of their large numbers, they get only a nominal price, i.e., nominal wages for their labour. That is why a labourer [*mazdoor*] is not appropriately described as a "wage-labourer," but as "proletariat." The meaning of this word is "*sarvahara*," i.e., one who has been deprived of everything. Karl Marx, in the book cited in the preceding chapter has compared the proletariat with the silkworm. Just as the silkworm is fed because it begets silk for its owner [*malik*], so too the proletariat are fed only because they work. If the worm has to live it must beget silk and the proletariat must work if it is to survive. Quoting Marx: "If the silk-worm's object in spinning were to prolong its existence as a caterpillar, it would be a perfect example of a wage-worker." He continues on this theme:

> The free labourer, on the other hand, sells his very self, and that by fractions. He auctions off eight, ten, twelve, fifteen hours of his life, one day like the next to the highest bidder, to the owner of raw materials, tools and means of life, i.e., to the capitalist. The labourer belongs neither to an owner, nor to the soil, but eight, ten, twelve, fifteen hours of his daily life belongs to whosoever buys them.[4]

In his world-famed book *Capital*, Marx has written much the same thing but more briefly: "He must be free from everything that is essential for the realisation of his labour power. . . [They are] persons who own nothing, but their labour power. . ." (*Capital*, Vol l; Chapt. III, Sec. 3). John Strachey makes the same point in his book *The Theory and Practice of Socialism* when he writes that: "A working class is composed of persons who are compelled to live by selling their ability to work in other men's factories or fields." (p. 302.)[5]

Now we must consider whether these formulations hold for the conditions of agricultural labourers in our country. We can divide agricultural labourers in India into two categories. One section consists of those who work on thousand acre "farms" cultivated by scientific methods. These labourers are found in the tea gardens of Darjeeling and the northern districts of Assam and on large coffee and rubber "farms" in the Nilgiris and elsewhere. Palme Dutt in his aforementioned book has written about them in the following terms:

> Akin to these [bonded labourers] in many respects is the condition of the plantation slaves, or over one million labourers on the great tea, coffee, and rubber plantations, owned up to 90 percent by European companies which pay high dividends. (*India Today*, p. 219.)

Labourers of this type can be found on large "farms" of provincial governments and the Government of India and on some non-government farms as well.[6] We have no accurate knowledge about these farms, but the case of the aforesaid plantation labourers is of a clear and unique type. For decades they have settled in the thousands at these several places. In this way they have become in very real terms a "proletariat" (*sarvahara*). This is not generally the case with those working on the large government and non-government farms. Hence, Palme Dutt writes about the plantation labourers as follows:

> From the standpoint of the potential strength of the organised labour movement, we should add over one million workers employed on the plantations, who are employed in fully large scale enterprise under the most scientific slave-driving conditions, and have already shown a high degree of militant activity in periods of unrest, although so far cut off from all organisation and held under conditions of complete isolation and subjection. (*India Today*, p. 349.)

Hence no one can object to these agricultural labourers being included in the category of labourers or the proletariat. This is clearly where they belong. Agricultural labourers found on such plantations or farms certainly in no way differ from the "proletariat" (*mazdoors*) who work in mines, large factories or other similar industries. The living conditions and struggles of both are similar, indeed they are fundamentally the same.

<25.7.41> There are, however, two categories of agricultural labourers. This point was made in a speech delivered by Lenin in the summer of 1921 on the occasion of the Tenth Congress of the Communist Party. Lenin conceded in that speech a proletariat category

of agricultural labourers. He writes on this issue as follows:

> In the countries of developed capitalism a class of hired agricultural labourers emerged over the course of some decades. . . Where this class is sufficiently developed, the transition from capitalism to socialism is possible. We have emphasized in a whole series of writings, in all our speeches, in all our press, the fact that in Russia the situation is not like this---that in Russia we have a minority of workers in industry and an enormous majority of petty land-owners.[7]

This assertion of Lenin shows that it is only by large scale farming that a proletariat class [*varg*] of agricultural labourers comes into existence and that this process requires that capitalism be fully developed. Even in these circumstances it takes considerable time for this class to emerge. On the other hand, Lenin has made no mention of other kinds of agricultural labourers. Except the class of agricultural labourers called proletariat [*sarvahara*], Lenin has included everyone else in the class of petty landholders [*tut pujiya khetihar*]. But it cannot be said that labourers in agriculture are found only on large farms and that there are no such labourers working in the fields of small peasant holders [*chote-mote kisans*]. Even Russian history bears witness to the fact that there were many such agricultural labourers in that country. Not only this, when agriculturally related "serfdom" was legally abolished in Russia on February 19, 1861, in theory these serfs became independent kisans having lands. But in fact the annual prescribed payment to the government for acquiring this freedom and land was substantially more than the actual production on the land itself. This problem has been examined by Professor Y. E. Yanson to the effect that in several localities the paucity of land was so acute that it was impossible for the peasants to produce on that land both their essential living requirements and also pay the government dues. Launcelot A. Owen, in his book *The Russian Peasant Movement, 1906-1917* has written specifically about this issue as follows:

> Even in 1877, the well known Professor Yanson, having statistically investigated peasant allotments and payments, showed that the total of peasant payments exceeded the return from their land. While he did not accept Professor Yanson's

> conclusions as being right with regard to some localities, yet it was impossible for the Procurator of the Kharkov Appeal Court to deny that "in certain areas there was a manifest insufficiency of land to satisfy their very pressing needs, both to secure their mode of life and to carry out their obligations to the Government." (p. 6.)[8]

On page seven Owen points out the meaning of these circumstances in clear terms: "The insufficiency of land compelled the peasants to supplement their earnings by renting land from the squires, by working on the squires' estates and by extra employment outside the confines of the village."

The November 9, 1906 proclamation of Stolypin, the Czar's Prime Minister, resulted in the creation of two kinds of peasants. One category of peasants were forced to sell their lands inasmuch as the holdings were uneconomically small or in the absence of the necessary tools of agriculture. The other category of peasants who were rich and wealthy, were now free to purchase these lands. Between 1907 and 1910 about one crore [10,000,000] acres (3,723,000 desyatines) of land was sold in this way.[9] The process is described explicitly in Owen's book:

> It seemed that the separation from the land commune resulted in the exit of two village elements---the pauperised layer giving up farming and thus securing its allotments simply for sale, and the more prosperous members who were freed from communal restrictions. . . Between 1907 and 1910, 3,723,000 desyatines of allotment land was subjected to sale, there being a consistent rise in the yearly figures. (pp.64-65.)

In addition to these examples, there were the "batraki" in the Baltic States who, though without lands of their own, used to work in the fields of others.[10] There were also those who cultivated lands on the condition of giving a fixed share of the produce to the landowner. In this way just as we have in our country agricultural labourers who do the physical work of agriculture in the fields, so too was the case in Russia. Then we need to understand why Lenin rather than referring to them as "agricultural labourers," has called them petty [*tut pujiye*] kisans and has included them in the category of cultivators [*khetihar*].

After all it was Stolypin's patronage which encouraged in Russia the growth of rich peasants [*dhani kisans*] called "kulaks," and there was no dearth of labourers to work in their fields. But according to Lenin, we cannot even call these agricultural labourers small landolding peasants, i.e., "*zamin wale chote chote kisan.*" <26.7.41> It is clear from Lenin's failure to mention them separately at such a significant period, that so far as the people's revolution was concerned, these agricultural labourers had no separate existence apart from the peasants. Instead of including them in the category of the factory proletariat or the proletariat of the large farms, Lenin regarded them as belonging to the category of peasants.[11]

But Lenin's assertion has another meaning as well. In fact, in his analysis of the revolution, he has indicated that the real revolutionary forces can be found only among the proletariat sector of the villages, as this group is most like the factory proletariat. The rest of the people will follow them and join the revolution when they find that their interests too will be served in the process. The proletariat is compelled to come to an agreement with these other groups for the success of the revolution. By this Lenin means that it is a great mistake to think of the proletariat as the all-powerful element of the revolution and to expect its success only from them. The factory proletariat are not to be found in the rural villages. Here it is the petty kisans who are found in very large numbers and if no compromise is reached with them, the revolution cannot be successful. Its potential achievements would be totally frustrated without such compromise. Lenin had made this point in explaining the need for the New Economic Policy (NEP) and in doing so gave substantial concessions to the petty or ordinary [*sadharan*] kisans and accordingly the principles of socialism were not entirely adhered to. Consequently a kind of compromise had been effected between these kisans and the proletariat class [*varg*]. Had he considered labourers engaged in agriculture in the category of the proletariat, the success of the revolution might have been illusive, inasmuch as their mentality is very much like that of the kisans. Hence, just after that assertion, Lenin in the same [1921] speech, makes the point in the following terms:

> The other condition is an agreement between the proletariat which holds the state power and the majority of the peasant population. Only an agreement with the peasants can save the socialist revolution in Russia.

The most characteristic feature of the proletariat is their power to secure their rights by united and organized struggle, what in English is referred to as their "collective bargaining power." It is a feature also found among the labourers working on large farms and plantations, whom we have already described as falling within the category of the proletariat. These plantation and large farm labourers number between ten and twelve lakhs [1,000,000 to 1,200,000] in India.

Let us consider the matter of organized struggle in the following way. Take the example of a mill or factory. Thousands of labourers will be found working there. They have a sense of community and a patterned life style, not unlike that of soldiers in the army. They develop a consistent regularity in their coming and going. Thus it follows that if they stop work with one mind, then it becomes impossible for the factory owners to go on. First, it is difficult to find replacements in such large numbers if all workers stay off the job and this can also not be done so quickly. Thirdly, the strikers themselves can stop any outsiders ("black-legs") by picketting at the factory gate and by other means. Fourthly, their union [*sabha*] can easily direct them because they all live at the same place with the facility to assemble as may be necessary. Fifthly, it is also the case that workers of other factories may strike in sympathy inasmuch as their circumstances will not be dissimilar from those of the initial strikers, hence they have a direct interest in what is happening. When occasion arises, such sympathy actions must of course be reciprocated. The most important fact is that by virtue of the factory's location, the strikers benefit from newspapers, other current literature and meetings, which means that they develop a clear sense of their duties and responsibilities in the strike situation. Furthermore, they also have access to railways, telegraph, wireless, and other kinds of communications facilities which provide the news of their strike to the outside world, and vice versa. This permits people on the outside to demonstrate their sympathy with the strikers. As a result of all these factors the struggle of the labourers is greatly facilitated and often achieves success.[12]

Thus far we have considered the conditions of factory workers and that section of agricultural labourers working on plantations and large farms. These agricultural labourers belong cent per cent to the working class. Hence their struggles, their organization, and their programme should be patterned exactly like those other labourers who work in mills and factories. But it must be remembered that these plantation and farm labourers form a very negligible portion of the five crores [50,000,000] or more of all agricultural labourers.[13] They constitute a mere two percent of this sector of Indian agricultural. So the question arises, to which category do the remaining 98 percent of agricultural labourers belong? That is to say, it is essential to consider this other and more significant section of agricultural labourers. As a matter of fact we are really concerned only with these 98 percent. Who knows in what remote places the other two percent live? This situation has been referred to by Lenin in the Russian case in the extract cited above. It is even more true for India. Here small fields are found scattered everywhere in which can be found one, two or four khet mazdoors either ploughing or doing other agricultural work. In some villages the kisan himself does all this work. He does not require ploughmen or other help. Again in some villages there are only two, three or four kisans who require the services of agricultural labourers. And there are still other villages with large numbers of agricultural labourers. In some places villages exist side by side while at others the distance from one village to the next is measured in miles. This means that agricultural labourers are widely scattered across the countryside, making it difficult to gather and meet, and almost impossible to do so with any frequency. Neither are their hours of work uniform nor is it settled that they will work only so long and no more. They work day and night like an ass and are consequently in a state of total exhaustion at day's end. This is the condition of most kisans and their labourers, both of them. And so where is the strength and energy to organize meetings when the day's work is done?[14]

Beyond this, differences of caste and religion also keep the khet mazdoors apart from one another. Old orthodoxies and social values prevent the idea from taking root that they are all agricultural labourers. Then how can the question of a united and organized struggle even arise? And if the agricultural labourers dare to raise their voices, the kisan can easily take work from others. Each kisan requires only one, two or four labourers and these can be easily found. And even if these are not available the kisan can himself carry on the work of cultivation. After all this work involves no sophisticated technical skills. The antiquated wooden plough can easily be used by anyone. In fact a false sense of self-respect or a mistaken notion of his religion has prevented the kisan from using his plough and doing other agriculturally-related work. But these notions will disappear when the kisans are faced with hunger or come under other kinds of pressure. This is not a matter of conjecture; it has already happened in hundreds of places.[15] In such circumstances there is no scope for united struggle or "collective bargaining" by the agricultural labourers. And if at some places they have threatened to stop work [*hartal*] or a particular strike or hartal was successful, in most places these efforts have failed. It should also be remembered that where these struggles have achieved any success, it is because the kisans themselves have not been fully awakened. But when such hartals will be attempted in an organized form, then the kisans will certainly also awaken and react, and the consequences will be unfortunate for everyone.[16]

All that has been stated thus far about the capacity for "collective bargaining" among labourers, cannot be applied in any sense in the case of agricultural labourers generally. There is an absence of railways, telegraph, and similar facilities in these far off villages and the availability of newspapers and other current publications is negligible. Rarely are meetings held and forming an organization is still more difficult. Mutual sympathy scarcely exists and there is no occasion to demonstrate it. In these circumstances little can happen. The relationship between one kisan or khet mazdoor and the other is not like that between one mill and another. Hence it is not correct to place them in the same category as [factory] labourers. There is no reason to do so. The most important fact is that these agricultural labourers have their own dwellings or hutments, and often they have a goat, cow, or pig, etc., and may possess two to four *katthas* of land.[17] If not this, at minimum they have the site of their dwelling place. The fact also is that till yesterday they were kisans. But as all their lands have been auctioned off by the zamindars or moneylenders, they have suddenly become landless, that is to say, they have become agricultural labourers. How then can they become proletariat so quickly? It has already been pointed out that the number of agricultural labourers is increasing very rapidly. Hundreds of thousands of them move into the category [*dal*] of agricultural labourers every year. Hence it is entirely appropriate that they be considered kisans, indeed, they must be included in this class [*varg*].

It is an issue which requires further consideration. The term kisan includes in its meanings many different kinds of peasants.[18] Even those who hold 20,000 *bighas* of *raiyati* lands dare to call themselves kisans. But correctly speaking, they are zamindars---true zamindars, as they can easily deceive people under the pretense of being kisans. Generally, only those whose chief means of livelihood is agriculture should be called kisans, which means that those who are not primarily dependent on agriculture cannot make this claim. Under such conditions those who have vast raiyati holdings and, while maintaining a few acres for their personal cultivation, and settle the remaining lands with others, such persons are obviously not directly dependent on agriculture for their subsistence. Secondly, they take lakhs of rupees or lakhs of maunds of grain from their subordinate tenure holders in the form of rent.[19] On the contrary, those who have some small bits of land or none at all but carry on the cultivation of others' lands on *batai*, or some other rent settlement arrangement, and per chance also work as labourers in others' fields---all these can be called kisans.[20] But that person whose family's principal means of livelihood is labour, though generally not regarded as a kisan, should not be taken out of the category [*shreni*] of kisan so long as he subsists by working at least in the fields of petty landholders [*chote mote khetihar*] and does not work on vast plantations or large farms. The sum and substance is that so long as there is any hope of acquiring even some small plot of land and subsisting by cultivating that land, he can be called kisan. But this possibility vanishes where modern farms are cultivated by tractors and capitalism sets its foot in agriculture. There the agricultural labourers instead of being kisans inevitably become labourers, or part of the proletariat. Consequently as these farms will grow in number so will the number of real agricultural labourers go on increasing.

As a matter of fact kisans can be divided into three categories [*dal*]: (1) the poor kisan, (2) the middle kisan, and, (3) the rich kisan. Stalin, the creator of present-day Russia, in an important collection of essays and speeches illuminates this issue clearly. So far as the question of kisans is concerned, the condition in Russia at that time was similar to that of India. So Stalin's observation on page 308 of his collected essays (*Leninism*) is of great value to us. It runs thus:

> The Russian peasants compromise three main categories: (1) rich peasants, or kulaks, whose farms are large and who employ wage-labour; these form a "rural bourgeoisie." The village money-lenders and liquor sellers under the old regime were also termed "kulaks." <27.7.41> (2) Middle peasants, who work their holdings themselves with the aid of their families, but do not usually employ wage labour. (3) Poor peasants,

> who have very small holdings or none at all, being mainly agricultural labourers (for wages) and half peasants or semi-proletarians (who work in the towns at certain seasons).[21]

There are many significant facts in this account. Firstly, in general terms the description of Russian peasants given here compares cent per cent with the kisans of India. The rich and poor kisans referred to here are exactly like those found in our country. There is absolutely no difference. In Russia agricultural labourers have been included in the category of poor kisans. This is the case in India as well. It is a different thing if we disagree or fail to understand this position. But the condition is the same in both places. Of course there is some difference between the condition of the middle kisans here and the middle kisans in Russia. Here because of false religious values, the middle kisans hire labourers for their agricultural work. Mostly it is Brahmans and some Kshatriyas who abstain from direct involvement in the work of agriculture.[22] Due to these false religious injunctions even poor Brahman kisans do not do ploughing themselves. But this in itself makes little difference in their economic condition, inasmuch as the middle peasants of India are engaged primarily in subsistence agriculture. Their harvest is very seldom sufficient to be sold in the market. By this I mean specifically food grains. Sugarcane, chillies, tobacco and such other cash crops are of course meant for sale. But the peasants do not do this to become rich, but rather to meet their basic subsistence needs.

The second important factor is that the third category of poor kisans is mainly composed of agricultural labourers. At most they are half kisans and half labourers, that is to say they work in their fields for a period of time and when free they go to the towns to work and earn. This is cent per cent found in India as well. By identifying "agricultural labourers (for wages)" as he does, Stalin means to suggest that poor kisans who work in the fields but are not doing so on wage payment are also in fact agricultural labourers. I have written about this issue earlier.

Thirdly, those who have no lands at all are also counted as poor kisans. I have already said that it is not necessary that they must possess lands to be considered poor kisans. Wherever there is scope for or hope of getting land, there the agricultural labourers should be called kisans. In Russia this was also true. Of course agricultural labourers of large farms who have no hope of getting lands are real labourers, there as well as here, and the rest are at the most half labourers.

Those who do not believe that the poor kisans of our country are also a kind of labourer will find more discussion about this issue further on. But here I give an extract from the enquiry report of Dr. Harold H. Mann, Director of the Department of Agriculture of the Government of Bombay. He had inquired into the economic condition of the kisans of a village in the Poona District in 1914-15. The government did not believe the results of the report which was too heartrending and for which they were quite unprepared. Hence they inquired into the condition of yet another village, the results of which were published in 1921. But when it was found that these results were even more painful than the first, they were inevitably obliged to accept it.[23] Whereas in the first village only eight out of 103 families could comfortably support themselves from agriculture, in the second case only ten out of 147 were able to do so. There is one further point. In the first village after taking away the eight families of the 103, of the remaining 95 families, 28 could sustain themselves only by combining their agricultural income with outside employment. But in the second case, after taking out the ten families from the 147, only twelve of the remaining 137 families were able to sustain themselves in this way. Whereas in the first village the remaining 67 families, comprising 65 percent of the total number of families, remained in a constant state of hunger, in the second case the remaining 125 families, comprising a full 85 percent of the total family population of the village, faced this dreadful circumstance. The report has mentioned still another heartrending fact about the second village. There out of a total of 732 persons, 664, that is to say nearly 91 percent of the total population were almost starving. Due to the location of an aluminum factory [actually a large ammunition factory] near the first village, 30 percent of the population worked there and were thus able to support themselves.[24] But in the absence of any such facility near the second village, conditions there were much worse.

But if we consider the minimum levels Dr. Mann used to define the villagers' living standards, in terms of the foregoing description, the extreme poverty of the kisans will be even more apparent. He has taken into account only the absolute minimum requirements of food and clothing scarcely adequate to cover the bodies of the kisans. Mann has excluded even lamps and lanterns from his list of requirements allowing the villagers to manage only by the light of the sun and the moon. He is quite clear on this: "This conclusion is reached on the basis of an estimate of the economic minimum for the ryots' standard of life, which touches the lowest level of scanty food and clothing, with no allowance for such a luxury as an artificial light." Dr. Mann apparently regarded lamp light as a luxury. He has given a full description of the two Poona villages in the two volumes of his book, *Life and Labour in a Deccan Village*, published in 1917 and 1921. He makes one further point of importance: "In the [second] village, where the minimum economic holdings would be about 20 acres, 77 percent of the holdings were below this level." "In the first village he [Mann] found that 81 percent of the holdings could not under the most favourable circumstances maintain their owners." This issue has been dealt with more fully at pages 222 and following in Palme Dutt's *India Today*, referred to earlier.[25]

The condition of agricultural labourers was also touched on by the delegation of the British Trade Union Congress which visited India in 1927-28. At page 347 of his book, Palme Dutt reports the delegation's estimate that the number of labourers capable of being organized in India is two and a half crores [25,000,000]. But out of this number at least two crores and fifteen lakhs [21,500,000] comprise only the agricultural labourers, of which nearly ten lakhs [1,000,000] belong to tea plantations, etc., and the remaining two crores and five lakhs [20,500,000] comprise those khet mazdoors who work on the small fields of Indian agriculture. It is they who have no assurance of finding regular work and mostly they are engaged by the very hungry and poorest kisans. There is simply no way they can be organized through "trade unions" in the normally accepted manner, though they can play a very significant role in the kisan movement [*andolan*]. The International Labour Office (I.L.O.) examined this matter a decade later in its 1938 report, titled *Industrial Labour in India*.[26] On page 30, the I.L.O. reported as follows:

> The total number of agricultural labourers, which was given [as] 21.5 million [two crores and 15 lakhs] in 1921, was shown by the Census of 1931 to be over 31.5 million [three crores and 15 lakhs], of whom 23 million [two crores and thirty lakhs] were estimated by the Indian Franchise Committee to be landless. . .

By landless is meant that they did not hold any raiyati or *maliki* lands. Of course they might carry on cultivation either on *batai* or *shikmi* lands or they may not be doing even that. But the Franchise Committee did accept that there were at least 85 lakhs [8,500,000] of such families of agricultural labourers at that time who possessed some lands of their own [raiyati or maliki]. Why have two crores and thirty lakhs [23,000,000] out of three crores and fifteen lakhs [31,500,000] been shown as landless? The fact that the I.L.O. includes both those who hold some land and those who are landless in the category of agricultural labourers supports my contention that agricultural labourers are in fact none other than kisans.

But some persons might still be reluctant to agree that agricultural labourers are in fact kisans. So we should examine the real condition of the kisans even more carefully. The Indian Agricultural Commission Report cites one Mr. Keatinge of the Bombay Government on this issue in the following terms: Mr. Keatinge has expressed the opinion that "the agricultural holdings of the Bombay Presidency have to a large extent been reduced to a condition in which their effective cultivation is impossible," and the economist Dr. Gilbert Slater found that similar conditions prevailed in parts of Madras. In other provinces conditions are much the same. (p.132.)[27]

Referring to Keatinge's estimate, Dr. Mann had investigated the condition of the two Deccan villages referred to above. Palme Dutt in his book writes about it in this way: "Following Keatinge's estimate that 'an economic holding of good dry land such as is most [common] in this village in the Western Deccan, and with an Indian ryot's standard of life, would be about 10 to 15 acres.'" Now let us again look at page 133 of the Indian Agricultural Commission Report. It is written there that:

> The Punjab figures, which are the only ones available for a province, indicate that 22.5 percent of the cultivators cultivate one acre or less; further, 15.4 percent cultivate between one and two and a half acres; 17.9 percent between two and a half and five acres, and 20.5 percent between five and ten acres. Except for Bombay, which would probably show a very similar result, and Burma, which would give higher averages, all other provinces have much smaller average areas per cultivator.

It is evident that in the Punjab which is regarded as the most prosperous of all provinces, 76.3 percent of kisans cultivate at most 10 acres, and as has been reported above, 10 to 15 acres are required to support a family. Hence they remain hungry. According to the Census of 1921 the average area available per family in the provinces is even less. It shows that only in Bombay the average holding is more than 10 acres. The rest are below this figure, i.e., (1) Bombay, 12.2; (2) Punjab, 9.2; (3) Central Provinces and Berar, 8.5; (4) Burma, 5.6; (5) Madras, 4.9; (6) Bengal, 3.1; (7) Bihar [and Orissa], 3.1; (8) Assam 3.0; (9) United Provinces, 2.5. This is also evident from the extract of the Agricultural Commission Report cited above that except Bombay, more than 76.3 percent of the kisans in all other provinces cultivate 10 acres or even less.

And when we take into account the fact that there are from two to fifty "intermediaries" between the land owner and the kisan who actually tills the soil, and that these many intermediaries collect rent and profit by it, then we can begin to understand how much in fact remains to the cultivating kisan.[28] In a true sense he is being looted.[29] This fact has been accepted in the recently published Report of the Floud Commission in Bengal [1940] and the point about fifty looting intermediaries also finds mention at page 340 of Volume I of the Simon Commission Report [1930] as well. It is very specific on this point:

> In some districts the sub-infeudation has grown to astonishing proportions, as many as fifty or more intermediary interests having been created between the zamindar at the top and the actual cultivator at the bottom.

When in this way a man takes land from another and "sublets" it to the third and the third to the fourth and when this process goes on, then there is practically no difference between the actual kisan and the agricultural labourers who work in the fields. In 1930 the Banking Enquiry Committee of Madras stated this fundamental issue in the following explicit terms:

> We find it difficult to draw a clear line between cultivation by farm servants and subletting. Subletting is rarely on money rental. <28.7.41> It is commonly on sharing system, the landlord getting 40 to 60 or even 80 per cent of the yield

> and the tenant the rest. The tenant commonly goes on from year to year eking out a precarious living on such terms, borrowing from the landlord, being supplied by him with seed, cattle and implements. The farmservant, on the other hand, uses the landlord's seed, cattle and implements, gets advances in cash from time to time for petty requirements, and is paid from the harvest either a lump sum of grain, or proportion of the yield. The farm servant may in some cases be paid a little cash as well as a fixed amount of the grain. The tenant may cultivate with his own stock and implements, but there is in practice no very clear line between the two, and when the landlord is an absentee, it is not always obvious whether the actual cultivator is a farmservant or a sub-tenant.

Rajni Palme Dutt makes much the same point when he writes as follows:

> But in fact the situation of the majority of small cultivators on uneconomic holdings, of sub-let tenants and unprotected tenants is not far removed from that of the agricultural labourers, and the line of distinction between the two is an extremely shadowy one. (p. 220.)

The Report of the Royal Commission on Agriculture elaborates the point as well. At page 292 of Vol. II, Part I of Evidence, figures are cited [for Bombay] showing how the number of kisans cultivating less than 15 acres is rapidly increasing. Citing a government witness, the report continues as follows:

> These figures referring only to a period of five years appear to me to show a very marked increase in the number of agriculturists cultivating holdings up to 15 acres, which excepted in a very few soils is not an area which can economically employ a pair of bullocks.

It is clear from what has been stated that there is no significant difference between the condition of the real kisans whom we call poor or middle kisans and the condition of 98 percent of agricultural labourers.[30] So far as the economic condition and the financial circumstances of both these groups, no distinction can be made. Indeed, there is no possibility of making any distinction between agricultural labourers and the poor kisans who constitute not less than 80 percent of all kisans. If some kisans can feed themselves, so must also be the case with some agricultural labourers. At the most we can say that as the condition of the kisans deteriorates those who are reduced to the lowest level are poor kisans; and in the same way generally when their condition deteriorates even further, they can then be called agricultural labourers. But it is difficult to say when the word kisan should be dropped and the term labourer begun. No such "demarcation line" (*koi sima*) can be drawn. Hence it is proper to regard the agricultural labourers, the khet mazdoors with whom we are here concerned, as kisans.

The reason for considering them as kisans has to do with the issue of their organization and movement. We must think of them as kisans so that their movement rather than being organized as a labour movement be organized like that of the kisans and only together with the kisans.

Editor's Notes to Chapter II

1. As Sahajanand makes immediately clear, this is essentially a chapter of definitions, first and foremost to clarify the meanings of the terms labourer and kisan explicitly in the Indian context, but doing so comparatively with the Russian experience and in the process drawing on a wide range of official British documentation and other sources as well. The value of this text is precisely this, that while appealing to a wide range of documentation, Sahajanand utilizes that evidence to reinforce his argument and then integrates it with his own deep experience on the ground to come up with a range of definitions and solutions that are finally his own.

As will be evident from the Hindi text which accompanies this edited translation and as I have explained in the introductory remarks to the glossary, Sahajanand seeks complete clarity and understanding in conveying his meanings, and he does so not only by elaborating his definitions in Hindi, but by using specific English terms where these will sharpen the clarity he seeks to achieve. He does this by placing either English or Hindi terms in quotation marks or parentheses. Where I have sought editorial clarification in the translation, those definitions will appear in brackets. There will be no such editorial emendations or explanations in the Hindi text itself, which appears without editorial comment, exactly as Sahajanand produced it in 1941. Indeed, the Hindi text of this brief tract is included here precisely to facilitate the Hindi reader's making his/her own assessments of Sahajanand's meanings, while the editorial notes, textual definitions, and the glossary are intended both to facilitate that process for readers of Hindi and English, and to provide as full an access as possible to Sahajanand's meanings for readers of English. Essentially, the effort is to place this document in as complete an intellectual context as can be achieved when working across two languages and more than fifty years of time.

2. This is simply to remind the reader that the 1941 dates which

appear marginally throughout this edited translation, as well as in the Hindi text are retained from the original and presumably reveal the day and the point in the manuscript where Sahajanand began work at a particular time. It is clear not only from the present text but from others of his major published works, that Sahajanand utilized his time in the Hazaribagh Central Jail in an almost non-stop effort at writing. For example, the last date entry in the manuscript copy of the *Khet Mazdoor* tract is 3.8.1941, that is, August 3, 1941 and the first date entry in his major *Kranti aur Samyukta Morcha* [Revolution and the United Front] (Patna: Shramjeevi Pustakmala, 1943), is 14.8.41, that is August 14, 1941. A partial second edition of this important book was issued at Varanasi in 1987 by the Sahajanand Shodh Sansthan, a Sahajanand research institute with CPI (M-L) Liberation connections. The editor of this partial edition is "Chandra Bhushan."

3. The exact citation is Manu 10.121. Professor Romila Thapar indicates that the reference is in the latter verses of the tenth chapter and that Sahajanand, possibly working from memory, inadvertently cited the eleventh chapter. The sloka is *bhrityanamuparadhya*.

4. With rare exception, Sahajanand has provided us specific citations for all of his quotes. In this case he simply refers to his reference to *Wage-Labour and Capital* in the preceding chapter. For a full bibliographic comment on this title please see Editorial Note 8 of Chapter I. Inasmuch as we are concerned here with Sahajanand's use of his sources and his intent in that use, we will neither attempt to track down every source he cites, nor to assess the interpretation he places on those sources. As we have indicated from the outset, *Khet Mazdoor* was written as a political tract to make a particular argument in 1941, and its interest in 1993 as a historical text or political tract is essentially to inform us of the thought and mind of one of the leading peasant activists of his day. Of course, where Sahajanand provides source references, we will utilize these explanatory endnotes to provide as complete a bibliographic citation as possible.

5. Which issue of *Das Kapital* Sahajanand had at his disposal in 1941 is of course quite impossible to estimate. Many English editions were single volume translations from the third or fourth German edition. The fact that Sahajanand refers here specifically to volume one, suggests that he might have had available the

two volume 1930 translation, reprinted in 1934 by J.M. Dent and Sons in London and Toronto and in New York by E.P. Dutton and Co. in the Everyman's Library series. This edition was translated from the fourth German edition and titled *Capital (A Critique of Political Economy*). The John Strachey title poses less of a problem inasmuch as there were two 1936 editions, London: V. Gollancz, Ltd. and New York: Random House, either of which may well have been available to Sahajanand in the Hazaribagh Central Jail. What we do know is that among the influential books in India in the 1930s, Strachey's had both the reputation and presumably the availability of a college text, or so it has been reported by a number of contemporaries. The book was very widely read and discussed in left circles in India at this time.

6. Sahajanand uses the term "farms" both in the English and in the Devanagri, sometimes in quotation marks, sometimes not. Whatever his usage, we have tried to retain his original form, whether in English or Devanagri. However, this will be the only endnote reference to the term in this edited translation.

7. As will be noted in comparing this translation with Sahajanand's original, I have taken the liberty of making a minor stylistic modification in the first sentence of this quote, where Sahajanand appears to have omitted a word or phrase. Please also note that Sahajanand has followed no consistent convention in his translation of references from the English. Often, as in the present case, there will be a fairly complete translation to the Hindi following the English quote. Sometimes that translation will precede the English quotation and sometimes Sahajanand will provide a summary translation. Rarely does he provide no translation at all. For purposes of this edited English translation, obviously I have not retranslated any of Sahajanand's Hindi translations but used only the original English as he has given it.

8. I have used the Russian Kharkov rather than the Anglicized Harkov appearing in Sahajanand's original quote from Owen. The full Owen citation is Launcelot A. Owen, *The Russian Peasant Movement, 1906-1917* (London: P.S. King and Son, Ltd., 1937).

9. For purposes of clarity I have retained Owen's spelling of the term desyatine, a Russian measure of land equaling 2.7

acres. The Russian spelling is dessiatina. For all Russian terms in this chapter and throughout the translation, I have relied on the standard *Russian-English Dictionary* compiled by Professor O.S. Akhmanova, et al., 11th edition (Moscow: Russian Language Publishers, 1977). For providing me access to this dictionary and especially for clarifying much Soviet and Russian history and reading the relevant portions of this tract where that history is an issue, I am especially indebted to Dr. Shashi Kant Jha of the School of International Studies, Jawaharlal Nehru University in New Delhi.

10. Batraki is the plural of batrak, defined in Akhmanova, *op.cit.*, as farm labourer, farm hand, hired man.

11. It is clear that Sahajanand is appealing to Lenin's logic in these pages to sustain his wider argument that in India agricultural labourers and petty kisans and poor peasants were part and parcel of the same social category on the land. The point essentially is that if compromise between the proletariat and the peasants was a necessary precondition for revolutionary success in Russia, at minimum such an accommodation must be reached between agricultural labourers and poor and even middle peasants in India if their more limited goals were to be realized.

This is incidentally, an argument Sahajanand had begun to make some years before his 1940 imprisonment and well before the writing of the *Khet Mazdoor* tract. See for example, the latter pages of his *Presidential Address*, All India Kisan Sabha, Third Session, Comilla, 13-15 May 1938 (Calcutta: Bankim Mukherji, 1938). It is also in this document that Sahajanand cites Trotsky on the relative uses of violence, that is by whom is violence used and for what purposes. Trotsky, of course, was making the point in terms of the Russian experience, Sahajanand in terms of the Gandhian idea as it related to agrarian violence in the rural countryside.

Sahajanand's Comilla address can be found in the Peasant Movements in India File, No.190 LXXXXV, Item 30, pp. 729-755, in the Manuscripts Division of the Nehru Memorial Museum and Library in New Delhi. This file, incidentally, contains a large number of other Sahajanand and Kisan Sabha materials of the thirties and forties. In addition to this bound xerox file, the NMML also holds a substantial microfilm collection of Sahajanand and related Kisan Sabha materials as well as uncatalogued files and newspapers awaiting preservation. The card catalogue at the NMML shows twenty-two published books and pamphlets under the Sahajanand listing. Apart from these specific Kisan Sabha sources, there are large numbers of Kisan Sabha and Sahajanand references both in the official collections at the National Archives of India and in the private collections of the NAI and the NMML, as the recent and forthcoming work of Amit Kumar Gupta and Bhagwan Josh make abundantly clear. For Gupta see his "The Leftists and the Rural Poor in India, 1934-39," Occasional Papers on History and Society, Second Series, No. XX (1987), NMML; and *The Agrarian Drama: The Left and the Rural Poor in India, 1934-1951*, (forthcoming, 1994); and especially the recent volume by Bhagwan Josh, *Struggle for Hegemony in India 1920-47: The Colonial State, the Left and the National Movement, Vol. II, 1934-41* (New Delhi: Sage Publications, 1992).

12. It might be noted that Sahajanand had some experience in organizing factory workers, so his observations here are not drawn entirely from second-hand reading about urban Indian or Western industrial experience. There was in Bihta, which is primarily an agricultural marketing centre, the Bihta Sugar Mill, processing sugar cane from the adjacent area and Sahajanand was long active in mobilizing those workers, most of whom were, of course, also peasants and khet mazdoors. The sugar mill is on the main railway line in the centre of Bihta, but not far removed from Sahajanand's ashram on the outer edge of the town. For an introduction to these issues in the latter part of Sahajanand's career, see the Peasant Movements in India File, No. 190 LXXXXV, Item 8, dated 1947, in the Manuscripts Division of the Nehru Memorial Museum and Library in New Delhi. This is Sahajanand's speech to the cane growers.

13. As indicated in the initial note of Chapter I, a crore in Indian usage is ten million.

14. It is here where Sahajanand brings to bear on his argument the social, cultural, and practical difficulties of rural life and the immediate experiences of the khet mazdoors, that his writing is at its descriptive richest and most potent. Few who have not experienced the demanding rigour of field work of any kind, can fully appreciate Sahajanand's question about the strength and energy that remains at day's end for mobilizing and organizing political activism.

15. Sahajanand's point here is obviously well taken especially as it relates to "other agriculturally-related work," if not yet to the use of the plough with a team of bullocks. The example of a Maithil Brahman using a *khurpi*, that is, a hand-held weeding instrument to clean the weeds in a field of young sugar cane in the early morning sun of a late March day in 1993, is revealing evidence of Sahajanand's observation. In the case cited, the Maithil landowner at some point presumably found it economically necessary to undertake this manual field labour rather than assign it to a khet mazdoor, and in his present more affluent circumstances he still finds it a rational economic decision little influenced by cultural constraints. He is, coincidentally, the owner of one of the wheat threshing machines in the village, which during harvesting season is in constant use at the rate of Rs.25/- per hour, or one bundle in ten of cut grain. See also Chapter IV, where Sahajanand returns briefly to this issue, especially at my Editorial Note 16.

16. Both Sahajanand's anxieties and his prescient sensitivity to the potential for conflict between peasant tenants and khet mazdoors comes out clearly in these pages, and of course, has been revealed in the sharp conflict and violence between newly organized khet mazdoors and newly rich middle peasants, bataidars, and owners in many parts of Bihar, including precisely those districts of South Central Bihar where Sahajanand and the Kisan Sabha were active in the 1930s. This suggestion is not meant to exclude owners whose social, political, and cultural history in the agrarian environment of Bihar involved them in the past and continues to involve them in precisely the conflict Sahajanand anticipated so many years ago.

For a more detailed comment on the historical background of agrarian radicalism in Bihar see my essay, "Violence, Agrarian Radicalism, and the Audibility of Dissent: Electoral Politics and the Indian People's Front," appearing as Ch. 15 in Harold Gould and Sumit Ganguly, eds., *The Indian Elections of 1989 and 1991* (Boulder: Westview Press, 1993).

17. A *kattha* is one-twentieth part of a *bigha*, which is itself a locally and regionally variable measure of land in India. In villages immediately neighbouring Madhubani town in North Bihar one acre equals one bigha, two katthas and eighteen *dhurs*, a dhur being one-twentieth part of a kattha. This means that in this region an acre is equal to approximately twenty-three

katthas, whereas in Patna District the bigha is a considerably smaller measure, one acre there being equal to thirty-three katthas. Apart from the implications one may draw from these local variations in land measurement, there is the further point that the measurements themselves are calculated in almost infinitesimally small sizes of ownership and especially cultivating plots and fields. The implications of this process of elaborated subdivision and subletting are touched on in the Editor's Notes to Chapter I and in Note 25 of this chapter.

18. It is in this and the immediately succeeding paragraphs and pages where Sahajanand comes to his most explicit definitions of the terms peasants and agricultural labourers.

19. A maund is an Indian measure of weight equaling 82.29 pounds or 37.32 kilograms. The Indian division of the maund is the *seer*, forty of which equal one maund.

20. Batai is a share-cropping arrangement arrived at on various terms, but most often in terms of a half/half division of the crop and locally varying agreements about production inputs. The sharecropper is hence a *bataidar*.

21. These were and are familiar agrarian categories and definitions. What Sahajanand provides us in these pages is a more subtle definition of these categories in the rural environment of India. For an elaboration of Sahajanand's definitions in terms both of caste and the critical issue of who does the actual work, see James R. Hagen, "Indigenous Society, The Political Economy and Colonial Education in Patna District: A History of Social Change from 1811 to 1951 in Gangetic North India," PhD Dissertation, University of Virginia, 1981. This manuscript is available at the Nehru Memorial Museum and Library in New Delhi. The assumption is that Sahajanand had available to him in Hazaribagh either one of the two current editions of Joseph Stalin's *Leninism*, the two volume set published in London by G. Allen and Unwin, Ltd., between 1928-33 or the 1940 edition, apparently in one volume by the same publisher.

22. On this issue of changing attitudes and practices to the actual physical work of agriculture, see my Editor's Note 15, above.

23. The first village Mann and his associates investigated was Pimpla Saudagar; the second more isolated village situated approximately twenty-five miles northeast of Poona was Jategaon Budruk. The publications emerging from these studies and to which Sahajanand refers were Harold Hart Mann, *Land and*

Labour in a Deccan Village (London and Bombay: H. Milford, Oxford University Press, 1917), and *Land and Labour in a Deccan Village, Study No. 2* (London: H. Milford, Oxford University Press, 1921). For a short and fascinating comment on Mann and his work in India by an especially sensitive observer of Indian agriculture see Daniel Thorner, "Social and Economic Studies of Dr. H.H. Mann," in Thorner, *The Shaping of Modern India* (New Delhi: Allied Publishers Private Ltd., 1981), pp. 339-48. There are many other essays in this collection of Thorner's work of directly related interest to readers of Sahajanand's *Khet Mazdoor* essay. Most of this writing relates to the Indian experience but some also goes beyond that experience in a direct sense, but nevertheless bears on the issues Sahajanand has raised both for India and Russia and the issue of the peasant economy generally. See for example Thorner's "A Post-Marxian Theory of Peasant Economy: The School of A.V. Chayanov," pp. 325-38. Tangentially, but important for the same reasons to readers of *Khet Mazdoor* are Thorner's lectures on land reform in India delivered in 1955 at the Delhi School of Economics under the title *The Agrarian Prospect in India*. Happily, that little volume, dedicated to Harold H. Mann has since appeared in a second edition, and reprinted by Allied Publishers Private, Ltd., New Delhi: 1981. Also of related interest will be the essay by G.G. Kotovski, "Indian Agricultural Labourer: A Soviet View," *Economic Weekly* (April 14, 1956), pp. 443-48.

24. This was the government arms factory at Kirkee. Sahajanand apparently misread or misremembered aluminium for ammunition in this case.

25. The critical point Sahajanand is trying to convey here in citing Mann and Palme Dutt is that more than size, it is the quality of the land, apart from any potential infrastructural inputs, that must be considered in evaluating the productive value and hence the economic, social, and political status or situation of a peasant on a given holding of land. It is an issue to which Sahajanand will return in later chapters.

26. This volume issued by the International Labour Office was published in Geneva in 1938 and concerned itself with labour and labouring classes, labour laws and legislation, wages, costs and standards of living, and hours of labour.

27. The Indian Agricultural Commission Report to which Sahajanand refers here and in the pages following is the *Report of the*

Royal Commission on Agriculture issued by the Government of India in 1928, and often referred to as the Linlithgow Commission for its chairman and the subsequent Viceroy (1936-1943), Lord Linlithgow. The first witness called by the Commission was none other than Harold H. Mann whose views by this time were beginning to gain even official acceptance. Indeed, he was encouraged to submit fresh evidence to the Commission on the two villages he had previously studied.

The Keatinge whom both the Commission and Dr. Mann cite was Gerald Francis Keatinge, who had a long background of experience in Bombay agriculture. His two books on the subject were *Rural Economy in the Bombay Deccan* (London: Longmans, Green and Co., 1912), and *Agricultural Progress in Western India* (London: Longmans, Green and Co., 1921).

28. The term intermediary does not quite carry the full richness of meaning of the Hindi in this case, that is, *ek upar ek*, literally meaning one above the other, which defines in clear and explicit terms the multi-tiered system of intermediaries which functions in economic, social and political terms between the land controller and the actual cultivator. It is an idea C.A. Bayly puts very nicely in a review article considering the first four volumes of the *Subaltern Studies* scholarship edited by Ranajit Guha (Delhi: Oxford University Press, 1982-1985). He makes the point that, "Down almost to the very bottom of society every subaltern was an elite to someone lower than him." (See C.A. Bayly, "Rallying Around the Subaltern," *The Journal of Peasant Studies* 16:1 (October 1988), p.119).

29. It is useful to recall here that the English verb, to loot is a direct etymological derivative of the Hindi term *lootna*.

30. Sahajanand has marshalled an impressive array of evidence in this chapter and in these concluding pages to make his point that the complex range of overlapping interests of rights, of subinfeudation, and ultimately of social and economic exploitation, allow for only the most subtle margins of difference between real kisans and agricultural labourers. At this stage real kisans include not only poor kisans on the economic margin but middle kisans as well, a conceptual, ideological, and political problem he will return to again and again. But for the moment the point is that there is no demarcation line, to use his English term, between khet mazdoors and peasants at the bottom of the system, and in his concluding paragraph Sahajanand explains exactly why this is and must be the case, in political terms.

CHAPTER III
Their Problems

[In this brief chapter Sahajanand pointedly examines what he considers to be some of the most serious of the problems facing the khet mazdoors, namely those of wages, indebtedness, and debt bondage. The only way to break this cycle, he argues is to meet the agricultural labourer's hunger for land, thereby to provide some minimum basis for a stable livelihood. He begins the chapter by identifying these problems as economic and touching the poor and destitute of all castes and religions, not simply Untouchables. But if the problems are economic, the attitudes which colour the general perception of khet mazdoors as base and low are social and cultural and these too must change. Ed.]

Inasmuch as we have identified the population of agricultural labourers as belonging to the category of poor kisans, some question might then be raised about the need for further inquiry into the condition of these labourers. It is a legitimate question. However, only by identifying the full realities of the day to day lives of agricultural labourers can we even think of finding serious solutions to the problems which confront them. Only when the disease has been correctly diagnosed, can the appropriate medicine be prescribed and a lasting cure effected.

It is also the case that many false and deceptive issues are raised in the name of agricultural labourers. Mistaken "approaches" to their problems are proposed and the suggestions for resolving them are thus also wrong. In the process everyone is deceived, a danger which must be avoided at all costs. It is for this reason that we raise here the full range of issues relating to the lives of agricultural labourers.

We have seen an effort for some time, both directly and indirectly, to confuse the movement of agricultural labourers with the caste movement of the socially most depressed members of the society. Those involved have assumed that there is no distinction between the *Dalits* or Harijans and the agricultural labourers. It is for this reasons that the leaders of Harijan organizations have for so long led the movement of the agricultural labourers. It is clear, however, that others have been behind them in this effort.[1]

The one unfortunate consequence of this development has been that the basic problems of the agricultural labourers have been ignored and in their place only some broad questions have been raised. This has limited to a few particular castes what is a large and complex range of issues involving all khet mazdoors. Secondly, the problem has in the process been coloured by questions of religion. It is our misfortune that the problems of the Harijans have intentionally been given a religious form in this country. And when the problem of the agricultural labourers is viewed only as a Harijan problem, then automatically it also gets a religious colouring, though perhaps not so deep. But this is wrong and dangerous. In fact, the problem of the Harijans instead of being religious is economic, and this is an absolutely fundamental point. But the problem of agricultural labourers is cent per cent economic. Agricultural labourers include the poor and destitute of all castes and religions. I have already established this fact in the first two chapters.

Though the question of agricultural labourers is economic, this is perhaps still not the most central issue. The truly fundamental issue is that this problem does not belong to a "fixed class" (*mukarrar dal*). Our greatest blunder would be to assume that agricultural labourers are persons limited to particular castes and communities and that their numbers are, in a sense, fixed. Doing so will prevent us from arriving at real solutions to this problem. The class (*jamaat*) of agricultural labourers is growing rapidly. Persons who until yesterday were prosperous kisans are being added daily to the numbers of khet mazdoors. Another critical issue, which has already been raised is that the class of agricultural labourers is not outside the larger class of kisans. Finally, to restate the argument yet again, instead of giving this issue a religious colour, it must be considered cent per cent economic, related to agricultural labourers and Harijans alike. If we mistakenly introduce religious considerations into the movement, its very soul will be desroyed. In our further considerations these several points must be clearly borne in mind.

<29.7.41> However important these larger issues are to the movement of agricultural labourers, by comparison with the daily adversities which they suffer, they are certainly distant and remote to the labourers themselves. Nor do their so-called leaders fully comprehend them. But our concern with resolving these immediate problems of the agricultural labourers must not preclude our placing them in the larger social, economic, and cultural context in which they occur. Yet this larger context can be understood only when we apprehend fully the problems faced by the agricultural labourers every day of their lives. What are these problems and what is their nature?[2]

The first question is that of wages. Agricultural labourers receive neither an annual or a monthly salary. They are paid daily wages and then only when they work. If there is no work they receive nothing. On the surface this seems as it should be. But if we probe beneath the surface, the truth is more painful. For example, when the agricultural labourer is sick or disabled his family and other dependants must starve. Of the demands of the [factory] workers, the first and foremost is that there should be a guarantee of their livelihood during illness and old age. But as we have shown, agricultural labourers are not in the same category as these workers. Hence, for them this has never been a consideration. But when the ox of a trader or kisan is not being used to carry a load or pull the plough, does it not then still get its fodder? Why then should human beings be treated any differently when there is no work or when they fall ill or become infirm. It is difficult to comprehend. Hence it can be argued that agricultural labourers should at least be similarly provided for in circumstances of illness, old age or at other times of need.[3]

The second question which arises with regard to wages, is what they should be? It is accepted by everyone that the wages of an agricultural labourer must at minimum be sufficient to provide for his basic requirements of food, clothing, and medicine, and those of his dependants. The problem is that neither government nor any other agency has established minimum wage norms designed to meet these basic needs. This is a great obstacle in determining what the "minimum living wage" of agricultural labourers should in fact be. This is one of the central questions, and it is the responsibility of the leaders of the agricultural labourers to help make this determination.[4] Failing this, unrealistic demands may be put forward which can never be fulfilled until far-reaching changes are made in the economic condition of the kisans themselves. Instead of being simply idealistic, we must also be practical. It should not be forgotten that by agricultural labourers

I mean those who work for and with the poor and ordinary kisans. These labourers who work for the petty kisans, constitute the majority of agricultural labourers and the most important thing is to determine what their wage should be. Hence we should not put forward demands which the kisans cannot fulfil even by selling their houses and fields. To do so would inevitably result in unwanted hostility and conflict between the khet mazdoors and the kisans.[5]

In considering the question of wages we must also take note of past experience as it relates to the circumstances which prevail today. After such a comparison we will be in a better position to make legitimate claims on behalf of the agricultural labourers. Some useful facts have been provided in the survey and settlement reports of the districts and in other documents as well. But especially valuable in this regard is the book of Dr. Radhakamal Mukerjee, *Land Problems of India*, in which he shows at page 222 how there was a rise and fall in the wages of agricultural labourers over the last hundred years in India.[6] He has taken the year 1842 as his starting point. In order to place this rise and fall in wages in a broader perspective, he has also provided the selling price of rice per rupee at the time. Wages were paid only in cash and on a daily basis. In his description, there was no other arrangement for providing food to supplement the cash wage. When the selling price of rice was 40 seers per rupee in 1842, wages were one anna per day. After ten years in 1852 the selling price of rice became 30 seers per rupee and the wage had become one and a half annas. In 1862 when it was 27 seers, the wage was two annas. Again in 1872 it rose to three annas when the selling price of rice was 23 seers per rupee. In 1911 when rice was sold at 15 seers the wage was four annas and in 1922 when rice was sold at 5 seers the wage was 4 to 6 annas. Dr. Mukerjee also cites the quinquennial wage report published by the United Provinces government in 1934 to show that the average wage in that province was three annas. In 326 villages it was only one and a half annas.

It is clear from Dr. Mukerjee's evidence that as the price of rice, i.e., foodstuffs, was becoming more dear, wages were also increasing to match those price rises. These figures also show that there was in fact a gradual increase in the wage level relative to prices, permitting a marginal improvement in the subsistence possibilities of the agricultural labourers. This trend is consistent for the period from 1842 to 1911. By the year 1911 when the wages had increased fourfold [over 1842], rice was available at 15 seers, although according to these calculations it should have been available at the rate of only 10 seers per rupee. This trend is more or less evident in 1852, 1862 and 1872 and this is as it should be. But this pattern does not continue in the year 1922. Whereas the price of rice had increased from 40 seers per rupee in 1842 to five seers in 1922, wages instead of rising eight fold from one to eight annas or more, at maximum remained at six annas and at some places wages were only four annas. How and why this should be the case is difficult to comprehend. It appears that the first war of imperialism which broke out in Europe after 1911 and which embroiled almost all the countries of the world, created confusion in every sphere, and consequently the natural upward trend in the rise of wages was also negatively affected. The accepted theory regarding mill labourers, as I have already indicated, was that wages must be at least sufficient to maintain the labourer and his dependants. But even this theory is not being implemented in this age of imperialism inasmuch as labourers are available in plenty. Hence they are paid the minimum possible wages. Perhaps the same thing is happening to agricultural labourers.[7] The reason is that their number is growing very rapidly; where one is required four are available. In these circumstances, why will anyone be concerned with questions of their wages or their general well-being? Whatever its cause, this state of affairs is deplorable and portends a terrible catastrophe in the years ahead. This prospect will be considered later.

Another relevant issue is that where the kisans pay wages both in cash and kind, even this combined amount seldom provides a minimum living wage. My personal experience is that at some places it is never sufficient. Yet another consideration is that the grain which is given is always of poor quality and this is true even if the labourers are provided with mid-morning food. I understand that this is so because of the helplessness of the very poor kisans themselves. They eat the same coarse grain. Still, this has become common practice and well-to-do kisans also follow it in imitation. What prompts them to do so is impossible to understand. Their behaviour takes undue advantage of the helplessness of the agricultural labourers. As if they were not be regarded as human beings.

The practice of paying the khet mazdoor a proportionate share of the cut crop is prevalent in many provinces with many variations and peculiarities in the system, whether the division is done in the field at the time of harvesting or at the *khalihan* [i.e., on the threshing floor] of the kisan. At some places out of 12 bundles of paddy or the winter *rabi* crop [wheat, pulses, gram, etc.], the labourer's share is one, at other places the ratio is 16 to 1 or 20 to 1 and in some cases 24 to 1, although this latter ratio is found very rarely. Twenty to 1 is found more often and the ratios of 12 to 1 and 16 to 1 occur commonly. Why such wide variation is found is diffcult to understand. It is not known how and when these distinctions were first introduced. This is a kind of contract system and must have begun at a time when the demand for harvesters and carriers was very great. But now these practices are found everywhere. This wage contract system is unjust in any circumstances and its dramatic variation from place to place makes it even more painful.[8]

After wages, the next question to be raised is that of indebtedness and the related practice of debt bondage.[9] It is a complex problem which has taken many different forms throughout the country. At some places it is referred to as *halwahi*, at other places as *kamiauti*, and at still other places it is known by yet other names. No one can say precisely when this practice of debt bondage was begun.[10] It appears to be a variation of an ancient form of slavery. Under this system, the *halwaha*, i.e., the ploughman or the khet mazdoor in fact becomes the slave of the kisan.[11] At some places he becomes the slave of even the moneylender or the village shopkeeper and that too along with his children for generations on end. The system of debt bondage purposely assumes no official or legal form. In many places there is no indication showing the initial amount of the loan made by the kisan. He might make some personal notation for his own purposes, but otherwise there is no formal record of the arrangement. It is entirely oral. But it remains a lifelong burden on the khet mazdoor from which it is virtually impossible to extricate himself. This bondage is literally without escape inasmuch as the *kamiauta* or *halwaha* have no means of paying off the debt they have assumed. It will not be cleared even in a thousand years, no matter if the labourer goes on working endlessly for his owner, or *malik* until the day he dies. Of course, in theory the debt is free from interest, with the peculiarity, however, that the principal remains always the same. An interest-bearing loan is something quite different and functions the same for the khet mazdoor as for anyone else.

Any ploughman or labourer might fall victim to these conditions of debt bondage. The forefathers of the mazdoor might have taken a loan either in cash or kind at a time of urgent financial need, or on the occasion of a marriage. That debt would then be carried over from generation to generation. If any other kisan wishes to engage a particular bonded ploughman or labourer, he must first assume his debt, that is, by paying it off to the first kisan. And if the latter wishes to engage yet another *kamiauta* he would advance that recovered amount to a mazdoor in order to enslave him as his agriculture labourer. Now the practice of bonded labour is gradually dying out and is being replaced by a simple loan system. But at one time it was widespread and even today it is found at many places. One of the reasons for this is that certain castes are obliged by custom to feast their kith and kin on the occasion of marriage and death ceremonies and to arrange for them wine and toddy [i.e., country beer] at these times. This is one of the ways in which bonded indebtedness may begin, whether the *kamiauti* system in Bihar or the *halwahi* system in the United Provinces. Similar systems are found in other provinces as well. In Gujarat the transition from kisan to bonded labourer occurred among the *halis*, or ploughmen and the *dublas*, or agricultural labourers. In the past, the *halis* and *dublas* were true kisans but through the long process of mortgaging their lands and becoming indebted, they have effectively been enslaved. The *hari* of Sindh is a true kisan and not unlike the *hali* of Gujarat before his bondage. <30.7.41>

Entire families, including husbands, wives, and children can become the lifelong "bond slaves" of the moneylender in this process of perpetuated indebtedness. They must go to the moneylender's house even before dawn, draw the day's water, boil it for bathing, then bathe their malik, wash his clothes, feed the cattle, do cultivation and all other work and take their leave only in the night. This is their daily routine. If per chance they are a bit late, they are slapped and abused. If they attempt to escape they will find no shelter. Wherever they go they are interrogated about their escape, as if the name *hali* and *dubla* is a stamp of slavery. Everyone regards them as having been someone's slave. They cannot become free. And not only this. The moneylenders and Parsi wine merchants who enslave them, employ one or two Pathan strongmen whose main function is to search out the escaped slaves and return them, no matter the distance. Beating and assaulting the *halis* is common. And the remarkable thing is that whereas in other provinces the *kamiauti* system and similar forms of bonded labour are dying out of their own accord, the *hali* system is gaining momentum. Now, however, through the agitations of the Gujarat Provincial Kisan Sabha even this system is being rooted out.[12]

Once a *dubla* youth in the area of Haripura in Gujarat, narrated to me his story. He explained that he worked like a slave in the home of a Parsi. He had to go there at four in the morning, boil the water and bathe him. The slave had to soap and rub his malik's body and wash him. In this process, if the Parsi felt the least irritation from the rough hands of the *dubla*, he would slap him. But the slave had heard speeches of the Kisan Sabha and this gave him courage and one day when his Parsi owner gave him a slap, he returned the slap and fled, and since that time he has been free.

In short, the bonded labourers are not only enslaved for life, but poorly fed and grossly mistreated as well. The *dubla* gets only a meager breakfast, a coarse meal in the day and a bit of grain and two to four pice at day's end. In illness they receive neither medicine nor clothes to wear, and indeed, then too they must work, as the *dubla* women do even when pregnant. And the small children are not spared. They too must work, tending goats and other animals of the field and otherwise they are treated like the oxen of the oilpresser. All of this the bonded labourers must do to eat, otherwise they will starve. And beyond that, as basic needs arise, they are obliged to take new loans deepening even further their bondage. Their only hope of liberation from this cycle of debt and slavery is revolt; only by becoming rebels, as in the kisan movement, are they now being freed.

Under these circumstances there is a persistent desire for land, to assure the agricultural labourer some minimum basis for a stable livelihood.[13] In Bihar and the United Provinces it is the custom for the kisan to provide some small amount of land to every *halwaha*. Though these small plots are cultivated with the kisan's plough and his oxen, they are never sufficient to meet the labourer's needs. Moreover, the kisan is under no obligation to provide such lands. And now at a time when the number of agricultural labourers is growing and there is no reason for the kisan to pay higher wages, he will likewise feel no need to provide land, no matter how little. Accordingly, however great the desire of the khet mazdoor for land, his desire will be fulfilled only with the greatest difficulty. This issue of land constitutes one of the major problems for the agricultural labourers. In the absence of some such small holding, the labourer is at the mercy of the zamindar and others who may demand *begar*, i.e., forced labour, failing which the mazdoor will literally be driven out of house and home. These conditions simply are not acceptable. They must be resolved by providing agricultural labourers some basic minimum holding thereby to enable them to sustain life and limb.

Finally but not the least, are the social attitudes which account for the crude maltreatment meted out to the khet mazdoors.[14] Among the agricultural labourers there are some castes which are regarded, though wrongfully, as base, low, and mean. They are not regarded as we regard ourselves. They are not presumed to have any sense of self respect. What a tragedy it is that those who are most indispensable to the very sustenance of society and without whom all its comforts would go unmet, should be viewed in these terms. Regarding these men and women and children as low and less than human is an act of gross ignorance; it is the height of lunacy. The result is that the *halwaha* of today is thought of as a *halwaha* forever. He is forever regarded as low, so much so that the word *halwaha* or ploughman has come to mean fool and illiterate, uncivilized and unwise. Hence, who will understand the need of educating the children of the khet mazdoors? Who can have in his heart any feeling of respect and honour for them? Who will respect the honour of their mothers and sisters? Who will think that they should participate in the experience of civilization? Who can be concerned to save them from a kind of gradual death, experienced only by the insects and worms? Who will assume the responsibility for dealing with this very complex range of issues? If these are the attitudes which prevail in the society at large, there is no escape, much as when bhang is dropped into the village well, then too there is no escape for anyone who drinks from that well.

In this way we have considered five fundamental problems in the lives of the agricultural labourers of India; those of wages, indebtedness and debt bondage, their hunger for land, the gross maltreatment to which they are subjected, and the attitudes which lead to this maltreatment. These problems urgently await solution. The sooner such solutions are achieved, the better it will be. Therein lies everyone's welfare.

Editor's Notes to Chapter III

1. This is a thinly veiled criticism of Jagjivan Ram as the main Harijan political actor in Congress politics in Bihar in the 1930s. While Sahajanand had no compunction about naming Vallabhbhai Patel as the chief opponent of the Kisan Sabha in the Congress, as he does in the Introduction to *Khet Mazdoor*, one can only presume that out of respect for Rajendra Prasad, with whom Sahajanand also had profound differences and who was one of Jagjivan Ram's key patrons, Sahajanand nevertheless thought better of in effect attacking Rajendra Prasad, Jagjivan Ram, and a set of Harijan interests Sahajanand differed with but did not wish to alienate.

The politics of these relationships are touched on in a series of khet mazdoor petitions to Jagivan Ram in 1938 when he was Parliamentary Secretary in Bihar. These petitions, from agricultural labourers in Patna and Shahabad districts and complaining of maltreatment and underpayment by the kisans who employed them, were forwarded by Jagjivan Ram to Jayaprakash Narayan with the request that he "please enquire into these alleged atrocities of the Kisans," and that he do so "personally or through some of your trusted lieutenants and get the grievances of the Khetmazdoors redressed." The degree of involvement of Jagjivan Ram in this episode appears to confirm Sahajanand's allegation that it was marginal at best. These documents also make amply clear the issue Sahajanand refers to again and again throughout this text, namely the potential conflict of interest between the agricultural labourers and the peasants who employ them, and the fact that some peasants presumed the Kisan Sabha to be a class organization which could be used in their conflict with the khet mazdoors. (See Jayaprakash Narayan Papers, Parts I and II, File 149, NMML, New Delhi).

It is also interesting to note that Sahajanand uses both the terms Dalit, a common usage of the 1990s, as well as Harijan, Gandhi's nomenclature for Untouchables. Dalit literally means depressed, downtrodden, and exploited, whereas Harijan means children or people of God. Sahajanand's critical distinction in these pages is that the exploitation of neither Untouchables nor agricultural labourers can be defined in religious and cultural terms, which in effect deflects attention from the economic, which is in Sahajanand's view ultimately the fundamental point. It will not pass notice that this argument about religion and economics is coming from a man of the saffron robe, deeply steeped in the classical traditions of Hinduism, who at the same time has been totally immersed in the lives of the rural poor and is defining his own social and religious values precisely at this time in more radical ideological terms. His preface to the *Gita-Hriday* [The Heart of the Gita] (Allahabad: Kitab Mahal, 1948), was written on January 1, 1942, while Sahajanand was still in the Hazaribagh Central Jail. The book is clearly an effort to compare and reconcile the Gita and Marxism. It is on this occasion after his decision on the "People's War" in consonance with the CPI, and less than three months before his early release from Hazaribagh that Sahajanand for the first time, identifies himself in the preface to *Gita-Hriday* as a political prisoner [*rajbandi*].

2. To repeat a point which emerges so often in everything that Sahajanand writes, while he is fundamentally concerned with the larger political and theoretical definitions of the human experience and the ideological form these definitions may take, his deepest concern is what this all means in the lives of the rural poor and how this reality of immediate day to day experience can be brought into some relevant conjunction with the wider world of theory and politics. So he turns to those issues of most direct concern to the khet mazdoors on the ground, namely wages, indebtedness, and debt bondage. And as will be obvious both in the original Hindi and in the English translation, he does so with a degree of vividness seldom seen in print. His descriptions do not come from library research but from the lived experience of knowing what it means to be a peasant and an agricultural labourer.

3. Sahajanand raises an issue here that has immediate relevance in 1993, namely what is described in the organized industrial

sector, which comprises approximately seventeen million workers, as the "exit", or retrenchment policy. These are workers covered by provident fund and gratuity schemes, who in 1993 continue to benefit from these programmes, though many of the industries which employ them may be non-productive, that is, "sick" industries. It is alleged that indeed a substantial percentage of these employees, while receiving full benefits and salaries do not in fact engage in productive labour. The suggestion is that not only is this a drain on the national exchequer, it is, as Sahajanand pointed out in 1941 discriminatory against the vast bulk of Indian labourers, namely agricultural labourers, who functioned then as they do now with few benefits of any kind, and who certainly are paid only for those days on which they work. It might be added coincidentally, that any attempts at retrenchement through a rational exit policy in industry is opposed by labour unions of all political and ideological persuasions, with concerns about election vote banks high on that agenda of opposition. For an introduction to the range of economic issues which impinge on retrenchment in "sick" industries in the organized sector and how this relates to agricultural labour, see the speech of Shri Dayanand Sahay in the Rajya Sabha, May 4, 1993, Mr. Sahay is a Congress Party MP in the upper house of India's Parliament.

4. Sahajanand raises two issues here, namely what should the wages of agricultural labourers be and who should make this determination? In fact, since his writing in 1941 there have been numerous government reports, recommendations, and legislations on the subject, and many of these have of course become grist for the populist politics of the day by all parties, especially at election time. However, it is also the case that it is precisely in those parts of the country where the issue of wages has become central to the programmes of radical agrarian activists at election time and beyond, that political movements of the rural poor have flourished, and at the same time raised vigorous opposition. Eastern U.P. and the districts of South Central Bihar are cases in point. The daily press and news journals are filled with stories of these reactions and counter reactions. To quote a recent report from *Sunday* (21-27 March 1993),

p. 42: "Whenever the agricultural labourers have raised their voice for a fair deal, they have either been implicated in criminal cases or killed by the landlords. The peasants have lost confidence in the government due to the nexus between the landlords, police and the administration."

The literature on agricultural wages is very substantial and can only be touched on here. However, for those who wish to pursue the matter, each of the titles cited carry detailed bibliographic references. One of the best historical points of departure remains Dharma Kumar, *Land and Caste in South India: Agricultural Labour in the Madras Presidentcy During the Nineteenth Century* (New Delhi: Manohar Publishers, 1992). Please see especially the references in the new introduction to this reprint of Professor Kumar's 1965 Cambridge book. For a more recent treatment, again focussing on Tamilnadu, see V.K. Ramachandran, *Wage Labour and Unfreedom in Agriculture: An Indian Case Study* (Oxford: Clarendon Press, 1990). At a more intimate level of inquiry and also concerned with South India is the work of M.Atchi Reddy. See for example his "Wages Data for Private Agricultural Accounts, Nellore District, 1893-1974," *The Indian Economic and Social History Review* 16:3 (1979), pp. 301-321; and "Work and Leisure: Daily Working Hours of Agricultural Labourers, Nellore District, 1860-1989," also in *IESHR* 28:1 (1991), pp. 73-95. On a related set of questions see Sumit Guha, "Labour Time in Agriculture: Two Essays," in the Occasional Papers on History and Society, Second Series, No. LX, of the Nehru Memorial Museum and Library, New Delhi, August 1992. For the view from Bengal see Dabjani Sen Gupta, "Khetmajoor Movement: A Case Study in West Bengal (1974)," *Social Scientist* 170 15:7 (July 1987), pp. 30-53. The story for Kerala, including the issue of wages can be found in Jose George, *Unionisation and Politicisation of Peasants and Agricultural Labourers in India* (New Delhi: Commonwealth Publishers, 1992).

For the basic data emerging from the All-India Agricultural Labour Enquiry conducted by the Ministry of Labour of the Government of India in 1950-51 see B. Ramamurti, *Agricultural Labour: How They Live and Work* (New Delhi: Ministry of

Labour, 1954). For an assessment of both the first enquiry and the Second Agricultural Labour Enquiry Report, 1956-57, see the collection of essays edited by V.K.R.V. Rao, *Agricultural Labour in India* (Bombay: Asia Publishing House, 1962). And for the brief Report of the Sub-Committee of the Parliamentary Consultative Committee For the Ministry of Labour For Studying and Reporting on the Problems of Unorganised Workers in Agriculture Sector, see the Communist Party of India pamphlet, *Problems of Unorganised Workers in "Agriculture Sector"*, (New Delhi: 1989). The Communist Party of India (Marxist) position is spelled out in the *Proceedings, Report and Resolutions of the General Council of the All India Agricultural Workers Union* (Khammam, A.P., May 1, 1989). For the most recent policy positions of the CPI (Marxist-Leninist), which through its Indian People's Front and the Bihar Provincial Kisan Sabha is the radical group most active in South Central Bihar, and as already noted, to a lesser degree in eastern U.P., see their *Basic Documents of the CPI (M-L)* and the *Political-Organisational Report*, both adopted at The 5th All-India Party Congress (Calcutta, 20-26 December, 1992).

5. Sahajanand reverts to the issue we may take as one of the central themes of this brief tract, namely that though poor peasants and agricultural labourers constitute essentially an identical agrarian category, among whom in fact there may be considerable overlap, nevertheless there is also an arena of potential conflict on this very issue of wages. His argument is that the demands of the khet mazdoors must fall within a practical range of what the poor peasants can pay, otherwise as he says, there is likely to be hostility. Sahajanand's solution, which he proposes in his last chapter is negotiated compromise. It is an issue incidentally raised in the petitions of agricultural labourers cited in Editorial Note 1 of this chapter.

6. The book Sahajanand cites here was based on the Calcutta University Readership Lectures by one of the most prominent and widely-published figures in the field. Also important in terms of the issue of availability we have raised with other titles is that *Land Problems of India* (London: Longmans, Green and Co., Ltd., 1933) was printed in India, and hence both well-known and easily available.

7. This is another fundamental point with many regional and local variations. For example in the South Central Bihar districts where agriculture is weak and the economy generally depressed, agricultural wages are dramatically below the norm, leave alone the legally established minimum. As Sahajanand explains, less work and more workers means lower wages. Wages are further depressed in a district like Palamau which is currently suffering a severe drought with an even more depressed agrarian economy than the rest of the state. Daily wages reported to be as low as Rs. 3.50 per day. In Madubhani District in North Bihar agricultural labourers are paid Rs. 12/- per day plus a meal by middle caste share croppers, that is bataidars, for a work day beginning at six in the morning and ending at noon. The share cropper in question reported that he demanded that at that wage, his labourers are required to "work harder than he does," and it is clear that he works very hard, and does extremely well. His family are *Barai*, traditional betel leaf growers, but in this case successful middle caste cultivators comparable to Yadavas in this village and in other parts of Bihar. Agricultural labourers are mostly from Untouchable castes or lower Backward castes, Hindu and Muslim.

The localness of khet mazdoor wages is demonstrated by the variation from one tola or part of the village to the next. Whereas agricultural labourers will be paid Rs.12/- and a meal by the share cropper who most often employs them, in the Brahman and Kayastha tolas, where they are less frequently employed directly, they will demand and get Rs.15/- to Rs.20/- per day and a meal. One final revealing point is that no one in the village was aware of the official minimum wage for agricultural labour in Bihar. The strong evidence obviously is that custom and practice are more relevant than the law in this as in so many other cases. The evidence cited in this note was gleaned in Bihar and Eastern U.P. during late March and early April 1993, which coincided with the *rabi* wheat harvest in that region.

8. The remarkable evidence from North Bihar at the time of the wheat harvest in late March 1993 is that agricultural labourers were being paid at precisely the rate Sahajanand reported in 1941. Of twelve bundles cut, they were paid one bundle.

9. In the remainder of this brief chapter Sahajanand is concerned primarily with debt bondage, which is intimately linked with the whole issue of indebtedness, an issue Sahajanand returns to often in these pages. An obvious but often misunderstood element of indebtedness in rural India is that in circumstances of unemployment, seasonal under employment, below minimum wages, and under education, apart from the social and cultural discrimination that define the very nature of agricultural labour and with which Sahajanand concludes this chapter, indebtedness is almost by definition a way of life. This is a caveat meant to qualify the common perception that toddy and ritual demands are among the chief causes of indebtedness in rural India.

10. Again the literature on debt bondage is enormous and the titles suggested here are meant to be no more than points of departure. Sahajanand's observations in fact make many of the basic points. Others may be found in the general literature on agricultural wages cited in Editorial Note 4 above. The best and most recent study on debt bondage which couches its argument in historical terms while at the same time reflecting on the contemporary present is Gyan Prakash, *Bonded Histories: Geneologies of Labor Servitude in Colonial India* (Cambridge: Cambridge University Press, 1990). The other value of Prakash's book is that it's inquiry is sited in Bihar and specifically in Gaya District and examines in close detail the kamiauti system of bonded labour in that place, the district where Sahajanand devoted so much of his activist career in the 1930s. See also Prakash's more recent edited volume, *The World of the Rural Labourer in Colonial India* (Delhi: Oxford University Press, 1992). Another Bihar specific title is that by Sudipto Mundle, *Backwardness and Bondage: Agrarian Relations in a South Bihar District* (New Delhi: Institute of Public Administration, 1979), sited in Palamau District. For a broader consideration of related issues see Sugata Bose, *Peasant Labour and Colonial Capital: Rural Bengal Since 1770* (Cambridge: Cambridge University Press, 1993). See also the collection of essays in Utsa Patnaik and Manjari Dingwaney, eds., *Chains of Servitude: Bondage and Slavery in India* (Madras: Sangam Books, 1985). Useful but unpublished is the contribution of Rani Dhavan Shankardass,

"Debt Bondage: the Survival of an Ancient Mechanism," in the Occasional Papers on Perspectives in Indian Development series of the Nehru Memorial Museum and Library, No. VI (May 1989). The survey sponsored by the Gandhi Peace Foundation conveys a wide range of regional and all India data. See Sarma Marla, *Bonded Labour in India* (New Delhi: Biblia Impex Private, Ltd., 1981). A number of these issues as they relate to labour generally and agricultural labour and bonded labour specifically, are raised in a recent volume edited by Peter Robb, *Dalit Movements and the Meanings of Labour in India*(Delhi: Oxford University Press, 1993). See especially Robb's introductory essay. Finally, the contribution of Dharma Kumar "Capitalism, Colonialism and Bondage," in Martin Klein, ed., *Slavery, Bondage, and Emancipation* (forthcoming), provides some of the most recent thinking of this long time student of the phenomenon.

11. Sahajanand makes very clear throughout this section on bonded labour that the malik, or owner of the kamia or bonded labourer is just as likely to be a kisan, or peasant as not. I make the point here simply to reinforce the terminological range of definitions Sahajanand employs in this text, and the potential conflict of interests which is at the heart of the relationships between cultivating peasant tenants or share croppers on the one hand and agricultural labourers, who may also be bonded labourers, on the other. This is not to suggest, as Sahajanand makes amply clear, that only peasant tenants are maliks or owners in this situation. That possibility is equally open to moneylenders, shopkeepers, and land controlling zamindars, among many others.

12. After 1936 and the formation of the All-India Kisan Sabha, Sahajanand moved widely throughout the country representing the interests of the AIKS, while maintaining his primary base and committment in Bihar. His travels took him often to Gujarat given his close association with Indulal Yagnik, who with Sahajanand and N.G. Ranga from Andhra were the three main activists on the peasant front in the 1930s. So Sahajanand wrote with some familiarity about systems of bonded labour in Gujarat and as late as 1941 he had the strong sense that the Kisan Sabha as movement had the capability of liberating the bonded labourers. For a more detailed description of the phenomenon

in Gujarat see the very rich interview with Dinkar Mehta, File No.300, in the Oral History Project of the Nehru Memorial Museum and Library in New Delhi. The interview was done on July 27, 1975 at a time when Mehta seemed to be at his reflective best in recounting the political and ideologicial history of the freedom movement and his involvement in it. On Gujarat see also Jan Breman, *Patronage and Exploitation: Emerging Agrarian Relations in South Gujarat* (Berkeley: University of California Press, 1974).

13. Sahajanand here raises the issue of land as the basis for providing some minimum degree of economic livelihood to the agricultural labourers, bonded labourers and the marginal poor. It is question to which he will turn in specific detail in the final two chapters of this tract.

14. Wages, debt, bondage, and land hunger are all key problems facing the rural poor, but no issue is more painful or more poignantly stated by Sahajanand in these pages than the cultural attitudes that reinforce the social maltreatment and economic exploitation of the rural poor. For Sahajanand, changing those attitudes is as central a part of the solutions he proposes as any others of an apparently more practical kind.

CHAPTER IV
Their Solution

[Sahajanand's concern in this chapter is to confront directly the inherent conflict in the relations between peasants and the agricultural labourers they employ. It is a matter of attitude and practice and Sahajanand makes a poignant appeal for a sense of decency, dignity, and humanity to be shown the khet mazdoors who ultimately produce the food that keeps the system going. He then turns to the "root causes" of social and economic deprivation in agriculture, namely land hunger and wages. Citing a range of scholars and official reports, Sahajanand defines the potential for the extension and more efficient use of cultivable land, which will enhance production and resolve the crisis of wages at the same time. In a set of proposals which sound remarkably like the 1970s and 80s, he appeals for the application of science, technology and capital to move India to the limits of its productive potential and to permit kisans and khet mazdoors to live in an environment free of conflict. Ed.]

How are we to deal with these issues? What means are to be adopted in resolving them? These are the difficult questions which now confront us. Anyone with eyes to see will realize that change is sweeping the world, a fact whose significance and meaning is not fully understood by those adherents of old and orthodox images of the times in which we live. It is clear to persons of vision that the days of tyrants and exploiters are numbered, the days when the tyrannized masses, the labourers, suffered silently the arbitrary acts of injustice to which they have for so long been subjected. This exploitation may not yet be ended, but how can it be that there will be no storm or rain, that people will not react to their agony and pain? It is a settled fact that those who have benefitted by these injustices, their end will come. This is the age of the exploited and the oppressed. They are awakening, indeed many have already awakened.[1] And as the oppressed become more and more conscious they gain a new sense of self respect and recognize their rights, which they are now determined to achieve. In such circumstances how long can the process of thieving and intimidation continue? Unless we stop these practices the exploited and oppressed will force us to stop them, and they will rest only when they have ended the atrocities and brought down their perpetrators and those who have stood silently by.

In our considerations, we must try to understand what is happening, to understand as fully as possible the sufferings of the khet mazdoors. If we or the kisans or their sympathisers feel any annoyance at these efforts, then this is not right. It is neither an issue of prestige or favouritism. It is not that the problems of the agricultural labourers are imagined or contrived; to the contrary, they are very real and our attempt to understand them is an honest effort to reach real solutions. It is not meant to create problems for others. Ultimately the full reality of their circumstances must be perceived. And not only this, we must impress this understanding on the minds of the kisans as well. If at first they are hesitant and not prepared to listen, or respond abusively, there is no reason for concern. They will do so because they do not fully understand and until they are more conscious, so long they will need our leadership. But as soon as they understand these issues, they will become leaders themselves and we will no longer be needed. Accordingly, we must consider the issues frankly and openly and allow the kisans time to reflect upon them as well. Only then will everyone's well-being be served. Then and only then will the agricultural labourers believe what we say and do, and accept our assurances that our efforts are for their benefit as well as for the benefit of others. The moment we begin to listen to their painful stories with sympathy, we will gain their confidence. By reaching out to them in this way, we will make our presence felt and our leadership accepted. After all, agricultural labourers are not blind, nor are they strange or different people. They are also kisans and an important part of the kisans. Then why this fear, or why do we think of them as our enemies? The kisans should understand the difficulties of the khet mazdoors and the khet mazdoors should understand those of the kisans. That will be the ultimate achievement. It should be our aim as Kisan Sabha workers and leaders to help both kisans and khet mazdoors to understand one another, and in that effort we must remain fully impartial.[2]

Let us now turn to these problems, try to understand them and to solve them. Some are of such a nature that little further needs to be said except to admit that they exist and then to move ahead in resolving them. For example, the issue of debt bondage of the *kamiauta* or the *hali* is one such problem. It is a matter of some satisfaction that this practice is dying out of its own accord. In this case time is working in our favour. But if there is even the slightest evidence that it exists at any place, or is being practiced secretly, we must make it an immediate public issue and force such persons to give it up forever. This must be done by whatever means of propaganda and special meetings might be necessary and only then can a favourable atmosphere be created to bring this evil to an end.

But in doing so we must also guard against the possibility of the khet mazdoors falling into the clutches of the moneylenders, a result which would be even worse. By adding interest, compound interest and in so many other ways, they can very quickly turn five rupees into fifty rupees. In the *kamiauti* system no interest is involved. The kisan should lend rupees to the khet mazdoor, even in the smallest amount, only at times of greatest need which will then be repaid gradually in two to four pice or anna bits towards the final payment of the principal amount. Rupees should not be advanced for toddy. If there is no interest moneylenders will no longer make unnecessary loans, and the whole *sharab* system, i.e., the country liquor industry will disappear as well. While seeking to limit unnecessary expenditure, we must take care not to hamper the essential work of the khet mazdoor. In a larger sense we must also root out the thinking that permits usury and slavery to exist at all. Unless we do this, our satisfaction with the decline of the *kamiauti* system will do more harm to the poor than good.

In the same way we must also deal with the issue of the kisans' treatment of the khet mazdoors. There can be no place for controversy here. If the kisans are not to face destruction, in a very real sense to cut off their own legs, if they do not wish that their real enemies should ruin them by instigating quarrels between themselves and the khet mazdoors, then they must inevitably treat the agricultural labourers on the basis of equality and brotherhood. Nobody asks that they take food together or enter into marriage relationships with the khet mazdoors and make them their kith and kin. This is an altogether separate question and has nothing to do with the manner in which one treats a fellow human being. We treat birds and animals with sympathy; do we not literally show affection to dogs and cats when we keep them as pets. Is it not therefore a matter of surprise that these agricultural labourers who are literally the arms and legs of the kisans are not also treated in this way? After all what do they lack which should give rise to the feelings of contempt and hatred which we find? In what respect are they inferior to others? The khet mazdoors sweat blood to produce the wheat and fine rice which they themselves are destined never to eat. Is it just that the kisan should mete out such inhuman treatment to those who in a very real sense sacrifice themselves and renounce the good things of life for everyone else? Unless this changes the heavens are certain to burst open. We have seen that the zamindars have grasped this opportunity of winning over these heart-rent agricultural labourers to their side. And by setting them against the kisans the zamindars have triumphed over these very kisans and that with the help of the khet mazdoors themselves. After all what would one expect given that those who are sacrificing their very lives for you, are treated like animals in return? They are also human. It is this which pains them. Still, immediately the kisans approach the khet mazdoors sympathetically and with understanding, they respond in kind. That is why I am constrained to say that when the kisan does not treat the agricultural labourers with a sense of decency and humanity, he is effectively cutting off his own limbs.

<31.7.41> The kisan of course carries on his cultivation with his bullocks and other animals. He loves them very much. Unless and until he has fed the cattle he will not eat himself. He may go without food but his cattle can never go hungry. If by chance they become ill or fail to eat, the kisan will know no sleep and his anxiety no bounds. Only when they begin to ruminate and eat again will the kisan be at ease. Then how is it that his ploughman or agricultural labourers have not this much claim on his sensibilities? The kisan should search his heart and if on this issue he is found wanting he must not only make amends but atone for his misdeeds. Only therein lies his welfare.

As a matter of fact unless the kisan regards the agricultural labourer and his children as members of his own family and treats them in this way, this age old neglect cannot be truly and properly atoned for. The labourer, his children, wife or old father are more indispensable for cultivation by the kisans than are their own fathers, children and wives. In ploughing, weeding the fields, and transplanting the paddy, the family members of many kisans are of absolutely no help. This work is done only by family members of the khet mazdoors. And how can the kisan survive without growing paddy or other crops of grain? In such a situation if he treats the family members of the agricultural labourers as his own, or even more sympathetically, it is no special thing. He would then be acting only with wisdom and foresight. The kisan should respect the mothers and sisters of the khet mazdoors just as he does his own. He must never tolerate their dishonour by anyone. If any of the labourers fall ill, he must see that they are cared for and made well. In their sickness they must not be made to work and they must be fed with the same food grains he himself eats. If these injunctions are followed, everything will be set right. On these questions of social justice and respect for the humanity of the khet mazdoors, there is no room for argument. It is a change that must come sooner than later.

Now we turn to the real and more important problems, namely those related to the desire for land and those of wages. If we resolve these fundamental questions, others will automatically be resolved. But their solution will not be easy. It is important to note here that the wage question and that of land are intimately linked. If the land problem is solved, that of wages will also be solved. It will require no great additional effort. I have included agricultural labourers in the category of kisans precisely because of this interconnectedness of the land problem.

It is a problem which is exceedingly complex and difficult. First, we need to consider the total land area of this country and how much of it is under cultivation. In 1936 the Government of India pointed out that the total acreage of land was then nearly 66 crores and 74 lakhs (667,400,000) out of which 8 crores and 95 lakhs (89,500,000) acres were covered by jungle; 14 crores and 50 lakhs (145,000,000) acres were uncultivable; 15 crores and 36 lakhs (153,600,000) acres though fit for cultivation remained uninhabited; and 5 crores and 10 lakhs (51,000,000) acres were fallow land. In this way the total land under cultivation was 22 crores and 79 lakhs (227,900,000) acres.

It is also a fact that land does not expand like rubber but human population is continuously increasing. Out of 40 crores of Indians today if we take 80 percent to be agriculturists, then the per capita acreage would be less than three-fourths of an acre. We have available for distribution only 22 crores and 79 lakhs (227,900,000) acres among 32 crores of people. The clear meaning of these figures is starvation for all.[3]

In 1911, an Englishman named Sir Thomas Holderness, wrote a book titled *Peoples and Problems of India.* At page 139 of that book he has made some interesting observations. It must be remembered that the population then was much less than it is today. Still his descriptions are heart rending. He writes:

> The total population of India including that of the protected native states is 315 millions. Three-fourths of this vast population is supported by agriculture. The area under cultivation is not accurately known as the returns from the native states are incomplete. But we shall not be far wrong if we assume that there is less than one acre and a quarter per head for that portion of the population which is directly supported by agriculture. . .
>
> Not only does the land of India provide food for this great population, but a very considerable portion of it is set apart for growing produce which is exported. . . In fact it pays its bill for imports and discharges its other international debts mainly by the sale of agricultural produce. Subtracting the land thus utilised for supplying foreign markets from the total area under cultivation we shall find that what is left over does not represent more than 2/3 acre per head of the total Indian population. India therefore feeds and to some extent clothes its population from what 2/3 acre per head can produce. There is probably no country in the world where land is required to do so much.[4]

This calculation is made on the basis of one and a quarter acres per head. But I have already pointed out that the cultivated land per head now is hardly three quarters of an acre. Hence, the deplorable condition of the kisans or those subsisting on agriculture can be recognised even more easily. But in practice this average of three quarters of an acres in fact does not operate. After all, everybody does not subsist according to this average. There are lakhs of people who appropriate or rather grab the produce of thousands of acres. Consequently crores of people are deprived of any land or a grain of its produce. Therefore the majority of peasants are extremely poor, depressed and faced with ruin. How then can they give land to their agricultural labourers? What justification is there that they should do this? After all there must be some basis for such a demand. When the kisan himself is dying and not only grasping every inch of his land, but also feverishly searching out more land, then how can he lend his ears to the plea of conveying land to the khet mazdoors? How can this appeal be made and who will have the courage to make it? When the produce is not sufficient to provide for the kisan himself then what will be achieved by such a distribution of land other than adding to the hunger of both the kisan and the khet mazdoor? Of course it would be a different thing if production were increased, full irrigation and other facilities were provided and the acreage of cultivable land increased. Accordingly, our attention should first be directed to these issues rather than to the demand for land.

Let us then consider whether the land available for cultivation can be increased and whether its production can be raised sufficiently to feed everyone. In giving a description of the total land area above, I have mentioned that 15 crores and 36 lakhs (153,600,000) acres of cultivable land had not yet been brought under cultivation, and that there were 5 crores and 10 lakhs (51,000,000) acres of fallow land. If we add both figures it comes to 20 crores and 46 lakhs (204,600,000) acres, that is to say we get nearly as much land as is at present under cultivation. In other words, about twenty and a half crores of acres of additional land is available for cultivation. However, there are substantial difficulties and major resource requirements not available to the kisans, in doing so. This is ultimately a responsibility of government, otherwise why does it exist?[5] If by making such an investment the government brings these lands under cultivation, then very quickly the land under cultivation would nearly be doubled, that is to say, the total acreage will be 43 crores and 25 lakhs (432,500,000).

But not only this, the Indian Agricultural Commission in its report has made reference to a very remarkable fact on page 605.[6] The above figures show that 14 and a half crore (145,000,000) acres of land are such as cannot be made available for cultivation. It is strange that more than one-third of the total land - 22 1/2 percent - will be permanently left out of cultivation. The commission writes: "It is difficult to believe that the whole of the vast area now classed as 'not available for cultivation', amounting as it does, to 150 million acres or twenty two and a half percent of the total area of British India is either not available or not suitable for cultivation."

It clearly means that about twenty and a half crore acres of land not now cultivated are however suitable for cultivation, a figure which is 35 1/2 percent of the total land, which is certain to increase up to as much as 40 percent according to knowledgeable observers. That is to say about three crore acres more land will become available. In this way every man will have one and one half to two acres of land. If suitable arrangements are made out of approximately nine crore acres of jungle land some additional land may also become available.[7] Extensive tracts of open space are found in the jungle amounting to lakhs of acres and if adequate monies are applied it will be possible to make available a per capita acreage of as much as two acres of land. Vast stretches of wetland (*chaur*) and marsh lands (*daldali*) can also be made suitable for cultivation.[8] Even barren lands can be converted in this way. Both science and capital are needed to do this and these can be provided only by government.

Let us go further. R.K.Das, an Indian scholar, published a book in English, *The Industrial Efficiency of India* in 1930. There he writes at page 13 as follows:

> The net area actually sown with crops amounts to 228 million acres, or 53 percent of the total arable land. But if the areas sown more than once are taken as separate areas for each crop, the total gross area sown would amount to 262 million acres. Thanks to the climatic conditions, a considerable proportion of the arable land is adaptable to more than two crops a year, but on the other hand a part of this area is not cultivable more than once and some may not be available for cultivation even once for some time to come. It may therefore be assumed that on the average all the arable land is fit for two crops a year. The potential area of arable land would thus amount to 864 million acres of which only 262 million acres or about 30 percent are utilised for productive purposes and 602 million acres or 70 percent are wasted.[9]

This description is of great significance, but before appreciating its value we must understand its meaning. The area of 22 crores and 79 lakhs (227,900,000) acres to which I have referred earlier, is given by Das as 22 crores and 80 lakhs (228,000,000) acres. He has also doubled my figure of the total potential of cultivable land from 43 crores and 25 lakhs (432,500,000) to 86 crores and 40 lakh (864,000,000) acres because he has presumed that all lands have on average the potential for growing two crops. With the application of both capital and appropriate technology, these assumptions are fully warranted. <1.8.41> In fact Das suggests that if the government becomes fully involved in these terms total available acres for cultivation could be tripled. If one accepts this view, then even if the per bigha production were not increased, there would be an equivalent improvement of arable availability to ten maunds from the present three maunds. If production were then also increased, these figures would accordingly increase as well. Mr. Das is calling for maximum utilization of all potential land and productive capabilities. In these terms the situation is perhaps not as hopeless as might appear on the surface.

Similar views have been expressed by Radhakamal Mukerjee at page 26 of his recent book *Food Planning for Four Hundred Millions*. Referring to Mukerjee, Palme Dutt writes at page 191 of his *India Today* as follows:

> It has been estimated even on the existing basis of small scale technique the available land area for cultivation in India given necessary measures of land-reclamation and irrigation, could maintain a population of 447 millions or 70 millions in excess of the existing population.[10]

It is clear that if Indian agriculture is fully "modernized," including the development of up to date irrigation facilities and the application of scientific fertilizers, the potential for a dramatic increase in crop production is entirly possible. Furthermore, if these developments are undertaken, one agricultural labourer will be able to do the work of several, and in this way with the increase in production, the cost of cultivation will be relatively less. The evidence from other countries shows this possibility. The statistical year book of the League of Nations for 1932-33 indicates the maximum produce per acre in particular countries. We must bear in mind that the production figures are given in pounds and 82 pounds make one full maund. The comparative figures are as follows: (1) India - paddy 1357, wheat 652; (2) Japan - paddy 2267, wheat 1508; (3) Egypt - paddy 2356, wheat 1688; (4) U.S.A. - paddy 2112, wheat 973; (5) Italy - paddy 4601, wheat 1241; (6) Germany - wheat 1740; (7) Britain - wheat 1812.

These statistics make it clear that despite the great fertility of the land and the ideal climate and weather as compared to other countries, agriculture in our country is still backward. Whereas our production per acre should be relatively much higher than that of other countries, we are actually miserably behind. Japan and Egypt grow 1 3/4 times more paddy per acre than India, the U.S.A. grows more than 1 1/2 times and Italy 3 1/2 times more. When we come to wheat growing we find that the U.S.A. produces roughly 1 1/2 times, Japan more than 2 1/4 times, Egypt 2 1/2 times, Italy roughly 2 times, Germany nearly 3 times and Britain 3 times more. Can our land not produce as much? In fact, it can produce even more. But we lack the necessary facilities to do so. Our kisans have no capital and the government is doing little to intervene. As has been suggested, if government were to take the lead, our production could increase as much as three times beyond what it is today. Our two main cereal crops are paddy and wheat. From the figures given above there is in fact a potential possible increase in production of nine to ten times. I have shown that we can achieve a three fold increase by ordinary processes and it will be trebled again by taking to modernized methods of agriculture. On this topic I think it proper to cite the opinion of an officer of the Government of India placed before the Indian Banking Inquiry Committee and which appears at page 700, Appendix 13 of the Committee's report. The name of the officer is A. P. MacDougall. In the same connection Rajni Palme Dutt has shown in a paragraph prior to quoting the MacDougall statement at page 198 of *India Today*, how labour is wasted in India. He indicates that whereas in other countries the work which is done by one labourer will require seven or eight labourers here. Palme Dutt writes as follows:

> The contrast is still more marked if taken in relation to number of workers employed on the land. In India there is one person employed in cultivation for every 2.6 acres of land, as against 17.3 acres in the United Kingdom and 5.4 acres in Germany. (*India Today*, p.198.)
>
> [Here begins McDougall] It has been stated that the soil of India is naturally poor. This is not correct. It has

> become poor. The great river valleys must at one time have been among the most fertile in the world. In Denmark and Germany the greater part of the land in its original state consisted of barren wastes of sand growing nothing but gorse and heather.
>
> If the output per acre [in India] were raised to that of France, the wealth of the country would be increased by Pounds 669,000,000. If the output were in terms of English production, it would be raised by Pounds 1,000,000,000 per year. Yet England is by no means highly cultivated. This does not make any allowance for part of the land in India producing two crops per year. In the other countries referred to only one can be grown. The advance should equal any loss from drought. In terms of Danish wheat production the increased wealth production would be Pounds 1,500,000,000 per year. It is not therefore the soil that is responsible for the poverty of rural India.

Here one pound is equivalent to 13 rupees 5 annas and 4 pie. Roughly speaking the total income from agriculture in this country is estimated to be nearly twelve hundred crores of rupees which is less than one hundred crores of pounds. But if agriculture is improved the income would be one hundred and fifty crores of pounds more. That is to say it would be two and one half times greater than it is at present. But as stated above, if all the lands were to grow two crops annually and the acreage is roughly doubled, the income must increase by a factor of ten. The statement of R. K. Das cited earlier demonstrates this same point. Das agrees that the soils of India match the most fertile lands in the world and if they have lost their fertility it is because the kisans cannot provide essential manure and the government has not concerned itself with this issue.

In our country labourers are employed seven and one half times less efficiently than in England and more than three times less efficently than in Germany. This is a sheer waste of manpower. On the one hand production is less, on the other hand, manpower employed is large and the kisans are literally caught in between. Inevitably they cannot derive full benefit from agriculture. If agriculture is carried out scientifically, obviously fewer agricultural labourers will produce more. But the one inevitable consequence will be that out of seven or eight persons only one will be required in cultivation and the rest will become unemployed. But there is no doubt that agriculture will become very profitable. Which, however, leaves the question of unemployment among the agricultural labourers. This problem will be solved in two ways. First, when the land area under cultivation will be more than trebled, fifty percent of the unemployed labourers will be absorbed in those newly cultivated lands. But half will still remain unemployed. They will find employment in new industries and workshops. The full introduction of scientific methods in agriculture means that there will need to be a large number of new factories to produce the necessary tools and equipment for engaging in scientific agriculture. It is impossible to meet these needs only through imports; in fact no country does this. It is an accepted fact that only when industries and trade are fully modernised in a country, can agriculture also be operated on modern methods.[11]

So it is clear from the foregoing that when arrangements are made for moving the whole country into full production in all spheres, only then can the land-hunger of the kisans be met and only then will the agricultural labourers also be able to get land. There is no other way. In the situation which exists today, the struggle between the agricultural labourers and the kisans is essentially one of fighting over crumbs.[12] It is a conflict which will benefit no one. Hence, I have attempted here to get at the root cause of this issue. In doing so I have tried to bring the kisans, which includes the agricultural labourers, face to face with reality. I want that they too should understand the fundamental root causes of the problem which confronts them. It is these root causes which must concern all of us. Grasping for leaves and flowers in these circumstances will benefit no one.

But even when the question of land and agriculture is settled as defined here, there remains the very real problem of crores of acres of land held by lakhs of zamindars as *zirat* and *bakasht* or *khudkasht*. They either do not cultivate themselves or if they do, it is in order to amass wealth and not for their own consumption. They snatch the lands of crores of people, bring it under their control and collect rent at their sweet will. What we need today is that government should dispossess those zamindars from all their *zirat* and *bakasht* lands who are not dependent on cultivation. By zamindars I mean those who let their lands to others on *bhaoli* and *nagdi*, i.e., "rent in kind or cash." After these lands are resumed they should be distributed first to agricultural labourers or others like them who subsist on agriculture or wish to do so.[13] Only such kisans and agricultural labourers who have either no lands or none worth the name should be the rightful claimants of these lands. Only then can any remaining land from this pool be utilized for other purposes. Furthermore, the illegal practice of some persons amassing wealth from lands while tens of millions are starving should be stopped. When these lands are given to the poor kisans which includes the agricultural labourers as well, they will have the opportunity of taking up *panchayati* cultivation, which should be a condition of land distribution. It is in fact the duty of government and the society at large that along with the distribution of land, it facilitate the setting up of *panchayati* cultivation.[14]

With the settlement of the land question, the question of wages will automatically also be solved. But until the question of land availability is resolved the wage question will remain an issue of deep concern. Even when the distribution of land takes place, elements of the wage question will remain. It is much more complex an issue than simply filling the belly, and only when it is satisfactorily resolved can agriculture function efficiently. Otherwise there will always be problems on the land. Ultimately the question of wages for khet mazdoors is one of rights. It is to that question which we now turn.

As indicated earlier, we must understand that agricultural labourers are not only engaged by rich kisans but by poor kisans as well.[15] In these circumstances if the poor kisans feel difficulty in paying proper wages, the rich kisans have no such difficulty. They can pay full and sufficient wages. But in imitation of the poor kisans, as I have indicated, they do not do so. They pay the same fixed wage. Most kisans are poor and what they pay is taken to be the standard wage. But this is wrong and we will have to fight against it. We should have no consideration at all for the rich kisans. After all, they too have weaknesses which we can use against them. They cannot do cultivation with their own hands. On the one hand they are led by a sense of pride not to plough themselves, on the other hand how they will manage to cultivate their vast fields? In fact, they require large numbers of labourers for this purpose. By this means we can force them to pay full and proper wages.

But if necessary the poor kisans can do the work of cultivation themselves. They are not so much obsessed by the idea of pride. It is also the case that they have very small holdings. Some do not do actual cultivation due to old customs and traditional religious values. But when forced by circumstances, they will.[16] But if too much pressure is put on the kisans on the wage issue, they may not agree, with the result that their agricultural labourers will starve. Hence we can make concessions to the kisans and because of compulsions on both sides some agreement can or should be reached, especially until the land question itself is resolved. After all somehow, one has to survive. Both the kisans and the khet mazdoors should look to each other's condition and find a middle way.

<2.8.41> The fact is that as the crocodile had nearly swallowed the elephant, similarly whatever these poor kisans grow is grabbed by the zamindar, moneylender, and others. Nothing is left with them. And if anything at all does remain it is certainly not sufficient to subsist upon. Secondly, the eyes of the crocodiles are fixed even upon this small remainder to see how and when to swallow it as well. The poor kisan himself is hungry and this is why he cannot feed his labourers well. Hence the first task for both the khet mazdoors and the kisans is to jointly protect what they have from these zamindars and moneylenders. Only then is their any hope of filling their bellies. But so long as both go on quarrelling, they cannot successfully oppose the zamindars and little will be gained. Hence it is necessary to have a mutually acceptable agreement between them. Therefore we need to consider the question of wages in these terms.

With that end in view I have myself made inquiries at many places and was able to achieve a positive settlement between the kisans and the khet mazdoors. At some places the demand of the labourers was a small one for a decent mid-day meal and the kisans were agreeable to this. At other places the demand for increasing the wage by a quarter to a half seer of grain was also accepted. These agreements were achieved by persuasion alone. The blunder of engaging in a *hartal*, or strike in these cases was not committed. That would have effectively been a direct attack at the very foundation of the kisan organization, inasmuch as the poor kisans are the very backbone of the Kisan Sabha, and a *hartal* by the khet mazdoors would have severely undermined their trust in the Sabha. Hence it would have been a gross mistake, a veritable blunder to go to that length.

At some places the kisans themselves raised questions about our stressing the issue of fixed wages. They explained that while almost half of the land-produce was taken by the zamindars, they were proposing that mazdoors could take half of the balance and one fourth they would retain themselves and bear the cost of agricultural operations as well. But the labourers did not agree. This proposal is of real significance inasmuch as it throws full light on the generosity and honest intentions of the kisans. In it is hidden the seed of compromise and the end of conflict. It gives hope that the future of the kisans as a whole is bright. There is also in it the confidence that we will succeed in our efforts.

Editor's Notes to Chapter IV

1. For Sahajanand the awareness of the marginal poor of their condition and turning that awareness into a mobilized reaction and political response, what he refers to as their awakening, is an ongoing process. It has happened and is happening and by Sahajanand's logic will continue to happen. As I have suggested previously, this descriptive definition of social and political change as an active, ongoing process, reflects not only Sahajanand's conceptual sensitivity to the realities as he perceives them; it is also a literary device Sahajanand uses in virtually everything he writes, thereby reinforcing his confidence that the system is changing and must change.

2. Sahajanand makes clear in this paragraph that he is engaged not in political games, but in serious efforts to resolve serious problems in rural India, and that this can be achieved only by a full understanding of the realities of those problems as they affect both agricultural labourers and peasants. Before turning to issues of wages and land, he makes his most elaborate appeal for a sense of decency and humanity in relations between peasants and the agricultural labourers whom they employ. It is a graphic suggestion that khet mazdoors are ultimately the arms and legs which keep the agrarian economy functioning, and that without at least the treatment and respect that peasants mete out to their bullocks, the system is in danger of self destruction. But Sahajanand is also committed to the idea of compromise, however difficult the social and cultural changes his solutions demand.

3. At this point Sahajanand draws an implication of doom, based on the cultivable land area of the country and its population. He does this to capture our attention and to anticipate the solutions which were already being proposed when he was writing in 1941, and which he endorses in this chapter in terms of a sophisticated, modernized agriculture and industrial economy that can only be described as years ahead of its time. Without citing the incredible range of official and unofficial statistics on population, land use, and production which are now available, we will nevertheless cite enough figures to provide a basis of comparison with what Sahajanand knew and with what he thought

might or should happen in the decades after his writing.

Sahajanand's 1936 figures, which it must be recalled included all of British India and what is now Pakistan and Bangladesh, but did not include Princely India, indicated land available for cultivation of 227,900,000 acres for a population of 400,000,000. Without accounting for the qualifications just indicated, the most recent figures for 1987/88 on cultivable land area and for 1991 on the population of India alone are as follows: the 1991 population figures including projections for Jammu and Kashmir where census operations were not held, are 846,302,688; while the total cropped area in 1987/88 was 172,880,000 hectares or 432,200,000 acres, with a hectare equal to 2.5 acres. Of the total land area of the country in 1987/88 of 328.73 million hectares, that is 821,825,000 acres, 304.85 hectares (in millions) were classified in the following ways: forests (66.86 million hectares), non-agricultural uses, barren and uncultivable land (41.2 million hectares), other uncultivated land, that is, permanent pasture and other grazing land, land under miscellaneous tree crops and groves, cultivable waste land, and fallow land (60.61 million hectares), leaving a balance of net sown area of 136.18 million hectares of which 36.7 million hectares were sown more than once, giving us a total cropped areas of 172.88 million hectares, or the 432.2 million acres indicated above. By these measures, again without incorporating all the obvious boundary and area qualifications, we may say that the relevant cropped area in the intervening fifty plus years has nearly doubled, whereas the relevant population has more than doubled. Closer statistical analysis will obviously render more sutble and meaningful results, an exercise rather beyond the limited purview of these explanatory editorial notes. An equally or perhaps even more critical consideration to which we will return later in this series of chapter notes, is the issue of agricultural production in the years for which we are providing rough comparisons. For the most current demographic data see Government of India, *Census of India, 1991* Series 1, India, Paper 1 of 1992, Vol. I, *Final Population Totals* (New Delhi, 1992). Land use data are available from many sources; those given here come from the Directorate of Economics and Statistics, Ministry of Agriculture, Government of India.

4. The standard citation for Holderness is Thomas William

Holderness, *Peoples and Problems of India* (New York: H. Holt and Company, 1912). It may well be that Sahajanand had a 1911 British edition at his disposal or referenced from a secondary source. In the following paragraph Sahajanand estimates what this given man/land ratio means generally and specifically for the poor peasant and the demands the khet mazdoor may make on him. The only alternative Sahajanand suggests is to increase production by providing additional irrigation, introducing other infrastructural inputs and increasing the acreage of cultivable land. Only then can land hunger and land distribution be intelligently considered.

5. This is a demand Sahajanand consistently makes of government, namely that investment in agriculture is first and foremost a responsibility of government.

6. This is the Royal Commission on Agriculture cited in an earlier note.

7. Professional estimates are that at least some of the 21.9 percent of the classified land area of India defined as forest (and which is under state control) is informally being encroached on for agricultural cultivation.

8. In 1941 when Sahajanand was writing, concerns about environmental degradation and its potential impact on the ecosystem, including the productive capabilities of agriculture, were essentially a non-issue. Vast areas of wetlands have in fact been brought under cultivation in the meantime with consequences specialists do not consider entirely positive in the short or long term. There is a wide new literature on this subject in India and abroad, but specifically on effects of biomass depletion see for example John Richards, James R. Hagen and Edward S. Haynes, "Changing Land Use in Bihar, Punjab and Haryana, 1850-1970," in *Modern Asian Studies* 19:3 (July 1985), and by the same authors on arable expansion, "Changes in the Land and Human Productivity in Northern India, 1870-1970," *Agricultural History* 59:4 (October 1985).

9. In 1993 the general estimate among agricultural economists is that India's cropping intensity is 1.3, that is, that India produces from all sources, including irrigation, 1.3 crops per unit of land. The assumption of Das in 1930 that intensity could reach two was optimistic then as it is now. Some of the most fertile and

water rich land in the world in parts of Indonesia achieves an intensity of 2.5, but this is uncommon. As production figures will reveal, there has been a dramatic improvement both in infrastructural investment and agricultural output in the years since 1941. See notes following. It must also be pointed out that abundant monsoonal rainfall makes irrigation unnecessary for at least one crop in much of the country. The Das citation is R.K. Das, *The Industrial Efficiency of India* (London: P.S. King and Son, Ltd., 1930).

10. See Radhakamal Mukerjee, *Food Planning for Four Hundred Millions* (London: Macmillan and Co. Ltd., 1938). The figures already cited suggest that Mukerjee's expectations have been more than fulfilled. A recent assessment of Indian agriculture based on a 1983/84 foodgrain production of 146 million tons, estimated even this "was seen as only a partial realization of the land's potential. According to experts, India could feed a population about three times its present size (about 2.1 billion people) if full use were made of the land. Indian planners have predicted that the total annual output of food grains could easily reach 210 million tons by the end of the century." (George Thomas Kurian, *Encyclopedia of the Third World* (New York: Facts on File, 1987), p. 889).

Given the most recent official figures those projections appear to be well within the realm of the possible. Quoting from the *Economic Survey, 1992-93*: "On account of the erratic behaviour of the south-west monsoon, foodgrains production in 1991-92 fell by 5.3 percent to 167.1 million tons from a record level of 176.4 million tons in 1990-91.... Production of foodgrains during 1992-93 is expected to be of the order of 176.7 million tons." (Government of India, Ministry of Finance, Economic Division, *Economic Survey, 1992-93* (New Delhi, 1993), p. 153). To repeat, these are foodgrain figures only and do not take into account oilseeds, sugarcane, cotton, tobacco, tea, jute, and livestock products, which in any total evaluation must obviously be included. Nor do they include fertilizer consumption, which the Economic Survey for 1992-93 expects to be around 12.7 million tons of nutrients for the year.

11. Sahajanand's concern in this chapter and in this tract is a fully developed Indian economy in which the agricultural labourers and the rural poor would be full participants. That is the jist

of the preceding paragraphs which have the tone of a 1941 version of a green and grey revolution twenty five years before the fact.

12. Sahajanand anticipated what would happen if there was no change in the agrarian environment or if the changes were qualified in social, economic, or political terms. What most raw statistics, however optimistic, fail to reveal is that ultimately the question of access to the benefits of increased production remain, unless issues of distribution and ultimately of social and political control and rights in the land and its product are also addressed. That "fighting over crumbs," is what is happening in South Central Bihar and other parts of the country in 1993, will be news to few observers, official or unofficial. Certainly the daily press devotes much ink to this continuing saga. Social conflict and agrarian radicalism have causes, most often related to economic inequity and social injustice. This is not the place to elaborate on the issue which is at the heart of Sahajanand's 1941 tract. For an attempt to link the events of the contemporary present in Bihar to their historical roots see my essay, "Violence, Agrarian Radicalism, and the Audibility of Dissent: Electoral Politics and the Indian People's Front,"cited in Editorial Note 16 of Chapter II

13. Zamindari abolition had been on the agenda of the Bihar Provincial Kisan Sabha since the mid-1930s but Sahajanand here spells out briefly yet explicitly that those resumed lands are to be distributed to agricultural labourers and the rural poor.

14. The term *panchayati* cultivation is precisely the term Sahajanand uses. The terms co-operative, joint, community, or collective farming are not used here. The closest English term for *panchayati kheti*, which is the full term Sahajanand invokes, might be community cultivation, but we will return to this issue in the Editorial Notes to Chapter V. It is in that final chapter where Sahajanand reinforces the logic he has now developed by resorting again to the Russian experience, but as we will see, with a distinctively Indian flavour.

15. In the concluding paragraphs of this descriptively rich chapter Sahajanand turns to the issue of wages, not simply as a function of resolving the land question as he has maintained, but in terms of the social and political relations between zamindars,

moneylenders, rich peasants, poor peasants, and agricultural labourers. Real wages must be paid by those who can, though not the minimal wage which only the poor peasants can afford. The poor peasants and the agricultural labourers must in fact ally against their dominant opponents, for they too have weapons, namely their work and their numbers against the rich peasants and zamindars who are totally dependent on the khet mazdoors to do the daily work of cultivation. Once such an alliance is forged then the potential conflicts between the poor peasants, who form the very backbone of the Kisan Sabha, and the agricultural labourer can and must and have been resolved by negotiated compromise. That prospect, Sahajanand allows, provides hope for the future.

16. On this issue see also Chapter II, and for a specific 1993 reference see especially Editorial Note 15 of that chapter.

CHAPTER V
How to Achieve These Solutions?

[The solutions proposed in the previous chapter will not be easily achieved in the face of opposition from government, the zamindars, and the rich kisans. But in this final chapter, Sahajanand returns to his point of departure in the Introduction, namely that only in a united movement of peasants and agricultural labourers, with the cause of the poor kisans and khet mazdoors as foremost, can the kind of political pressure be brought to realize the objectives that will serve both the khet mazdoors and the kisans, and ultimately the nation. Here again, Sahajanand cites the Russian experience but makes clear that Indian solutions will ultimately be defined in Indian terms. Ed.]

The solutions proposed in the previous chapters to the problems of the khet mazdoors appear on the surface to be especially attractive. They will not only solve the problems of the agricultural labourers but also of the kisans. But how in fact to achieve them? Just as in theory this effort may appear simple and easy, by the same token its implementation will be intricate and difficult. Government and the zamindars are certain to oppose these recommendations. Government will place thousands of hurdles and obstructions in our path and the zamindars will rage with fury. In this situation there must be some course to compel them to move in the direction of change. Similarly we must compel the rich kisans to pay full wages inasmuch as they too are not likely to come to terms in any other way.

These are the fundamental questions and the answers are ready, namely that the desired results can be achieved only with the support of the people and the influence of a powerful movement. The main thing is to persuade government to accept these proposals and this can be done by no other means than the force of public opinion. And that is our task, to mobilise a strong public opinion in support of our proposals. There is no other way, save this. As I have indicated before, this can be done only with the united force of both the kisans and the agricultural labourers. It is for this reason that I spoke about compromise. After all when the interests of both the kisans and khet mazdoors are identical then why should this effort not be undertaken unitedly? The zamindars, moneylenders and even the government would prefer that the kisans and agricultural labourers should engage in internicine conflict, leaving them open to easy exploitation. But the kisans and the agricultural labourers and we ourselves must be fully alive to this danger.[1]

So the question naturally arises whether the khet mazdoors and the kisans should have two separate organizations or only one between them. This question has already been answered, but perhaps more explanation is needed. It is of course absolutely essential for both that they be in one great organization. This is a fundamental principle. We can on no account forsake it. But we cannot also forget that the agricultural labourers are constituted chiefly of castes which have been suppressed for centuries, whose backbone is already broken and hence they cannot stand up easily by themselves. But even among them there is a sense of hierarchy, of being high or low born. Society treats them even worse than animals, an attitude which is changing, however slowly. Furthermore, society is presently so constituted that the feeling of exploitation and oppression cannot be uprooted without a radical social transformation. Until its basic foundation is changed, the feeling of exploitation will remain to some degree in everyone, whether high or low. Up to this time personal property has been its basis. Hence this feeling of exploitation has penetrated to the very marrow of our social bones. It will be eradicated only when joint property becomes the basis for our social relationships, but this will take time.

Until then this kind of exploitation will continue. Just as the frog before being swallowed by the snake will go on snatching insects, so too the kisan in the clutches of the zamindar and moneylender will continue to exploit his agricultural labourers. And strangely enough, he will not realize that he is doing so. This is the tragedy of the poisonous atmosphere of the times in which we live. Even among agricultural labourers the low castes discriminate between one another as high and low, touchable and untouchable and they have not the least hesitation in doing so. Do they pay full wages to their barbers, washermen, and others? Never. Do they understand that they are exploiting them? Never. Why so? Because of their poverty and helplessness. The psychology of the society is such that they do not realize that this is exploitation. But they cry aloud when they are exploited by others. This is true for the kisans who are poor, not to speak of those who are rich.

Therefore, whereas on the one hand we are deeply concerned with keeping the agricultural labourers and kisans within a single peasant organization, i.e., the Kisan Sabha, at the same time we must find ways to prevent their exploitation by the kisans and encourage them to raise their powerful voices against it. Their voices of protest can as well be raised from within the Kisan Sabha. But the danger is that within the Kisan Sabha they may face obstacles and their voices may be less powerful and their influence limited. Over the course of time this possibility poses the danger that an independent organization may be formed in an attempt to set them against the kisans. While this may be an honest effort, on the other hand it will be a foolish one. But mostly these efforts will come from the henchmen of the zamindars. In this way they will seek to derive undue benefit from the new awakening of the khet mazdoors. One further thing will certainly happen. As I have already mentioned, when government will seize *zirat* and other lands from the zamindars or resume waste lands into the pool of cultivable land, there will be clever efforts to grab these lands and thereby prevent them from going to the intended recipients, the poor peasants and the khet mazdoors. In these circumstances if the agricultural labourers were not to raise their voices in opposition and do so promptly, they would inevitably suffer the consequences, and in the process get none of the newly distributed land or very little. Because they have neither the courage nor experience to make their voices heard, there is the danger that their protest will be drowned out by the uproar made by others, and they will continue to be the sufferers.

The question then naturally arises, should the khet mazdoors have a separate organization? But this inevitably suggests that they should be totally separated from the Kisan Sabha. And as I have already said, this will be a completely wrong approach. But if it is suggested that they be in the Kisan Sabha and also have an organization of their own, this possibility can be discussed. But it is strange to belong to some organization and simultaneously to have an independent organization. These are in fact two opposite things. In the event of strained or opposing positions between the two, one side must become subordinate to the other. But can there be independence in case of subordination? Being in the Kisan Sabha and also being independent will then be only so much talk. It is also true that those who are outside the kisan movement, or opposed to it will want to encourage the creation of opposing organizations, thereby to serve their own ends. What is the remedy for this? It is ultimately not a question for our determination.

However, let us pause briefly and search more deeply. When we consider the issue in broader terms, some arguments of Lenin and his party come to mind. First, he and his party explained in a resolution at the Sixth Congress of the party in July 1917, the meaning of the term "dictatorship of the proletariat" in this way: "the dictatorship of the proletariat is the conquest of power by the workers and poorest peasants." It should be remembered that the use of the term "poorest peasant" means that middle or rich kisans were clearly not included in the category of the proletariat.

Likewise, R. Page Arnot in his *History of the Russian Revolution* has written as follows: "Thus the dictatorship of the proletariat in alliance with the poorer peasantry," "and to the building up of the organization of poor peasants." (Vol. 2, pp. 42, 43).[2] This means that the proletariat will be comprised of the very poorest kisans. "In the villages of Russia, the Bolsheviks formed organizations for the poor kisans." This is where mention is made of "poorer" and "poor" kisans. In the essays of Lenin these three words - "poor, poorer and poorest" have been referred to thousands of times. In the fifth and sixth chapters of his famous *April Theses*, he refers to "a Republic of Soviets of Workers', Agricultural Labourers' and Peasants' Deputies" in place of the parliamentary system, i.e., there will be a combined republic of the proletariat (*sarvahara*), khet mazdoors, and panchayats of kisans ("soviets"). He goes on: "The agrarian programme must be centered around the Soviets of Agricultural Labourers' Deputies," This means that our programme should be framed chiefly with the agricultural labourers at its centre. But soon after he again writes that all lands should be vested in the society and the management should be handed over to local panchayats of khet mazdoors and kisans, i.e., quoting Lenin, "The disposal of such lands to be in the charge of the local Soviets of agricultural labourers' and peasants' deputies." At the same time he again says that the new model farms should not be more than 100 to 300 desyatines and control should be handed over to panchayats of khet mazdoors: "The creation of model farms on each of the large estates varying from 100 to 300 dessatines . . . under the control of the agricultural labourers' deputies." At the same place he refers to the separate organization of panchayats of the poor kisans, i.e., "the organization of separate soviets of deputies of the poor peasants."[3] The striking point is that having mentioned the panchayats of agricultural labourers separately from those of the kisans, he is actually talking of the organization of the poor kisans. Over and above this, at page 313 of the book *Leninism*, Stalin writes as follows:

> There is distinct exploitation of wage-labour, or semi-wage-labour by the peasant proprietor (kulak). It would therefore, be unsuitable if we embarked upon a policy of mitigating or of moderating the fight. What we have to do is to organize the poor peasants for the struggle against the kulaks, and ourselves to act as leaders in the fight.

One thing more. In his *April Theses* Lenin has written that unless the reins of government were in the hands of the kisans and labourers, he would not become involved in support of the imperialist war. The war would be treated as being waged in defence of the revolution only when the reins of government had come into the hands of the labourers and kisans and when two conditions had been met. While referring to the making over of the reins of government into the hands of labourers and kisans he has written that by kisans he meant those poor kisans who are almost like labourers. "(a) That the power of government pass to the proletariat and the poor sections of the peasantry bordering on the proletariat." In his *Letters from Afar* he has also addressed the poor kisans as "semi-proletariat." All this makes it clear that Lenin regarded both the poor kisans and the agricultural labourers in the same category, the category of kisans.

When considered together these extracts bring out a number of facts clearly. Firstly, apart from the rich and middle kisans, there are three kinds of poor kisans, i.e., poor, poorer, and poorest. But in practice these differentiations are not adhered to and at one time or another the three terms are all used in describing poor kisans. Anyone who reads these extracts closely would agree. Secondly, it is the poor kisans who are in fact the agricultural labourers or semi-agricultural labourers. Stalin writes in the extract just cited about the exploitation of these very labourers and explains that the eradication of this exploitation can only be carried out, in the end by struggle, a struggle which must be led by the organization of these poor kisans. What can be more explicit than this? This is also evidenced in the extracts taken from Lenin's theses. In April, 1917 Lenin for the first time suggested the formation of an organization of the poor peasants quite separate from the overall peasant organization. In such an organization, middle and rich kisans may be included, particularly the middle kisans must be there. In Russia at that time the rich peasants were also there in this wider peasant organization. Not only this, it was they and the middle kisans whose voices predominated in that association. And so the voices of the poor were drowned into insignificance. Consequently it was essential to have a separate organization for them. But at the same it is also written that all programmes concerning agriculture or the peasants must be prepared principally with a view to benefitting the agricultural labourers. It is clear that Lenin considered these agricultural labourers and the poor kisans as one and the same. If they were separate social categories with separate organizations, how could programmes then be devised in this way? I have already mentioned that in the lengthy extract given above, Lenin meant precisely this. Of course it is true that very often the term agricultural labourers implies the idea of landless kisans. Hence Lenin has suggested that the model farms be handed over to the panchayats of these landless kisans and labourers. But they have no means of doing cultivation. Hence it would be right if the agricultual labourers seized the *zirat* and *bakasht* lands of big zamindars and started cooperative farming [*sammilit*] on these lands with the equipment and tools of the zamindars.[4] This was what Lenin meant. And in Russia it would have facilitated the process of communism.

In the letters written by Lenin from outside his country after the February Revolution and before the October Revolution with a view to preparing for the latter, there is some indication of having a separate organization of the peasants apart from that of the agricultural labourers. Yet if one reads the whole chapter closely it becomes clear that he meant to separate the poor kisans from the rich and middle kisans and not to separate the poor kisans from the agricultural labourers. He writes:

> Soviets of peasant deputies, soviets of agricultural workers, these are among our most urgent tasks. We shall thereby strive not only that the agricultural workers should establish separate soviets of their own, but also that the poorest and propertyless peasants should organize separately from the well-to-do peasants.

He has written this at the end of a long paragraph and its last sentence clarifies that the organization of the poor kisans should be separate from the rich ones. Those who are the poorest and propertyless kisans are in fact agricultural labourers.

When the agricultural labourers have to struggle against their exploitation by the rich kisans and when we lead them, then it will be natural for them to organize. After all how else will the struggle take form? Stalin made this same point. In this way and only during the course of struggle, can the organization of the agricultural labourers be formed. Only then will it be a strong and firm reality. Furthermore, there is the danger of undesirable elements coming into an organization formed outside the experience of struggle. That is why it was during the course of such struggle that the soviets in Russia were formed in 1905. After that as soon as the struggle ended, these soviets also ended. Again they came into being during the February Revolution of 1917. Hence we shall not form the khet mazdoors into a separate organization. And certainly this will never be done in opposition to the poor kisans.

It is true that others are attempting to create a separate organization of the khet mazdoors. It is impossible to stop them. Our efforts so far as possible should be to assure that they proceed in the right direction in the interests of the agricultural labourers and that they do not become opponents of the Kisan Sabha. If there are obstacles to our involvement, then it is essential to be vigilant from the outside. But it cannot be that true servants of the kisans will not find entrance into such organizations. But though we may lack effective control of these organizations we must protect the khet mazdoors from all dangers, and this can be done only when we continue to carry on their struggles in an organized and determined way against the rich kisans. This is the real and essential task. In this way their own organization will emerge and the ordinary kisans will have no opportunity to bear ill will against them. But such an organization of the agricultural labourers can and must only be formed in the experience of struggle, otherwise it is certain to arouse suspicion among the kisans.

<3.8.41> There can be no scope for mutual opposition between such an organization of agricultural labourers and the Kisan Sabha, because when this will be done by the leaders of the Kisan Sabha and that too through the medium of struggle, the occasion for such opposition will not arise. In an organization formed in struggle there will also be no room for artificial and self-seeking leaders. They will rather be far removed from it. Who then will be creating problems? This will be the organization of the most exploited kisans. It will be a matter of pride for kisan leaders to raise up those who are the worst sufferers and the most depressed at the very bottom of the kisan world. It is these who are the real kisans.[5] Consequently on the one hand, the world will come to know our real intentions. Secondly, this very sabha, this very organization will ultimately become the true organization of all kisans, those kisans who are themselves exploited and do not want to exploit others, who on the contrary want to eradicate exploitation and atrocities from this world. They will all gradually join this new organization. Those who are associated with the present Kisan Sabha with a view to maintain exploitation in one form or another, will in the course of time leave it. Hence both the sabhas constituted of the same kinds of people will gradually merge together. In the circumstances which presently prevail, this is not yet possible; it will still take time.

Whenever there will be any friction between the poor kisans and the agricultural labourers on the question of wages and other issues, these two organizations will by mutual discussions easily resolve them. Agreements with the middle kisans will also be reached. As all these kisans are at present associated with the Kisan Sabha, they may all express their views, but in the end they must abide by the decisions reached. Those who presume from Russian history that there should be no separate organization of any kind of agricultural labourers, nor should any effort in that direction be made, do not fully realize the [Indian] situation. Certainly we must learn from the Russian experience but that experience cannot be adopted in any total sense in India. During the last twenty to twenty-five years there have been great changes in our circumstances and we will have to react accordingly.

We must remember that in India we live in a time of complex imperialism. If we do not adapt accordingly we will be lost. Hence Lenin pointed out "the necessity of manoeuvering and retreating." It is these kinds of accommodations we must also be prepared to make.

If we consider seriously the issues raised in the foregoing chapters and the solutions proposed, and implement them with whatever changes may be needed, then not only the problems of agricultural labourers but of all kisans will be resolved, with the result everyone will benefit. Thus we will clear the way for transforming this vast nation and participating fully in this great enterprise when the time comes. The need for us is to give up all parochialisms and old ideas and to march forward with honesty and determination.[6]

Editor's Notes to Chapter V

1. In these initial pages of his final chapter, Sahajanand restates the central theme of this tract and he does so in unambiguous terms entirely consistent with his perceptions of the rural experience over the years. The central issue for him in 1941 was that exploitation of all kinds must end, social, economic, and cultural. To achieve that object he argues for an end to conflict among the poorest of the poor, the peasants and agricultural labourers on the margins of society, but who are ultimately its economic backbone. Because that exploitation of the rural poor has a history of centuries, the task of mobilizing this critical sector of agrarian society will not come about easily. The solution is a single Kisan Sabha organization where the concerns of the rural poor are foremost and the potential exploitation of the khet mazdoors by peasants of any kind must be guarded against. Only in that way can the confidence of the agricultural labourers in these efforts at political mobilization against exploitation be assured.
2. The full citation for the Arnot book is R. Page Arnot, *A Short History of the Russian Revolution from 1905 to the Present Day* (London: V. Gollancz, Ltd., 1937). As Sahajanand indicates, this was a detailed two volume history of the revolution. It is also clear from these pages that Sahajanand continues to reinforce his argument about the role of the poor peasants and agricultural labourers by a consistent appeal to the logic of Lenin. Where bibliographic citations have been noted in previous chapters, they will not be repeated in this final set of Editorial Notes.
3. Please note that a desyatine is a Russian land measure equal to 2.7 acres. For sources on Russian terms see Editorial Note 9 in Chapter II. Also please note that we are using the standard desyatine spelling, but where the term is spelled differently in quotes, that spelling will be retained.

4. See also Editorial Note 14 in the previous chapter on this issue. It is important to note here that Sahajanand is invoking Lenin and not Stalin on the organization of Russian agriculture. Given his grasp of the literature on the Russian revolutionary experience, Sahajanand was certainly familiar with the terms *kolkhoz* for collective farm, and *sovkhoz* for state farm, neither of which he uses in this tract. He rather felt more comfortable appealing to Lenin's revolutionary slogan of land to the tiller, peace to humanity, and all power to the Soviets. This position makes sense in terms of Sahajanand's logic of not only arguing the case of the agricultural labourers but of the poor and indeed, middle peasants as well, none of whom he was seeking to dispossess. It was zamindars and other large and non-productive holders whose lands were to be resumed, and within that framework distribution of lands to the rural poor to take place for the purpose of panchayati cultivation, the exact form of which Sahajanand does not spell out with any specificity. But it is clear that small holders, whether poor peasants or agricultural labourers were not to be deprived of their lands in any collective sense.

Finally, while we are not concerned in this text with Russian history, two points are worth noting. First, to cite Dr. Shashi Kant Jha of Jawaharlal Nehru University, Sahajanand apparently had a brilliant grasp of the Russian literature and the revolutionary experience in that country as it related to his agrarian, political objectives. Secondly, considering that Sahajanand had not imbibed Socialism, Marxism, or Leninism in Europe or America as had many of his contemporaries, it is notable that his familiarity with that theoretical history, given his background in the world of classical Hinduism and peasant activism, was so profound. It is equally notable that however impressed he may have been by the revolutionary experience of Russia, he persistently sought to understand it in the context of the social, cultural, and political environment of India within which he worked. Some of his intellectual and political contemporaries were perhaps less sensitive than he on this issue.

5. This is Sahajanand's most explicit definitional statement on the issue of who is a kisan, who is a peasant and who isn't. There is still some ambiguity in Sahajanand's idea of creating one unified Kisan Sabha, a peasant organization that will have

at its core the poor peasants and agricultural labouers, and others must inevitably become a part of this one peasant organization. In the meantime there will be two organizations, but the final goal and result must be a merged movement and organization, for only in that way can the interests of the true kisans, the rural poor of all definitions be fully served. Sahajanand is under no illusion that this will be an easy task; it will take time, he tells us. Again his logic here of agrarian change being part of an ongoing process is apparent. Final solutions do not happen today or tomorrow in the world of human experience. And that process as he reveals shortly will require not only compromise but also accommodation to the real world within which these changes will happen.

For a definition of peasant classes that bears many similarities to those of Sahajanand but differs in one critical direction, see P. Sundarayya on "The Land Question," All-India Kisan Sabha, 1976. He maintains that "A poor peasant never employs wage labour and hence does not exploit it." This is not a view entirely consistent with Sahjanand's descriptions. (See Utsa Patnaik, *Peasant Class Differentiation* (Delhi: Oxford University Press, 1987), Appendix A). Sundarayya's evidence is from Andhra Pradesh, and his most notable activism was in the Telengana movement, 1948-52.

6. In this concluding peroration of this brief text, Sahajanand's commitment to the idea of transformational change comes out clearly, as does his determination to achieve that kind of change for the benefit of the nation and the rural poor who constitute its agrarian core.

Addendum

(The following note appears on the last page of the copy book in which Sahajanand had written the Hindi text of Khet Mazdoor. He does not refer to this Eastern Economist quote in the text itself, but it clearly was additional evidence for the economic proposals he was making in Chapter IV. Ed.)

The Eastern Economist, 311 page
Postwar Employment

Here is a proposal from Mr. D.K. Sanyal, Secretary of the Appointment Board of the Calcutta University who can undoubtedly speak with authority on the subject. According to Mr. Sanyal's estimate immediate employment must be found for nearly 3,000,000 persons. The immediate avenues of employment which he suggests are: the road transport development scheme to be completed in 10 years instead of 20 years as recommended by the Nagpur Conference; 250 million acres of land classified as cultivable waste or fallow to be brought under cultivation according to the recommendations of the Imperial Council of Agricultural Research.

"The agrarian programme must be centred around the Soviets of Agricultural Labourers' Deputies" (Lenin, "April Theses").

Swami Sahajanand Saraswati

प्रवेशिका।

यों तो खेत-मजदूरों, खेती के मजदूरों (Agricultural Labourers) यानी हलवाहे, चरवाहे वगैरह का सवाल शोषित एवं पीड़ित जनता, मजलूम जनता के सवाल का एक बहुत ही महत्वपूर्ण अंग है, बड़ा हिस्सा है। इसलिये जब कभी यह प्रश्न उठे और उठते हैं, इसका ठीक ठीक हल हो जाना निहायत जरूरी है। इसीलिये जो लोग कमाने वाली जनता के हामी हैं और जो इसकी सभी समस्याओं एवं गुत्थियों को सुलझाने में दिन रात लगे हैं उन्हें इन खेत मजदूरों के प्रश्नों का स्वागत करने को तैयार ही नहीं रहना चाहिये, बल्कि खुद भी उनकी दिक्कतों और तकलीफों को ढूंढ निकालना चाहिये। अगर वे लोग सचमुच किसानों का उद्धार करना चाहते हैं, मजदूरों का निस्तार करने पर तुले बैठे हैं, तो उनकी ईमानदारी की परीक्षा और जांच सिर्फ इसी बात से हो जायगी कि वे इन खेत-मजदूरों की बातों को किस नजर से देखते हैं और क्या इनमें उन्हें खास दिलचस्पी है या नहीं। अगर किसानों का ताल्लुक खेती और उसके सवालों से है तो खेत-मजदूरों का तो और भी ज्यादा है। वही तो खेती की जड़ हैं, मूलाधार हैं, हाथ-पांव हैं। इसीलिये खेती और किसानों की बात उठते ही

PART II

Khet Mazdoor

Swami Sahajanand Saraswati

(As indicated in the Editor's Preface and the Editor's Introduction, what follows is the original Hindi text, exactly as written by Sahajanand in 1941. It should be noted that this is often rural, colloquial Hindi usage. The colloquial forms have all been retained as in the original. There are no editorial interventions or emendatioins in these pag[illegible] except in the one or two places where there are clearly omissi[illegible]s in Sahajanand's English quotations. At those infrequent points the editorial (*sic*) has been introduced to indicate an omission. As is explained in an Editorial Note to Chapter II in the English translation, Sahajanand, when he was referring to the two villages studied by Harold H. Mann, mistakenly describes a nearby ammunition factory as an "aluminium" factory. Other infrequent editorial changes can be located in the edited translation. But, to repeat, the text which follows, is exactly as Sahajanand wrote it. Ed.)

खेत—मजदूर

—स्वामी सहजानन्द सरस्वती—

प्रवेशिका

यों तो खेत-मजदूरों, खेती के मजदूरों (Agricultural Labourers) यानी चलवाहे, चरवाहे वगैरह का सवाल शोषित एवं पीड़ित जनता, मजलूम जनता के सवाल का एक बहुत ही महत्वपूर्ण अंग है, बड़ा हिस्सा है। इसलिये जब कभी यह प्रश्न उठे ठीक ही है। इसका ठीक ठीक हल हो जाना भी निहायत जरूरी है। इसीलिये जो लोग कमाने वाली जनता के हामी हैं और जो इसकी सभी समस्याओं एवं गुत्थियों को सुलझाने में दिन रात लगे हैं उन्हें इन खेतमजदूरों के प्रश्नों का स्वागत करने को तैयार ही नहीं रहना चाहिये बल्कि खुद भी उनकी दिक्कतों और तकलीफों को ढूंढ निकालना चाहिये। अगर वे लोग सचमुच किसानों का उद्धार करना चाहते हैं, मजदूरों का निस्तार करने पर तुले बैठे हैं, तो उनकी ईमानदारी की परीक्षा और जांच सिर्फ इसी बात से हो जायगी कि वे इन खेत-मजदूरों की बातों को किस नजर से देखते हैं और आया इनमें उन्हें काफी दिलचस्पी है या नहीं। अगर किसानों का ताल्लुक खेती और उसके सवालों से है तो खेत-मजदूरों का तो और भी ज्यादा है। वही तो खेती की जड़ हैं, मूलाधार हैं, हाथ पांव हैं। इसीलिये खेती और किसानों की बात उठते ही उनकी समस्या सबसे पहले आ खड़ी होती है। ऐसी हालत में उसे अच्छी तरह हल किये बिना ही यह समझ बैठना कि खेती से सम्बन्ध रखने वाले प्रश्न हल हो गये, निरी नादानी और बेईमानी है।

मगर आज की बात कुछ निराली सी है। जहां एक ओर सचमुच गरीबों के लिए चौबीसों घंटे मर मिटने वाले और उनकी सारी तकलीफों को मार भगाने की धुन वाले मस्तानों की टोली इन खेत-मजदूरों से सम्बन्ध रखने वाले सभी मसलों की उधेड़ बुन कर रही है, तहां दूसरी ओर शोषक और शासक या यों कहिये कि मिहनतकशों तथा श्रमजीवियों के खून पीने वाले ओर उनके पिट्ठू भी परीशान हैं। उनकी नींद हराम है। इसलिये वे लोग भी इन खेत-मजदूरों के प्रश्नों को उठाते हैं—इसलिये नहीं कि इन गरीबों की तकलीफों को दूर करें या उन्हें कुछ आराम दें दिलायें। बल्कि केवल इसलिये कि शोषितों एवं पीड़ितों के भीतर ही आपस में लड़ाई लगवादें। जिससे दलबन्दी की दलदल में फंस जाने पर शोषकों के खिलाफ लड़ी जाने वाली उनकी लड़ाई का संयुक्त मोर्चा खत्म हो जाय और वह लड़ाई इस

तरह खटाई में पड़ जाय। क्योंकि मजलूमों और पीड़ितों का तो एक ही बल है और वह है उनकी सम्मिलित शक्ति या मजमूई ताकत। फलतः इसमें गड़बड़ी हुई कि सारा मामला चौपट हुआ, सारी लड़ाई हवा हुई।

असल में किसान सभा की बढ़ती हुई ताकत और किसान आन्दोलन की तेजी को देख के जमींदारों और उनके भाई बन्धुओं के होश ठिकाने रही नहीं गये हैं। उनके दिल और दिमाग में कुछ ऐसा खौफ और आतंक छा गया है कि उसका बयान किया नहीं जा सकता है। नतीजा यह हुआ है कि वे सभी तरह की बन्दिशें किसान आन्दोलन को कुचलने के लिए करने लगे हैं। कानूनी और गैर कानूनी एक भी उपाय काम में लाने से चूकते नहीं। बिहार में खासकर तथा अन्य प्रान्तों में भी कानून और शांति के नाम पर किसानों एवं किसान कार्यकर्त्ताओं का जो दमन इधर कुछ वर्षों के भीतर हुआ है वह निराला है। सच्चे और झूठे मुकद्दमों की जो लड़ी लग गई थी वह किसान सभा के इतिहास में पहली बात थी। इसी के साथ जो गुंडेबाजी, जो लाठी राज, जो बेतहाशा मारपीट और लूटपाट जमींदारों ने जगह-जगह की, कराई वह भी सोलहों आने नई बात थी। मालूम होता था, कोई सरकार हई नहीं। मजलूमों का पुर्सा हाल कोई भी नजर न आता था सिवाय किसान सभा वालों के।

एक ओर तो यह किया गया। दूसरी ओर जमींदारों के पैसे, उनकी कोशिश पैरवी और उन्हीं के बल पर खेत-मजदूरों में आन्दोलन किया गया। बिहार में तो यह बात खूब ही की गई। मगर एकाध और प्रान्तों में भी यही चीज पाई गई। जहां किसान आन्दोलन तेज था वहीं यह बात देखी गई। जमींदारों के अलावे कुछ ऐसे चलते पुर्जे लोगों ने भी यह काम किया जो सस्ती लीडरी और नामधाम कमाने की इच्छा के साथ ही नगद नारायण के जमा करने की भी फिक्र रखते हैं। उन्होंने देखा कि यही तो मौका है। चूकने से पछताना होगा। उन्हीं को पक्के अवसरवादी कहते भी हैं जो मौके से फायदा उठाने से कभी बाज नहीं आते । नतीजा यह हुआ कि खेत-मजदूरों के बरसाती नेताओं की भरमार हो गई, जगह-जगह। उनकी सभायें होने लगीं, उनमें बड़े-बड़े प्रस्ताव पास होने लगे, किसानों के सामने असंभव मांगें भी पेश की जाने लगीं कुछ उचित मांगों के साथ ही, और उनके पूरा न होने पर हल वगैरह का काम बन्द कर देने की धमकी भी दी जाने लगी। कई जगह तो काम बन्द भी करवा दिया गया।

इसी के साथ-साथ एक बात और भी हुई। बिहार में जब किसानों के विराट प्रदर्शन पटने में तथा हजारों अन्य स्थानों पर होने लगे तो देखादेखी

खेत-मजदूरों के प्रदर्शन की भी नकल की गई। पटने में एक प्रदर्शन जैसे तैसे किया भी गया। बिहार प्रान्तीय किसान कान्फ्रेंस के समय मोतिहारी में भी एक छोटा सा दल ऐसा कर रहा था। इसमें कुछ उन महानुभावों का भी हाथ था जो अपने को गांधीवादी कहते हैं। या यों कह सकते हैं कि जितने लोग और जितने दल किसी कारण से किसान सभा और उसके आन्दोलन के विरोधी हैं और उसे बर्दाश्त नहीं कर सकते उन सबों का किसी न किसी रूप में इस खेत-मजदूर आन्दोलन में हाथ रहा है। यहां तक कि किसी वजह से जो इसमें कुछ भी हाथ बंटा नहीं सके वह दिल से इसका समर्थन तो करते ही रहे। इसे देख-देख के खुश भी होते रहे। जब हमने अंग्रेजी में छपी एक पुस्तिका देखी जिसके ऊपर लिखा था कि खेत-मजदूर आन्दोलन की यह रिपोर्ट है, तो हमारे ताज्जुब का ठिकाना न रहा। यह तथाकथित रिपोर्ट जहां तक हमारी जांच से पता चला हिन्दी में या और भाषाओं में न छापकर सिर्फ अंग्रेजी में ही छपी थी। गोया खेत-मजदूर अंग्रेजी के अलावे दूसरी भाषाएं या तो जानते ही नहीं, या उनके बिना इनके काम में हर्ज नहीं होता। ये अपना काम सिर्फ अंग्रेजी से ही चला लेते हैं।

इस रिपोर्ट से साफ पता चला कि असल में बाहरी दुनियां की आंखों में धूल झोंकने ही लिये इस आन्दोलन का रूप ख़ड़ा किया गया है। खेत-मजदूरों की सेवा से इसे कोई मतलब नहीं है। यह केवल प्रचार और प्रोपैगैन्डा के लिये एक नया जरिया बनाया गया है। इसीलिये तो सिर्फ अंग्रेजी में ही रिपोर्ट छापी गई, ताकि बाहरी दुनियां पढ़ सके। इतना हीं नहीं। हरिपुरा में जो कांग्रेस का अधिवेशन 1938 में हुआ था उसी समय आल इन्डिया खेत-मजदूर सम्मेलन के अधिवेशन की बार-बार खबर अखबारों में छपी थी। सरदार बल्लभ भाई पटेल ही उसके सभापति होंगे यह भी प्रकाशित हुआ था। मगर कुछ बातें ऐसी हो गई जिससे न तो वह कान्फ्रेंस ही हो सकी और न सरदार बल्लभ भाई सभापति ही बने। मगर इससे साफ हो जाता है कि खेत-मजूदर आन्दोलन के पीछे कौन हैं और इसका मकसद (लक्ष्य) क्या है। कौन नहीं जानता कि सरदार बल्लभ भाई से बढ़के शायद ही कोई किसान सभा का दुश्मन हो ?

यह भी बात है कि कौंसिल, असेम्बली आदि के चुनाव में सफलता का साधन भी यह आन्दोलन बनाया गया है। इसीलिये तो ऐन उसी मौके पर इसमें तेजी आती है और चुनाव के आगे पीछे कुछी समय तक वह कायम रहती है। बाद में कुछ पता ही नहीं चलता कि आया वह जिन्दा है या

मर गया। यह भी देखा गया है कि अकसर वही लोग उसमें ज्यादातर शरीक होते हैं जिन्हें चुनाव की गर्ज है। हमने खुद देखा है कि जिन लीडरों और उनके साथियों के रोजमर्रा के कामों से खेत-मजदूर तबाह और बेईज्जत होते रहते हैं, भूखों मरते रहते हैं, उजड़ जाते हैं वही लोग उनकी सभाओं में प्रायः शरीक होते रहते हैं। आखिर उन्हें अमली तौर पर तो कुछ करना है नहीं। बल्कि उलटे ही करना है। मगर बातें बनाने और रस्म अदाई की तौर पर बाहरी हमदर्दी दिखाने में वे क्यों चूकने लगे?

इसका यह मतलब कतई नहीं कि जो लोग इस आन्दोलन में शमिल हैं वे सौ फीसदी-सभी के सभी- ऐसे ही हैं, उनमें एक दो चार भी ईमानदारी के साथ इस काम में नहीं पड़ते। जरूर ईमानदार लोग भी यह काम करते हैं। मगर उन्हें हम उंगलियों पर गिनने लायक भी शायद ही पाते हैं। वे एकाध ही होते हैं—बिरले होते हैं । उनकी नीयत भी दुरुस्त रहती है। उनका यकीन है कि ऐसा करके वे वाकई खेत-मजदूरों को असली फायदा पहुँचा रहे हैं। मगर यहीं उनकी भारी भूल है। जिस फायदे के खयाल से वे उसमें पड़ते हैं वह तो होता नहीं। क्योंकि उस आन्दोलन के असली चलाने वाले दिल से चाहते नहीं कि वैसा हो और खेत-मजदूरों को जल्द से जल्द कुछ आराम मिले। उन्हें तो अपना उल्लू सीधा करना है। फिर उन गरीबों का काम हो तो कैसे? लेकिन उनके हजार न चाहने पर भी इस आन्दोलन के चलते धीरे धीरे जब इन पीड़ितों की नींद टूटेगी और असलियत को वे ठीक-ठीक समझने लगेंगे कि उनकी सारी विपदा और तकलीफों, उनकी बेइज्जतियों और अपमानों, उनकी भूख और बीमारी के असली कारण हैं कौन और वे दूर होंगे कैसे, तब उनका असली लाभ हो के ही रहेगा। इसे कोई रोक नहीं सकता। इसलिये इस दृष्टि से हरेक आदमी को, जो शोषितों और पीड़ितों की सेवा और मदद करना चाहता है, इस आन्दोलन का दिल से स्वागत ही करना चाहिये। उनके जगने में यह भी कुछ न कुछ मदद देगा ही और बिना जगे कुछ हो सकता नहीं।

तब तो इन यारों की भी आंखें खुलेंगी और ये अपने किये पर पछतायेंगे भी। मगर इससे क्या? तब तो वह काम रुक न सकेगा। बल्कि वे लोग तो इस खतरे से आज भी सजग हैं। इसीलिये वो इस आन्दोलन को हर तरह से अपने ही हाथों में रखना चाहते हैं और इसमें तेजी भी आने देता नहीं चाहते। मगर उन्हें याद रखना चाहिये कि इससे कुछ होने जाने का नहीं। यह उनकी या किसी की भी ताकत के बाहर की चीज है कि मजलूमों और पीड़ितों के आन्दोलन को शुरू करके आखिर में उसे अपने

कब्जे में रख सकें, चाहे उसका आरम्भ कितनी ही होशियारी और चालाकी से क्यों न किया जाय और चाहे वह कितना ही धीरे-धीरे या फूंक-फूंक के क्यों न चलाया जाय। असल में ऐसे आन्दोलनों का जन्म तो इसी तरह प्रायः होता ही है। अकसर इन्हें आरम्भ करते हैं वही लोग जो पीछे चलकर इनसे घबराने लगते हैं, यहां तक कि मिटा देना चाहते हैं। मगर तब उन्हें केवल कलेजा मसोसना ही हाथ लगता है। ये आन्दोलन तो मर सकते नहीं, जब तक वे शोषितों और पीड़ितों का पूरा उद्धार न कर लें। यह दूसरी बात है कि बीच बीच में परिस्थितिवश से दब जाया करें।

यह भी बात है कि बहुत से किसान किसान सभा और उसके आन्दोलन में शरीक होकर भी मन ही मन यह समझे बैठे हैं कि किसान सभा से फायदा उठ लें। मगर खेती के मजदूरों के साथ अपना रवैया न बदलें -उनके साथ सख्ती और बेमुरव्वती से ही पेश आते रहें। उन्होंने शायद यह समझ लिया है कि किसान सभा एक खास जमात की चीज है, ठीक उसी तरह जैसे जमींदार-सभा। मगर उन्हें जान लेना चाहिए कि किसी बंधीबंधाई जमात की चीज न हो के यह सभा खेती से संबंध रखनी वाली और उसी के जरिये गुजर करने वाली शोषित एवं पीड़ित जनता की चीज है। इसीलिये जो जितना ही ज्यादा पीड़ित और दुखिया है उतना ही ज्यादा वह किसान सभा के नजदीक है–किसान सभा भी उसके उतना ही निकट है। जुल्म और अत्याचार चाहे किसान करे या जमींदार या और ही कोई। मगर सभी बराबर हैं और किसान सभा उसे हर्गिज बर्दाश्त नहीं कर सकती। खेत मजदूर सब से अधिक दुखिया होने के कारण किसान सभा की नजर सबसे पहले उन्हीं पर जानी चाहिये और जाती भी है।

ऊपर लिखी बातें तथा इन जैसी ही और भी कितनी हीं हैं जिनपर प्रकाश डालना और जिन्हें अच्छी तरह समझा देना निहायत जरूरी है। खेत-मजदूरों का मसला मामूली न होकर बड़ा ही पेचीदा है। इन्हें किसान समझें या मजदूर यह भी एक बड़ा सा सवाल है और इसके हल कर लेने पर ही इस ओर हम बहुत कुछ आसानी से पांव बढ़ा सकते हैं। इस संबंध में आगे लिखी गई पंक्तियों का यही मतलब है कि सारी बातों का स्पष्ट विवेचन हो जाय।

सेन्ट्रल जेल, हजारीबाग
महाशिवरात्रि
24.2.1941

स्वामी सहजानन्द सरस्वती

1

खेत—मजदूर - - - तब और अब

आज जब जिधर ही देखिये सदियों से पददलित तथा युगों से शोषित जनता न सिर्फ अपने सवालों को ही मुस्तैदी से संसार के सामने पेश कर रही है, किन्तु उन्हें अपने अनुकूल हल करने के लिये भी या तो कमर बांध चुकी है या बांध रही है, तो खेती के मजदूरों की समस्याएं और उनके बहुत ही पेचीदे मसले, जिनके करते वे पिस रहे हैं, घुल-घुल के मर रहे हैं, न उठें न उठाये जांय यह बात तो दिमाग में आने की ही नहीं। जब किसानों और मजदूरों की रोटी, कपड़े वगैरह के सवालों को हमेशा के लिये एक ही बार ठीक कर डालने के खयाल से हजारों नहीं लाखों जन सेवक युवक और वृद्ध, स्त्री तथा पुरुष कमरबांधे मैदानेजंग में कूद चुके और कूद रहे हैं, तो फिर खेती में काम करने वालों का इसी सम्बन्ध का प्रश्न यों ही खटाई में पड़ा कैसे रह सकता है? इस पहेली को हमें सुलझाना ही होगा और इसीलिये सबों के सामने इसे अपने असली रूप में ला के खड़ा करना पड़ेगा ही। ताकि इस पर पूरा प्रकाश पड़े । और अगर हमने यह काम नहीं भी किया, या इससे मुँह मोड़ लिया तो सिर्फ बदनामी और पछतावा ही हमारे हाथ लगेंगे। ये प्रश्न और ये सवाल तो खुद ब खुद उस हालत में हमारे सामने क्या हमारे सर पर आ खड़े होंगे। हम इनसे भले ही भागना चाहें मगर ये तो हम से भागने के बजाय जबर्दस्ती हमारा पल्ला पकड़ेंगे, हमारा पीछा करेंगे। और नहीं तो इन खेत-मजदूरों के दिली दुश्मन ही इनको ला धमकायेंगे। समय की गति जो ठहरी।

और आखिर यह सवाल उठें क्यों न? यही नहीं कि खेती में काम करने वाले ये लोग अत्यन्त दीनदुखिया और सताये हुए हैं और न सिर्फ यही कि वर्त्तमान समाज में कल कारखानों के मजदूरों या किसानों की ही तरह वे एक महत्वपूर्ण स्थान रखते हैं। ये कारण तो हईं और उनकी समस्याओं को हमारे सामने जबर्दस्ती ला धकेलने के लिये ये दोनों ही वजहें काफी भी हैं। मगर सब से बड़ी बात है कि उनकी तादाद बहुत बड़ी है जो कल कारखाने के मजदूरों की संख्या से तो कहीं जबर्दस्त है। इसी के साथ बहुत बड़ी खूबी यह है कि इनकी यह संख्या शैतान की अंतड़ी की तरह बराबर

ही बढ़ रही है। सो भी जमीन रखने वाले किसानों को हटाकर उन्हीं की जगह जहां एक ओर मुफ्तखोर जमींदार नामधारियों की तादाद बेतहाशा बढ़ रही है तहां दूसरी ओर इन खेत-मजदूरों, या यों कहिये कि बिना जमीन वाले किसानों का नम्बर ऊपर सर उठाये चला जा रहा है। हम अच्छी तरह देख रहे हैं कि किसानों के हाथ से जमीनें धड़ाधड़ निकली चली जा रही हैं। वे या तो निर्दयता के साथ ज्यादे से ज्यादा लगान वसूलने और उसी पर सदलबल गुलछर्रे उड़ाने वाले जमींदारों के हाथों में चली जाती हैं जो उन किसानों से बहुत ही दूर और खासकर बड़े-बड़े शहरों में ही ज्यादातर रहते हैं, या सूदखोर बनियों और महाजनों के कब्जे में, जो उन जमीनों को उन्हीं के साथ बन्दोबस्त करते हैं जो अधिक से अधिक लगान देते हैं। सो भी यह बन्दोबस्त अधिकांश में अस्थायी या चन्दरोजा ही होता है। ताकि उनने जभी चाहा ये जमीनें निकाल के फिर दूसरों को दे दीं जो और भी ज्यादा पैसे दे सकें या जिनसे कुछ ज्यादा काम निकल सके। इसका यह भी नतीजा होता है कि किसान इन जमीन वाले बनियों या जमींदार-साहुकारों से हर घड़ी थर्राते रहते हैं। उनके खिलाफ चूं कर सकते नहीं। यह बात अभी-अभी साफ हुई जाती है।

असल में खेतों में कमाने या काम करने वालों की संख्या तो उस समय भी बहुत ज्यादा थी जब पहले पहले खेती करने की विद्या और तरकीब मानव समाज ने जानी और धीरे-धीरे इस काम को खूब फैला दिया। मगर उस दशा में और आज की हालत में जमीन आसमान का फ़र्क था। जहां खेती की तरक्की और उसका व्यापक विस्तार होने के साथ-साथ पहले जमाने में खेती में काम करने वालों की तादाद क्रमशः घटने लगी और लोग धीरे-धीरे दूसरे प्रकार की जीविकाओं और कामधन्दों में जाने लगे, तहां आज इनकी तादाद फिर बढ़ने लगी है। दूसरे कामधन्दों से ये लोग जबर्दस्ती बाहर निकाले जाने लगे हैं और अपने पुराने खेतों से भी। इस तरह आज तो उलटी गंगा बहने लगी है। वह न जानें क्या गजब ढायेगी और किसे-किसे उजाड़े बसायेगी। कमाके खुद खाने तथा गैरों को खिलाने वाले और इस प्रकार अपने खून को पानी बना डालने वाले इन लोगों की जीविका के सभी साधनों से होने वाली आहिस्ता आहिस्ता की यह बेदखली बहुत ही खतरनाक है। हमें बहुत ही ठंडे दिल दिमाग से इस भीषण परिस्थिति पर न सिर्फ विचार ही करना होगा, बल्कि बहादुरी के साथ इसका सामना भी करना पड़ेगा। नहीं तो यह सभी को ले बैठेगी।

आइये जरा इस हालत की और भी सफाई कर लें। ताकि इसका असली

और विकराल रूप हमारी आंखों के सामने अच्छी तरह नाचने लगे। तभी इसे हम बखूबी समझ सकेंगे। तभी इस बात की जरूरत भी महसूस करेंगे कि इसका सामना खामखाह करना चाहिये। तभी हममें सामना करने की पूरी हिम्मत भी आयेगी। हम उसी के मुताबिक अपनी तैयारी भी तभी कर सकेंगे। अभी तो हालत यह है कि जोई उठता है सोई इस समस्या के सुलझाने के लिए कुछ न कुछ बातें बोल ही देता और कुछ उपाय सुझाई देता है। आगा पीछा वह सोची नहीं सकता। क्योंकि सारी बातें तो उसे मालूम नहीं हैं। उसके सामने इस गहन समस्या के सभी पहलू आये ही नहीं हैं। इसीलिये वह सोच भी नहीं सकता कि उसके इन उपायों का असर दूसरों पर क्या होगा, ये उपाय कारगर हैं या नहीं आदि-आदि। यदि पूरी बातें उसे मालूम हों तो वह खुद सोचेगा कि उसके ये रास्ते शायद स्थिति को और भी बदतर बना देंगे। अतएव जल्दी में बिना अच्छी तरह छानबीन किये ही वह कोई बात इनके मुतल्लिक उस दशा में बोल सकेगा नहीं।

हां, तो हम उस बात को लें। यह तो सभी मानते हैं कि जब धीरे धीरे मनुष्यों की संख्या इस भूमंडल पर बढ़ने लगी तो उनकी जीविका का प्रश्न जटिल होने लगा। फलतः मुस्तैदी से खोज शुरू हुई कि जंगली जीवों या घासपात और फलफूल आदि के सिवाय क्षुधानिवृत्ति का कोई और भी जरिया है या नहीं। इस माथापच्ची तथा जांच पड़ताल में पड़े लोगों को जब पहले पहल खेती करने की सूझी, जब यह बात दिमाग में आई कि जमीन के भीतर बीज के रूप में जौ, गेहूं आदि के दाने डालकर उनसे दस बीस गुना पैदा किया जा सकता है, तो मानना होगा कि जीविका के उपाय के सम्बन्ध में एक बड़ी क्रांति हो गई। जमीन तो लम्बी और पैदावार थी ही। फिर चाहे जितनी दूर में फसल बोओ। केवल जंगलों को काट कूट के साफ करने की जरूरत थी। परिणामस्वरूप, एक बार खेती का खूब ही विस्तार हुआ। प्रायः सभी प्रजा, सभी जनता इस काम में लग गई। आज की तरह न तो जमीन पर कोई बन्धन था और न जमींदार या सरकार की तरह लगान या माल वसूलने वाले ही थे। तब रूकावट कैसी? जिससे जितनी बन पड़ी उतनी जमीन जोतता बोता था। एक बार तो सभी लोग प्रधानतया खेती में ही काम करने लगे, उसी के द्वारा प्रधान रूप से जीविका चलाने लगे। वेदों, वैदिक ग्रन्थों और महाभारत आदि इतिहासों में जो 'विशः', 'विशांपति' आदि शब्द पाये जाते हैं वे इसी बात के सूचक हैं।

बेशक पीछे चलके 'विश' या 'वैश्य' शब्द एक खास जाति या श्रेणी का वाचक बन गया और उसी के जिम्मे खेती का कारबार सौंपा गया। बाकी

लोग दूसरे दूसरे कामों में लग गये। यह बात तब हुई जब समाज के विकास के साथ उसकी रक्षा एवं समुन्नति के लिए वर्ण और आश्रम के विभाग बनाये गये। सारांश यह है कि जब समाज के कई दल बना के उन्हें अलग-अलग जवाबदेही सौंपी गई उसी समय वैश्य नाम का एक वर्ण खसतौर से खेती में लगा दिया गया। अब तो यह भी बात लापता है। पता ही नहीं चलता कि कौन वैश्य है, कौन नहीं। क्योंकि खेती सभी करते हैं। पहले यह बात न थी कि दूसरे वर्ण बिल्कुल ही खेती करते ही न थे। थोड़ी बहुत खेती तो ब्राह्मण तक भी करते थे। इसीलिये तो वेदों में भी यह बात मिलती है। मनु ने तो अपनी स्मृति के चौथे अध्याय के शुरू में ही "अमृतंकर्षराांमतम्", "तेनचैवापिजीव्यते" आदि के द्वारा ब्राह्मण के लिये भी खेती बताई है। दूसरे स्मृतिकारों ने भी ऐसा ही किया है। फिर भी यह प्रधान काम तो वैश्य का ही माना गया है। यह उसी का काम बताया गया है कि खेती के जरिये सबों के लिए अन्नादि पैदा करे।

मगर शुरू में यह 'वैश्य' या 'विश' शब्द प्रजा या जनतामात्र का ही बाचक माना जाता था। दरअसल प्रजा शब्द का वही अर्थ है जो जनता या जनसमूह का। 'विशांपति' शब्द का अर्थ है प्रजापति या राजा। मालूम होता है जमीन में बीज का सामूहिक रूप से प्रवेश कराने के कारण ही यह 'विश' शब्द पहले पहल प्रचलित हुआ। उस समय सभी लोग यह काम करते भी थे। क्योंकि एक तो यह नई बात थी, दिलचस्प थी। दूसरे इस प्रकार खेती करने से घर के पास ही खाने पीने के लिए अन्न हो जाता था। फलतः जीविका के लिये दूर दराज के देशों में जाना न पड़ता था। फिर तो सबों का खेती में लग जाना स्वाभाविक ही था। इसीलिये विश या वैश्य नाम सभी लोगों का, जनसमूह का, प्रजा या जनता का ही पड़ गया।

खेती में काम करने वालों की, या यदि कहें तो कह सकते हैं कि खेती के मजदूरों — खेत-मजदूरों की यह पहली दशा थी। हां, इस दशा में आज के उनके सम्बन्ध के प्रश्न उठी नहीं सकते थे। इनकी तब गुंजाइश थी ही कहां? "नविशेषोऽस्ति वर्णानां सर्वं ब्राह्ममिदं जगत्। ब्रह्मणा पूर्वं स्टष्टंहि कर्मभिर्वर्णतां गतम्" (मोक्षधर्म अध्या. 188/10), महाभारत के इस कथन का भी कि "ब्रह्मा की पैदा की हुई सृष्टि में कोई भेद या दल न था। सभी बराबर थे। यह तो पीछे चलकर विभिन्न कामों के करते ही वर्णों की जुदी-जुदी रचना हुई।" यही मतलब है कि शुरू में सभी लोग एकी तरह के काम करते थे।

इस प्रकार कुछ समय यों ही गुजर जाने के बाद ऐसा भी मौका आया

कि नये-नये उद्योगधन्दों की खोज हुई। जनसंख्या की वृद्धि के साथ ही उनकी जरूरतें भी बढ़ने लगीं। परस्पर संघर्ष और शत्रुओं के हमले भी होने लगे। ज्ञान की वृद्धि के साथ ही उसके लिये खास विभाग बनाने की भी जरूरत समाज ने महसूस की। लड़ाई दंगे होने पर भी खेतीबारी का काम न रुके और न अन्वेषण या खोज का। नहीं तो आफत होगी और सभी लोग यों ही तबाह हो जायंगे। इसीलिये जहां लड़ने भिड़ने का काम एक खास दल, विशेष वर्ण को सौंपा गया, तहां पढ़ने सोचने और खेतीबारी का काम भी ब्राह्मण और वैश्य वर्ग को क्रमशः दे दिया गया। इस प्रकार अब विश या वैश्य शब्द प्रजा या जनता के मानी में न बोला जाकर मानव समाज के एक खास दल, वर्ण या विभाग के अर्थ में प्रयुक्त हो गया।

हां, एक चौथा दल भी बनाया गया जिसे संरक्षित (Reserve) दल या शूद्र कहने लगे। इसका यही काम तय पाया कि जरूरत पड़ने पर शेष तीन दलों की सहायता हर तरह से करे। ज्यादातर दौड़ धूप और शारीरिक काम ही इस दल के जिम्मे था। तभी तो सभी दलों को इससे सहायता संभव थी। मगर यह बात न थी कि यह चौथा दल दिमागी काम करता ही न था। अनेकों प्रकार के कारीगर और मिस्त्री भी प्रायः इसी दल में होते थे। स्मृतियों में इन्हें भी शूद्र नाम से ही पुकारा गया है। इस प्रकार समाज के लिये शूद्र वर्ण एक रक्षित सेना (Reserve force) का काम करता था। एक ओर तो कला कौशल और कारीगरी के सम्बन्ध के जितने काम समाज के लिये जरूरी होते थे उनकी पूर्ति शूद्र ही करते थे। यहां तक कि रसोई बनाने का काम भी शूद्रों का ही माना जाता था। ऐसा स्पष्ट लिखा है। इसीलिये पाचक (रसोइया) का काम करने वाले ब्राह्मण को शूद्र के समान ही माना है, जैसा कि "पाचकश्चैव षडेते शूद्रवद् द्विजाः" से स्पष्ट है। दूसरी ओर शेष तीन वर्णों में जहां जिसे आदमी की जरूरत हुई कि इसी रक्षित सेना ने उसकी पूर्ति की। बिना दिमागी काम किये ही वे लोग कारीगरी आदि के ज्ञाता कैसे हो सकते थे? और अगर शूद्र शब्द का यही अर्थ न माना जाता रहता तो छान्दोग्योपनिषद (4/2/3/5) में जानश्रुति नामक क्षत्रिय राजा को रैक्व ऋषि बार बार शूद्र क्यों कहके पुकारते, जैसा कि "अरेत्वा शूद्र", "आजहारेमाः शूद्र" आदि वाक्यों से स्पष्ट है? उस ऋषि के द्वारा बोले गये इस शब्द का जो भी अर्थ भाष्यकारों ने किया है उससे ही साफ है कि शूद्र शब्द का पहले वह संकुचित अर्थ नहीं था जो दुर्भाग्य से आज माना जाता है।

यही बात वैश्य के बारे में भी शुरू में जरूर थी जबकि वर्णों की रचना

नहीं हुई थी। बेशक उस रचना के बाद वह शब्द प्रजा या जनता के अर्थ में प्रयुक्त न हो कर उसके एक अंश मात्र का बोधक रह गया। लेकिन उसी के साथ शूद्र वर्ग की भी रचना हुई जो व्यापक अर्थ में प्रचलित थी। साथ ही एक बात और भी हुई। जब खेती का अधिकार आमतौर से सब के लिये न होकर एक हद तक सीमित हो गया, तो दूसरों के द्वारा खेती करवाने का भी श्रीगणेश हुआ। कही चुके हैं कि वैश्य वर्ण के साथ खेती का आम अधिकार सीमित हो जाने पर भी दूसरे वर्ण इससे सोलहों आने वञ्चित न किये गये। खास कर ब्राह्मणों को तो यह अधिकार था कि वह खुद अपने काम के लिये खेती से भी अन्न पैदा कर सकते हैं, करें। मनुस्मृति का उल्लेख हो चुका है। दूसरी स्मृतियों ने भी इस पर काफी जोर दिया है। इस बात का विस्तृत विवेचन मैंने "ब्रह्मर्षिवंशविस्तर" नामक पुस्तक में किया है।

लेकिन खेती की आज्ञा देने पर भी ब्राह्मणों के लिये यह नियम था कि भरसक वे अपने हाथों खेती न करके औरों से ही करायें। हां, जब वे इस बात के लिए समर्थ न हों और या तो उन्हें खेती के लिए मजदूर तथा काम करने वाले मिलें ही न, या अगर मिलें भी तो उन्हें उचित मजदूरी वगैरह वे किन्हीं कारणों से दे के सन्तुष्ट न कर सकें, तो खुद अपने हाथों भी खेती कर सकते हैं, ऐसा नियम बनाया गया। इन दोनों प्रकार की खेतियों को क्रमशः अस्वयंकृता और स्वयंकृता कहते थे। स्वयंकृता के मानी हैं अपने हाथों की गई और अस्वयंकृता का अर्थ है दूसरों से कराई हुई। जिन पुरानी पोथियों में ब्राह्मणों को खेती करने का अधिकार मिलता है उन्हीं में ये ब्यौरे भी लिखे गये हैं।

चाहे इसका मतलब शुरू में कुछ भी क्यों न रहा हो। फिर भी यहीं से खेती के मजदूरों का श्रीगणेश उस मानी में होता है जिस मानी में आज हम यह शब्द बोलते हैं। भारत से बाहर के मुल्कों में जो सर्फ (Serf) या खेतों में काम करने वाले गुलामों का जिक्र पहले जमाने में पाया जाता है वह कुछ इसी ढंग की बात है। व्यवहार में या अमली तौर पर चाहे उसमें और भारत की व्यवस्था में प्रारम्भ में बहुत ज्यादा फर्क क्यों न रहा हो, फिर भी सिद्धांत के रूप में दोनों बातों, दोनों व्यवस्थाओं को एक ही स्थान मिलता है। आखिर खेती में काम करने वालों (Serfs) तथा दूसरे गुलामों में, जो उनसे पहले पाये जाते थे और इन "सर्फ" लोगों के समय में भी जहां तहां थे, मगर विलुप्त हो रहे थे और उनकी जगह ये खेती के काम करने वाले ही ले रहे थे, अन्तर तो था ही। सो भी महान् अन्तर। जहां गुलामों

की देह और आत्मा सर्वथा उनके स्वामियों के आधीन थी कि जब चाहें जो करें, वहां "सर्फ" या खेत-मजदूर ऐसे न थे। वे तो कुछ समय तक अपने ही लिये मालिक के द्वारा दिये गये खेतों में काम करते थे, और कुछ निश्चित समय तक मालिक के खेतों में उसके लिये भी। मालिक जब जो चाहे उनसे करवा नहीं सकता था। कभी कभी तो ऐसा भी होता था कि मालिक के खेतों पर काम न करके अपनी कमाई का एक निश्चित अंश ही मालिक को नजर या भेंट के रूप में वे लोग दिया करते थे। फलतः गुलामों की अपेक्षा उन्हें आंशिक स्वतंत्रता, कम से कम, बाहरी तौर पर, तो थी ही। ठीक इसी प्रकार देश-भेद से इन खेतमजदूरों में और उनकी दशा में भी भेद होना स्वाभाविक था। शोषितों और पीड़ितों के मसीहा श्री कार्लमार्क्स ने "पेट के लिए मजदूरी और पूंजी" (Wage-Labour and Capital) नामक ग्रन्थ में बहुत ही विशद रूप से इसका वर्णन यों किया है :

"The slave did not sell his labour-power to the slave-owner, any more than the ox sells his labouring force to the farmer. The slave, together with his labour-power, was sold to his owner once for all. He is a commodity that can pass from the hand of one owner to that of another. He himself is a commodity, but his labour-power is not his commodity. The serf sells only a portion of his labour-power. It is not he who receives wages from the owner of the land; it is rather the owner of the land who receives a tribute from him. The serf belongs to the soil, and to the lord of the soil he brings its fruits."

इसका अर्थ है, "जिस प्रकार खेती का बैल किसान के हाथ अपनी श्रम-शक्ति को नहीं बेंचता, ठीक उसी तरह गुलाम लोग अपनी श्रम-शक्ति को मालिकों के हाथ बेंचते न थे। किन्तु सदा के लिये एक ही बार अपनी उस शक्ति के साथ ही वे लोग उसके हाथ बेंच दिये जाते थे। किसी भी पण्य या विक्रेय वस्तु की तरह वे एक मालिक के हाथ से दूसरे के पास चले जाते थे। वे स्वयं तो खरीद बिक्री के पदार्थ माने जाते थे। मगर उनकी श्रम-शक्ति ऐसा मानी जाती न थी। विपरीत इसके खेती में काम करने वाले "सर्फ" अपनी श्रम-शक्ति का केवल एक अंश बेंचते थे। जमीन के मालिक के हाथ से इन्हें मजदूरी नहीं मिलती थी। बल्कि जमीन के मालिक लोग ही उलटे उन्हीं से एक तरह की भेंट पाते थे। असल में 'सर्फ" लोग जमीन के मातहत थे और उसकी पैदावार उसके मालिक को पहुँचाते थे।"

इस वर्णन में खेत-मजदूरों की आंशिक स्वतंत्रता साफ दिखाई गई है।

जहां गुलामों के भरण पोषण आदि की सारी जिम्मेदारी मालिक पर ही थी, वहां खेतमजदूर उलटे मालिक को ही खिलाते पिलाते थे। मालिक उस जिम्मेदारी से बरी था।

इस प्रकार हम देखते हैं कि खेती में काम करने वालों की—खेत-मजदूरों की- यह दूसरी दशा हुई। इसमें जहां एक ओर पहले की अपेक्षा खेती में काम करके जीविका करने वालों की संख्या अपेक्षाकृत कम हो गई और समाज के कुछ लोग अन्यान्य कामों में जा लगे, तहां दूसरी ओर ऐसे लोग भी पैदा हो गये जो दूसरे के खेतों पर काम करते थे, जिसके बदले में या तो उन्हें जमीन ही मिलती थी, या निर्वाह योग्य मजदूरी ही। यद्यपि खुद अपने खेतों पर काम करने वालों को आज की भाषा में मजदूर कहने की परिपाटी नहीं है। तथापि हम तो उससे पूर्व की दशा के मुकाबिले में उन्हें खेती के मजदूर या काम करने वाले ही कहते हैं। यही ठीक भी है। वे सचमुच ही मजदूर या श्रमजीवी (labourer) थे। लेकिन जिस मानी में आज मजदूर शब्द बोला जाता है उस मानी में भी तो आखिर कुछ लोग उसी समय पैदा हुए।

<21.7.41> इसके बाद तीसरी दशा में ये खेती पर काम करने वाले पहुंचे। मगर इस हालत में पहुँचने में बहुत लम्बी मुद्दत लगी। असल में अब प्रवाह उलटने की बारी आई। पहले जो खेती पर निर्भर करने वालों की संख्या क्रमशः घट रही थी अब उसके क्रमशः बढ़ने की नौबत आ पहुंची। इसीलिये इस हालत की शुरूवात को, आरंभ को एक प्रकार से खतरे की घंटी समझना चाहिये। पहली दो हालतों का जो संक्षिप्त वर्णन ऊपर आया है उससे साफ है कि उनकी तादाद घटने लगी थी। इस कमी के दो मानी होते हैं।। एक तो सर्वथा या हर सूरत से (Absolute) कमी; दूसरी अपेक्षाकृत (Comparative) कमी। खेतों पर कमाने वालों की यह कमी दूसरे प्रकार की या अपेक्षाकृत ही थी। क्योंकि जनसंख्या तो धीरे-धीरे बढ़ती ही थी। इसलिये जितने लोग हजारों वर्षों के दर्म्यान खेती छोड़ के और धन्दों में लगे उनकी तादाद समूची जनसंख्या के मुकाबिले में जरूर ही बहुत ही कम या सिर्फ उसका एक टुकड़ा थी। फिर भी यह तो मानना ही पड़ेगा कि यदि यही बात हजारों साल पहले होती तो जो संख्या खेती वालों की इस प्रकार होती उससे तो कहीं ज्यादा हजारों वर्ष बाद होई गई होगी। आखिर कम और ज्यादा जनसंख्या को एक ही प्रकार के टुकड़ों में बांटने पर ज्यादा संख्या का टुकड़ा बड़ा तो होगा ही। मगर फिर भी समूची संख्या के मुकाबिले में छोटा ही होगा। इसीलिये इसे अपेक्षाकृत कमी हीं कह सकते

हैं। मगर यह ठीक है कि इससे सभी लोगों की भीड़ खेती पर ही नहीं रह गई। फलतः जीविका में दिक्कतें न आईं।

मगर जब तीसरी हालत आई तो बात कुछ और ही हो गई। एक तो धीरे धीरे खेती लायक सभी जमीनें प्रायः जोती जा चुकीं। बच रहीं सिर्फ वे जिन पर आसानी से खेती करना गैर मुमकिन था। जब तक किसी वैज्ञानिक तरीके से काम न लिया जाय और बहुत ज्यादा पूंजी न लगाई जाय तब तक जिन जमीनों में खेती न हो सकती थी वही बच रहीं। इसलिये जो दल, वर्ण या कौमें खेती के लिए मुकर्रर की गई थीं उनकी भी जनसंख्या बढ़ते बढ़ते अब खेती के लायक जमीन की कमी महसूस होने लगी। दूसरे, कुछ लोगों ने अनेक तरकीबों से अपने कब्जे में ज्यादा जमीनें कर लीं। क्योंकि सभ्यता के विकास के साथ छीनाझपटी की भी उत्पत्ति हुई, उन्नति हुई। व्यक्तिगत सम्पत्ति जमा करने की होड़ सी लग गई। सभी जमीनें कब्जे में आ जाने पर ऐसी जमीन जो बिना खेती की बची हो (virgin soil) रही न गई। फिर तो जिनके पास पहले से जमीनें हों उन्हीं से छीनाझपटी करना लाजिम हो गया। नतीजा यह हुआ कि कुछ के पास जहां जरूरत से ज्यादा जमीन हो गई तहां बहुतों के पास या तो थी ही नहीं या बहुत ही कम। फलतः वे लाचार हो कर ज्यादा जमीन वालों के या तो हलवाहे वगैरह बनके गुजर करने लगे, या सख्त से सख्त शर्तो और ज्यादे से ज्यादे लगान पर उनसे जमीनें लेने लगे। इस प्रकार आज के मानी में खेत-मजदूरों की तादाद बढ़ी और उत्तरोत्तर बढ़ने लगी।

तीसरी और सबसे बड़ी बात यह हुई कि जहां पहले नये नये और आसान उद्योगधन्दे या गुजर बसर के रास्ते निकला करते थे, वहां अब नयों की तो बात ही छोड़िये, जो पहले से भी थे वह भी बन्द होने लगे। आधुनिक ढंग के कल कारखानों की उत्पत्ति और वृद्धि का गत चार पांच सौ वर्षों का इतिहास जिनने पढ़ा है वह इस बात को बखूबी समझ सकते हैं। इंगलैंड वगैरह सभी मुल्कों में किस तरह चरखे और करघे चलाने वाले या दूसरे पेशेवर लोगों को मजबूरन उन कामों से भाग के या तो खेती का लाचार सहारा लेना पड़ा, या चोरी, डकैती, भिखमंगी वगैरह का। हिन्दोस्तान में भी किस तरह जुलाहों ने अपने अंगूठे काटे-कटवाये, उनके तथा औरों के धन्दे कैसे तबाह हुए, तबाह किये गये यह बात सभी जानते हैं। आज भी तेल पेरने वाले, आटा पीसने वाले, चीनी बनाने वाले और इसी प्रकार के हजारों पेशे वाले कल कारखानों के मुकाबिले में दिवालिये बनके धीरे-धीरे उनसे भाग निकले हैं, भागे जा रहे हैं। गुजश्ता चार पांच

सौ सालों से जो यह नये ढंग की छीनाझपटी पुराने धन्दों के बारे में नये कल कारखाने कर रहे हैं वह रोज रोज बढ़ती ही जा रही है। उस छीनाझपटी के नये-नये रूप खड़े हो रहे हैं। यह सवाल आज हमारी आंखों के सामने नाच रहा है। पहले तो हाथ से किये जाने वाले उद्योगधन्दों को कल वाले छीने लेते हैं। फिर छोटे मोटे कल कारखानेदारों को बड़े-बड़े भगा देते हैं। अन्त में मुठ्ठीभर बड़े-बड़े मालदारों का गुट्ट बड़े-बड़े हजारों कारखाने खोल के बाकियों को बेकार बना देता है। इस प्रकार आज एकाधिकार (Monopoly) का एक छत्र राज्य या तो हो चुका, या होने जा रहा है।

अब सोचना यही है कि जिनके धन्दे और रोजगार छिन रहे हैं वे आखिर करेंगे क्या? अपने तथा अपने बाल बच्चों के पेटों पर पत्थर तो बांध लेंगे नहीं। हवा पी के भी गुजर कर सकते नहीं। नौकरी चाकरी भी आखिर कितने पायेंगे। ये कारखाने सभी को नौकर तो रख सकते नहीं। यह भी बात है कि जो लोग पढ़े लिखे न हों, निपुण न हों उन सबों को काम मिल भी नहीं सकता। और गरीबों के लिये पढ़ने का सामान कहां? उन्हें पूछे कौन? आज तो यह हालत है कि या तो बड़ी कला वाले विशेषज्ञों की पूछ है या स्त्रियों और बच्चों की। कलों ने कुछ ऐसा कर दिया है कि लड़कियां, लड़के या ज्यादे से ज्यादे औरतें ही वह काम कर सकती हैं जो पुष्टमर्दों के बिना पहले हो नहीं सकते थे। लड़के बच्चे वगैरह सस्ते मिलते भी हैं। उन्हें ज्यादा मजदूरी देनी नहीं पड़ती। नतीजा होता है कि मर्दों को कम काम मिलता है। सिर्फ बच्चों या औरतों की कमाई से गुजर भी होती नहीं। <22.7.41> ऐसी दशा में वे कहां जांय, क्या करें यह बड़ा सवाल उनके सामने चौबीसों घंटे खड़ा रहता है। दूसरा रास्ता मिलता भी नहीं। इसलिये हार के खेती की ही शरण लेना चाहते हैं, लेते हैं। खेत भी मिलते नहीं कि जोतें। वे भी तो बहुत मंहगे हो गये हैं। यह मंहगी भी आये दिन बढ़ती ही जाती है। फिर भी इतना जरूर है कि मंहगी से मंहगी कीमत या अधिक से अधिक मालगुजारी दे के खेत तो मिली जाते हैं। मगर नौकरी चाकरी या दूसरे धन्दों का तो दरवाजा उनके लिये सदा के लिये बन्द है। जिस तरह महान समुद्र, जिसके आरपार का कुछ अन्दाज ही न हो, के बीच में पड़े जहाज के मस्तूल पर बैठे कौवे के लिये कोई चारा नहीं, सिवाय इसके कि उसी मस्तूल पर खामखा बैठे, चाहे हजार बाधायें हो और अनामे मरना भी पड़े। आखिर मस्तूल छोड़ के जाय तो कहां जाय? ठीक वही हालत किसानी करने वाले इन गरीबों की है। हार के खेती का ही सहारा

लेते हैं। फिर चाहे वह कितनी भी मंहगी क्यों न हो।

जमीन वाले भी कैसे भले होते हैं। उन भलेमानसों को तो मौका ही मिल जाता है कि खूबही कसके कीमत, लगान या मालगुजारी वसूलें। मैं तो ऐसे खूनी और रक्त पीने वाले जमींदारों को जानता हूं जो जमीन की पैदावार का तीन चौथाई खुद ले के सिर्फ एक चौथाई ही किसान के लिये छोड़ते हैं। खूबी तो यह है कि उसी चौथाई में उसे खेती का समूचा खर्च भी चुकाना पड़ता है जो सरासर असंभव है। यह तो सभी मानते हैं कि कुल पैदावार का प्रायः एक तिहाई खेती के खर्च में चला जाता है, और उन्हें मिलता है केवल एक चौथाई ही। ऐसी दशा में वे खुद अपने परिवार के लिये क्या बचायेंगे? नतीजा होता है कि उन्हें अपनी मजदूरी भी हासिल नहीं होती। फलतः वे बनिये महाजनों या सूदखोरों के चंगुल में रोजरोज फंसते जाते हैं। ऐसे ही किसान सूदखोरों के क्रीतदास (Slave) बन जाते हैं। यों तो कहने के लिये वे किसान हैं। किंतु खेतों में बैलों से भी ज्यादा मिहनत करते रहते हैं। इतने पर भी जब पूरी मजदूरी भी उन्हें नहीं मिलती तो वे खेत-मजदूर से भी गये गुजरे हैं। यह भी नहीं कि थोड़े हैं। ऐसे किसान करोड़ों हैं और उनकी संख्या बेतहाशा बढ़ रही है, जैसा कि आगे बतायेंगे।

एक बात और होती है। खेती करने वाले किसानों के परिवारों की जब वृद्धि होने लगती है और इसी के साथ सम्मिलित परिवार की जगह उसके टुकड़े-टुकड़े हो जाते हैं तो इसका परिणाम खेतों पर बुरा पड़ता है। जो खेत पहले बड़े-बड़े थे वही अब बंटते बंटते बहुत ही छोटे हो जाते हैं गोया पानी पटाने की क्यारियां हैं। जहां एक ओर परिवार बड़े होते हैं तहां दूसरी ओर ये खेत छोटे । जैसे जैसे परिवार की वृद्धि होती है तैसे तैसे खेत छोटे होते जाते हैं। यह छुटाई कहां जाके टिकेगी कोई कह नहीं सकता है। इसके परिणाम स्वरूप कम से कम अस्सी फीसदी किसानों की जमीनें अब ऐसी हो गई हैं कि उनसे उनके परिवार के भरण पोषण की तो बात ही दूर रहे, आधा या चौथाई पेट भी नहीं भरता, सो भी मोटे से मोटे अन्न को खाकर। इस प्रकार की जमीनों (uneconomic holdings) की यह बीमारी किसानों को मटियामेट करने पर तुली बैठी है। फिर भी उसके रोकने का कोई उपाय हो नहीं रहा है। ये प्रायः अस्सी फीसदी किसान और कहीं कहीं तो नब्बे फीसदी भी, इतने गरीब और तबाह हैं कि उन्हें मजदूर कहने में भी शर्म आती है। क्योंकि मजदूर होने पर कम या बेश एक बंधी बंधाई मजदूरी तो मिलती है। मगर यहां तो वह भी नहीं है।

यह इतनी प्रत्यक्ष और सभी जानकारों की मानी हुई बात है कि इसमें किसी भी शंका की गुंजाइश नहीं। फिर भी खून पीने वाले जल्लाद लोग दलील कर बैठते हैं कि तो फिर किसान ऐसी खेती के पास जाते ही क्यों हैं? वे खामखा क्यों खेती में पड़ते हैं जब मजदूरी भी नहीं पाते? उसे वे छोड़ बैठते क्यों नहीं? बिना फायदे के तो कोई भी काम इन्सान कभी करता ही नहीं। तो क्या ये किसान पागल हैं जो ऐसा करते हैं? आदि आदि। इन सवालों के जरिये ये भलेमानस यह दिखाना चाहते हैं कि नन्हें-नन्हें खेतों के टुकड़ों के पीछे अपने खून को पानी बना डालने वाले ये किसान परिवार जरूर फायदे में रहते हैं। ये लोग दूर की कौड़ी लाते हैं। इसे ही कहते हैं असंभव को संभव साबित करने की हिम्मत और कोशिश। ये लोग अपने को काफी चतुर समझते हैं। मगर इनकी हालत उन बड़े हिसाबी मुंशी जी जैसा ही है, जिन्होंने नदी की गहराई का इसी तरह की दलील और अक्लमन्दी से ऐसा हिसाब लगा लिया था कि उनके छोटे-छोटे बच्चे आसानी से बेखटके पार हो जांय। उनने लड़कों को इसी के बूते पर नदी पार कर जाने को कह भी दिया था। मगर जब बीच में ही सभी लड़के डूब मरे तब कहीं जाकर मुंशी जी को अपने हिसाब की गलती का पता चला। ठीक यही बात ये लोग करना चाहते हैं। जब किसानों की हड्डियां तक लापता हो जायंगी तब ये लोग चेतें तो चेतें। मगर पहले नहीं। इन्हें क्या मालूम नहीं कि मिट्टी या बालू से आदमी की न तो भूख जाती, न वह जिन्दा रहता और न वह उसका खाद्य है? मगर भयंकर अकाल वाले प्रदेशों में सैकड़ों-हजारों ऐसे आदमियों और जानवरों की लाशें मिली हैं जिनने भूख से व्याकुल हो के बालू या मिट्टी खा ली थी। फलतः मर जाने पर उनके पेटों में वही चीजें पड़ी निकलीं। मस्तूल के कौवे की बात तो कही चुके हैं। कोई और उपाय न देख के लाचार किसान ऐसी दिवालिया खेती का सहारा लेते हैं यही सोचकर कि पीछे जो कुछ होगा देखा जायगा, तत्काल तो काम चले। इसे ही कहते हैं "डूबते को तिनके का सहारा"। फायदे का हिसाब लगा के वे इस काम में हर्गिज नहीं पड़ते। वे तो हिसाब लगाना जानते भी नहीं। वे यही सोचते हैं कि चलो और नहीं तो मिहनत करने के लिये एक साधन तो मिला—इससे और नहीं तो मजदूरी तो मिलेगी। मगर उन्हें क्या पता कि यहां मजदूरी तक को पहले से ही लूट लेने की बन्दिश करके यार लोग ताक में बैठे हैं। उन्हें कफन खसोटी करने वालों से ही पाला पड़ा है। इस बात पर आगे और भी प्रकाश डाला जायगा।

किस प्रकार किसानों की जमीनें लुट रही हैं और उसी के फलस्वरूप किस प्रकार खेती के मजदूरों की, जिनमें पूर्वोक्त किसान नामधारी भी शमिल हैं, संख्या शैतान की अंतड़ी की तरह बढ़ रही है इस बात की सफाई कुछ और भी करने की जरूरत है। तभी इसका नग्न चित्र हमारी आंखों के सामने आयेगा। यदि कोई भी आदमी सेन्सस (मनुष्यगणना) की तथा दूसरी सरकारी रिपोर्टों को, जिनमें इस बात की छानबीन की गई है, देखे और उसी के साथ साथ प्रामाणिक गैर सरकारी आंकड़ों की भी मिलान करे तो उसे आसानी से पता लग जायगा किस तेजी से खेती के मजदूरों की संख्या बढ़ती जा रही है और उसी के साथ सिर्फ लगान वसूलने वाले जमींदारों की भी। सन 1911 ई. की मनुष्यगणना में समूचे देश में लगान पर मौज मारने वाले जमींदारों या जमीन के मालिकों की तादाद 28 लाख लिखी गई है। फिर दस वर्ष बाद सन 1921 में वही बढ़ के 37 लाख और सन 1931 में पूरे 41 लाख हो गई। यानी कुल बीस ही साल में ये डयोढ़े हो गये। यह प्रायः पचास फीसदी की वृद्धि इतनी थोड़ी मुद्दत में गजब की है। इसी के साथ साथ सन 1921 में खुद खेती करने वाले किसानों की संख्या, जिनकी अपनी जमीन हो, जो सन 1921 में 7 करोड़ 46 लाख थी वही घट के सन 1931 में 6 करोड़ 55 लाख पहुंच गई। यानी दस साल में पूरे 91 लाख किसानों की जमीन छिन गई। इसका सीधा अर्थ यह है कि हर साल 9 लाख से ज्यादा किसानों की जमीनें छिनी गई। यह तेज चाल साफ बताती है कि अगर यही हालत रही तो कम-बेश सत्तर साल बीतते न बीतते सभी किसान बिना जमीन के हो जायगे। इनमें 14-15 वर्ष तो बीत भी चुके हैं।

अब देखना यह है कि किसानों की जमीनें जब यों तेजी से छिनी जा रही हैं तो जैसे एक ओर मुफ्तखोर लगानचट्ट जमीन वाले (जमींदार) बढ़ेंगे उसी तरह दूसरी ओर खेती के मजदूर भी बढ़ेंगे ही। यानी ऐसे लोग जिनकी अपनी जमीनें तो होंगी नहीं। इसीलिये या तो जमीन वालों से शिकमी, बटाई वगैरह के रूप में बहुत ज्यादा लगान दे के ये लोग जमीनें लेंगे और खेती करेंगे, या दूसरे के खेतों पर सिर्फ बहुत ही थोड़ी मजदूरी पर काम करके जैसे तैसे आधा-चौथाई पेट खाके और चिथड़े लपेट के गुजर करेंगे। हर हालत में वे खेतमजदूर ही होंगे। दूसरे हो सकते नहीं। इस बात पर ज्यादा विचार अगले प्रकरण में करेंगे। यहां यही जान लेना है कि सरकार की ही रिपोर्टों के मुताबिक इन खेत-मजदूरों की तादाद किस तेजी से बढ़ती बढ़ती आज कहां जा पहुंची है। सचमुच एक बार तो यह बात

दिल दहलाये देती है।

श्रीयुत आर. पामेदत्त (R. Palme Dutta) ने सन 1940 ई. में प्रकाशित अपनी पुस्तक "आज का भारत " (India Today) के 218 वें पृष्ठ में इसके बारे में इस प्रकार लिखा है :– "In 1842 Sir Thomas Munro, as Census Commissioner, reported that there were no landless peasants in India (undoubtedly incorrect picture, but indicating that the numbers were not considered to require statistical measurement). In 1882 the census estimated 7 1/2 millions "landless labourers" in agriculture. The 1921 census returned a total of 21.7 millions, or one-fifth of those engaged in agriculture. The 1931 census returned a total of 33.5 millions, or one-third of those engaged in agriculture. Since then it has been estimated (as in the debates in the Bengal Legislative Assembly on the amendment to the Tenancy Act in 1938; the Madras figures given above also indicate the same) that the real present proportion is nearer one-half."

इसका मतलब यह है कि "सन 1842 ई. की मनुष्यगणना के कमिश्नर सर टामस मुनरो ने लिखा था कि भारत में बिना जमीन का किसान एक भी न था (बेशक यह अत्युक्ति कही जा सकती है। मगर इससे स्पष्ट होता है यदि ऐसे किसान थे भी तो उनकी संख्या इतनी कम या नगण्य थी कि उसे लिखना फिजूल समझा गया)। फिर सन 1882 की मनुष्यगणना में "बिना जमीन वाले खेत-मजदूरों की तादाद 75 लाख आंकी गई। सन 1921 ई. की गणना ने तो उनकी कुल तादाद पूरे 2 करोड़ 17 लाख, या खेती में लगे लोगों का पांचवां हिस्सा ठहराई। सन 1931 में वह बढ़के 3 करोड़ 35 लाख, या यों कहिये कि खेती में लगे कुल लोगों की तिहाई हो गई। उसके बाद से लेकर आज तक (1940) में) यह कूता गया है (जैसा कि सन 1938 में बंगाल असेम्बली में काश्तकारी कानून के संशोधन के बहस मुबाहसे और पहले बताये गये मद्रास प्रान्त के आंकड़ों से भी सिद्ध हो जाता है) कि बिना जमीन के खेत मजदूरों की कुल संख्या खेती में लगे सब लोगों की आधी हो गई हैं।" स्थानान्तर में यह संख्या पूरे पांच करोड़ आंकी गई है, जिसका मतलब है कि खेती में लगे हुए किसान परिवारों की संख्या प्रायः दस करोड़ है। ऊपर केवल परिवारों की ही संख्या से मतलब है या ज्यादे से ज्यादा कमाने वाले व्यक्तियों से ही, न कि सभी व्यक्तियों से। परिवार के आश्रित बूढ़े, बच्चे आदि उस संख्या में शामिल नहीं हैं। किन्तु

केवल कमाने वाले ही लिये गये हैं। नहीं तो किसानों की संख्या 80 फीसदी होने के कारण कुल तादाद 28 और 32 करोड़ के बीच में होगी। इस प्रकार खेत-मजदूर बाल बच्चे सहित दस से लेकर चौदह-पन्द्रह करोड़ के बीच में पहुंच सकते हैं। कम से कम दस करोड़ तो जरूर ही। क्योंकि उनके तो बच्चे वगैरह भी कमाते ही हैं। केवल बहुत ही नन्हें बच्चे और निहायत बूढ़े वगैरह छूटते हैं।

जिस मद्रास प्रान्त के आंकड़ों का जिक्र ऊपर आया है उसकी हालत यों है कि सन 1901 में जहां सिर्फ लगान लेने वालों की तादाद फी हजार आदमियों में सिर्फ 20 ही थी, तहां तीस ही साल के बाद बढ़ के पूरी 50 यानी ढाई गुनी हो गई।इसी के साथ बिना जमीन वाले खेती के मजदूरों की संख्या 345 से 429 यानी एक तिहाई से प्रायः आधी हो गई। <23.7.41> इसी प्रकार यदि बंगाल की हालत का मुकाबिला सन 1921 और 1931 में करते हैं तो दस साल के भीतर ही भयंकर परिवर्त्तन पाते हैं। जहां बंगाल में 1921 में सिर्फ 390562 ही लगान वसूलने वाले जमीन के मालिक थे तहां 1931 में पूरे 633834 हो गये। यानी 61 फीसदी (sic) बढ़ गये। ठीक इसके उलटा अपने खेतों में खेती करने वाले किसान परिवार घट के 9274924 से 6079717 रह गये। अर्थात 50 फीसदी (sic) की कमी हो गई। खेत-मजदूरों की संख्या भी 1805502 से 2718939 तक जा पहुंची, जिसका मतलब है कि 34 फीसदी [sic.] की बढ़ती हुई। इसी तरह यदि पंजाब की ओर नजर डालते हैं तो भी इसी तरह की बात पाई जाती है। संयुक्त प्रान्त तथा मध्य प्रान्त और बरार भी कुछ ऐसे ही पथ के पथिक नजर आते हैं। पंजाब में लगान पर ही गुलछर्रे उड़ाने वाले (rent-receivers) सन 1911 और 1921 के दर्म्यान 626000 से बढ़के 1008000 हो गये। पूरे 62 प्रतिशत की वृद्धि हुई। मध्यप्रान्त में भी इसी मुद्दत में 52 प्रतिशत की और युक्तप्रान्त में 46 प्रतिशत की वृद्धि हुई। यह दशा बेशक निहायत ही खतरनाक है। इस सम्बन्ध में ज्यादा ब्योरा और विस्तार देना फिजूल है। ऊपर लिखी बातें काफी हैं।

खेती पर आधिकाधिक लोग क्रमशः किस प्रकार निर्भर होते जा रहे हैं इसका पता इसी से लग जाता है कि भारत की जनसंख्या की 61.1 फीसदी 1891 में खेती से गुजर करती थी। वही बढ़के 1901 में 66.5, 1911 में 72.2 और 1921 में 73 हो गई। बेशक 1921 की मनुष्यगणना में खेती से जीने वालों की तादाद में गोलमाल हुआ है। इससे पूर्व की तीन

गणनाओं के आंकड़े 61.1, 66.5 और 72.2 ही इसके सबूत हैं और संकेत करते हैं कि यह संख्या 78 के करीब होनी चाहिये। फिर भी वृद्धि तो मानी ही गई है। अगर इसी हिसाब से आगे के बीस वर्षों का भी हिसाब लगायें तो मानना पड़ेगा कि आज 80 से लेकर 85 फीसदी तक जनसंख्या का आधार एक मात्र खेती है। दूसरी ओर पुराने उद्योगधन्दों और दस्तकारी के क्रमशः खत्म हो जाने से खेती के अलावे दूसरे उद्योगधन्दों से गुजर करने वालों की तादाद क्रमशः घटती ही जा रही हैं। हालांकि नये ढंग के कल कारखाने और बड़ी-बड़ी मिलें इधर ज्यादा खुली हैं। इसका साफ मतलब यही है कि दस्तकारी वगैरह के चौपट हो जाने से जो लोग बिना जीविका के हो गये हैं नये ढंग के कारखाने उन सबों को काम देने में असमर्थ रहे हैं। इसीलिये जो लोग यह दलील करते हैं कि लोगों की एक जीविका यदि छूटती है तो दूसरी नये ढंग की मिल जाती है नये करखानों में, वे गलत रास्ते पर हैं और पूंजीवाद की असलियत को समझते ही नहीं। हां, तो उद्योगधन्दों से जीने वाले इस देश में जहां 1911 में 5.5 प्रतिशत थे, वहाँ 1921 में 4.9 ही रह गये और 1931 में तो और भी घटके 4.3 प्रति हो गये।

हमने पहले हिसाब लगा के बताया है कि अगर यों ही लोगों की जमीनें छिनती रहीं तो कम-बेश अगले सत्तर सालों में ही सारी जमीनें उनके पास चली जायंगी जो खुद खेती करते नहीं। फलतः खेती करने वाले सोलहों आने बिना जमीन के हो जायंगे और जमीन वालों की मनमानी शर्तों पर ही उन से जमीनें लेके या तो खेती करेंगे, भूखों मरेंगे, कहीं मजूरी करेंगे या चोरी डकैती आदि। मगर हमें यह न भूलना चाहिये कि वैज्ञानिक ढंग से लम्बे पैमाने पर खेती (Large scale farming) का यह युग है। इसलिये एक ओर तो हजार उपाय करके किसानों की सारी जमीनें जल्दी ही छिन जायंगी और भय है कि इस काम में सत्तर साल की आधी मुद्दत भी शायद ही लगे। दूसरी ओर वे जमीनें शिकमी ढंग से भी किसी को फिर मिल न सकेंगी जैसा कि अभी तक होता रहा है। नतीजा यह होगा कि बाकी लोगों को ठीक वैसे ही खेत-मजदूर बन जाना होगा जैसे कि आसाम वगैरह के चाय बगानों एवं कहवा या रबर की खेती में काम करने वाले करीब-करीब दस लाख मजदूर बन गये हैं, जिन्हें मोटी भाषा में कुली कहते आते हैं। सब लोग तो वैसे मजदूर भी बन न सकेंगे। कारण, सबको काम तो मिल न सकेगा। इसलिये कुछ या तो भूखों मरेंगे या दूसरे रास्ते में जायंगे। मगर बाकी लोग बड़े बड़े फार्मों पर मजदूरी करेंगे, जैसा कि अमेरिका आदि देशों

में होता है। वहां एक ओर मुट्ठीभर करोड़पति लोग बड़ी बड़ी मिलों और बड़े बड़े फार्मों के मालिक हैं। दूसरी ओर असंख्य जनसमूह उनका गुलाम है और मजदूरी के नाम पर उन्हीं के दिये टुकड़ों पर दिन काटता है।

इस प्रकार अब तक के बयान से यह साफ हो गया कि खेती के मजदूरों—खेत-मजदूरों का सवाल पेचीदा है। उनकी न तो कोई बंधी बंधाई तादाद हीं है, और न यही बात है कि किसी एक ही तरीके से उनका नम्बर बढ़ता है। उसके बढ़ने के तो अनेकों रास्ते हैं। खूबी तो यह है कि कल जमीनें पास होने से किसान थे और आराम से गुजर करते थे, तो आज एकाएक उनके छिन जाने से मुहताज बन गये। कल किसी धन्दे में लगे थे तो आज कोई पूछने वाला नहीं है, पुर्सा हाल नहीं है। हर जाति, कौम और मजहब के लोगों को आये दिन इसी घाट उतरना पड़ रहा है। जो लोग माने बैठे हैं कि खेत-मजदूर तो हरिजन या पिछड़ी जातियों के ही लोग हैं उनने देखा कि यह बात गलत है। इस दल में तो सभी लोग लाचारी से धड़ाधड़ शमिल हो रहे हैं, सबों शामिल होना है।

2

मजदूर या किसान?

खेतमजदूरों की हालत का जो नकशा अब तक खींचा गया है उससे उनकी असलियत की बहुत कुछ जानकारी हो जाने पर भी उनके बारे में एक निहायत ही जरूरी बात का जान लेना बाकी ही है और इसके बिना उनसे सम्बन्ध रखने वाली उनके दुःख सुख की बातों का ठीक ठीक समझना या उनका कोई हल सुझाना आसान हो नहीं सकता। इसीलिये आगे बढ़ने से पहले उस बात का विचार कर लेना आवश्यक है।

खेत-मजदूर या खेती के मजदूर (Agricultural labourers) कहने से ही यह बात एकाएक दिमाग में घुस जाती है कि ये लोग भी ठीक वैसे ही मजदूर हैं जैसे कल कारखानों और खानों वगैरह में काम करने वाले। इसीलिये लोग समझने लगते हैं कि दूसरे मजदूरों के उद्धार की जो तरकीबें हैं उन्हीं को अमल में लाने से खेतमजदूरों की भी भलाई होगी और वे अपना मकसद - अपना लक्ष्य - हासिल कर लेंगे। ऐसा खयाल हो आना स्वाभाविक है। सिर्फ खयाल ही नहीं, बल्कि उसी के मुताबिक कुछ नये-नये मजदूर-नेता अमल भी करने लगे हैं। नतीजा यह हुआ है कि एक तो इसके चलते खुद खेतमजदूरों की, और किसानों की भी, दिक्कतें बढ़ गई हैं। दूसरे उन्हें कामयाबी भी नहीं मिली है। आमतौर से आगे बढ़ने के बजाय ऐसे कामों से वे लोग पीछे चले गये हैं। यह ठीक है कि कुछ ने तो अनजान में ही ऐसा किया है। क्योंकि मजदूर नाम से ही वे धोके में पड़ गये हैं। मगर ज्यादातर ऐसे भी लोग उनका नेतृत्व करने आये हैं जिन्हें अपना उल्लू सीधा करना था। बस, उनने एक रास्ता यही पा लिया। फलतः सारा गुड़ गोबर कर मारा। पता नहीं कि उनका मतलब भी सधा या नहीं। हां, इतना तो जरूर देखा कि कुछ दिनों बाद वे मौन हो गये।

<24.7.41> दिक्कत यह है कि लोगों ने मजदूर शब्द का निराला मानी मान लिया है। इसी की जगह जो श्रमजीवी तथा मिहनतकश शब्द बोले जाते हैं उनका मतलब बहुत ही साफ है कि परिश्रम करके या हाथ पांव चलाके जो अपनी जीविका करे। अंग्रेजी में इसी अर्थ में 'वर्कर' और

'लेबरर' (Worker and labourer) शब्द आते हैं। उनका अर्थ है काम करने वाला या मिहनत करने वाला। यही अर्थ ठीक ठीक मिहनतकश या श्रमिक शब्दों का है। ये शब्द यह बताते हैं कि निठल्ले बैठे हुए माल उड़ाने वालों की तरह ये लोग नहीं हैं कि दूसरों की कमाई पर भरपूर हाथ साफ करें। यह काम तो जमींदार, साहुकार और पूंजीपति या सरमायेदार ही करते हैं। श्रमिक या श्रमजीवी तो अपनी मिहनत की ही कमाई खुद खाते तथा औरों को भी खिलाते हैं। यही ठीक भी है और यदि इसी मानी में मजदूर शब्द लिया जाय जैसा कि चाहिये, तब तो खेत-मजदूर का अर्थ समझने में धोका या गड़बड़ की गुंजाइश ही न रह जाय।

मगर गड़बड़ होती है इसीलिये कि मजदूर के मानी में ही एक शब्द अंग्रेजी में और भी आता है जिसे 'वेज-वर्कर' (Wage-worker) कहते हैं। 'वेज-लेबरर' शब्द भी इस अर्थ में प्रयुक्त होता है। इन दोनों शब्दों का अक्षरार्थ है "मजदूरी या वेतन के लिए काम (मिहनत) करने वाला"। प्रायः नौकर और भृत्य शब्द इसी माने में बोले जाते हैं। हालांकि भृत्य शब्द का असली अर्थ है कि जिसका भरण पोषण किया जाय। किसी कमाने वाले के आश्रित जितने लोग होते हैं उन सबों को भृत्य कहते हैं। मनु ने अपनी स्मृति के ग्यारहवें अध्याय में "भृत्यानामुपरोधेन" श्लोक में भृत्य शब्द का यही अर्थ लिया है। हां, तो 'वेज-वर्कर' के मानी में ही मजदूर शब्द को समझके लोग ऐसा मानने लगे हैं कि जो मजदूरी के ही लिये खेतों पर काम करे वही खेत-मजदूर है। जों अपने खेत को जोते कोड़े, जैसा कि शुरू में सभी करते थे और आज भी बहुतेरे करते हैं, उसे खेत मजदूर अब न कह के सिर्फ गैर के ही लिये उसी के खेतों को जोतने कोड़ने आदि का काम जो करता है और उसके बदले में अन्न या पैसे पाता है उसे ही खेत-मजदूर मानने से बहुत सी भूलें हो जाती हैं। अंग्रेजी के "ऐग्रीकल्चरल-लेबर्रर" या "ऐग्रीकल्चरल प्रोल्तारियत" का भी ऐसा ही अर्थ माना जाता है।

बात असल यह है कि आज संसार में, जिस मानी में मजदूर शब्द बोला जा रहा है उसके अर्थ को 'वेजलेबरर' (Wage-labourer) शब्द भी ठीक ठीक जाहिर कर नहीं सकता। इससे तो सिर्फ इतना हीं पता चलता है कि कोई आदमी गैरों के खेत या कारखाने वगैरह में इसीलिये काम करता है कि उसके बदले में एक बंधी-बधाई रकम या गल्ला वगैरह मिल जाय। इससे यह कतई मालूम नहीं होता कि काम करने वाले के पास खुद भी ख़ेत, काम के दूसरे साधन, घरबार वगैरह, या कुछ सम्पत्ति हैं या नहीं। आज तो इस प्रकार काम करने वालों का एक बड़ा दल बन गया है जो बाबू

कहलाता है और जिसे निम्न मध्यम वर्गीय भी कहते हैं। औफिसों के किरानी वगैरह इसी श्रेणी में आ जाते हैं। उनके अपने मकान, खेत वगैरह भी होते हैं। वे कमबेश सम्पत्ति भी रखते ही हैं। जिनके पास कुछ भी नहीं है और जो कमायें तो खायें, नहीं तो भूखों मरें ऐसे लोग भी 'वेज-वर्कर्स' हैं।

लेकिन आज तो आमतौर से मजदूर शब्द इसी मानी में बोला जाता है कि जिसके पास "न तो तर धरती और न ऊपर बज्जर" हो, जो हर प्रकार की छोटी बड़ी सम्पत्ति से सर्वथा रहित हो, जो दूसरों के खेतों या कल कारखानों में काम करके गुजर करे और पराये के मकानों में ही रहे, जिसे मकान मालिक या कल कारखानेदार जभीं चाहे निकाल बाहर करे। ऐसे लोगों को आज कल 'फ्रीलेबरर' (free-labourer) या स्वतंत्र श्रमिक कहते हैं। इसके मानी हैं कि हर चीज से उनका सम्बन्ध टूटा हो। क्योंकि सम्बन्ध बन्धन का कारण होता है। उसके चलते पूरी आजादी नहीं रहती। इसलिये उनके पास केवल श्रम-शक्ति ही रहती है। उनकी यही एक सम्पत्ति रह जाती है। बाकी सभी गायब। हां, स्त्री, बच्चे, पिता आदि ऐसे व्यक्ति भी हो सकते हैं जिनकी जीविका का दार मदार उसी एक कमाने वाले पर ही हो। हालांकि पूंजीवादी व्यवस्था अमली तौर पर आज यह भी नहीं मानती कि श्रमशक्ति या काम करने की ताकत के सिवाय मजदूर के पास या उसके सम्बन्धी स्त्री बच्चे आदि भी हैं। सिद्धान्त के रूप में भले ही यह बात मानी जाती हो कि यदि स्त्री, बच्चे उसे न होंगे तो उसके मरने या अशक्त हो जाने पर फिर मजदूर मिलेंगे कैसे? इसीलिये काम के बदले में उसे इतनी मजदूरी जरूर मिलनी चाहिये कि वह खुद सशक्त रहे, संतान उत्पन्न कर सके और स्त्री, बच्चों का भरण कर पाये। मगर व्यवहार में तो यही देखा जाता है कि जहां तक हो सके कम से कम मजदूरी ही उसे दी जाती है जिससे उस अकेले की भी गुजर असंभव है।

आज के कल-युग (कलकारखानों के युग) में वह एक प्रकार से खरीद बिक्री की चीज (Commodity) माना जाता है। जिस प्रकार कपड़े लत्ते वगैरह बाजार भाव पर बिका करते हैं और उनकी कीमत कभी घटती और कभी बढ़ती है, कभी-कभी तो ऐसा होता है कि उनका पूंछने वाला कोई होता ही नहीं, जिससे वे पड़े सड़ा करते हैं। ठीक यही दशा उस मजदूर की या यों कहिये कि उसकी श्रमशक्ति (labour-power) की है। वह भी 'कमोडिटी' (Commodity) ही है। उसकी भी कीमत घटती बढ़ती रहती है। कभी-कभी तो उसे कोई पूछता भी नहीं। गुलाम लोग तो बिक जाते

थे और जिसके पास वे जाते वही उनके खान पान वगैरह का प्रबन्ध सदा के लिये करता था- उसके लिये जवाबदेह बन जाता था। अगर उसने कदाचित् गुलाम को बेंचा भी तो जोई खरीदता वही उसके खान पान आदि के लिये उत्तरदायी बन जाता। यह बात पहले प्रकरण में ही कही जा चुकी है। मगर वर्त्तमान समय के 'वेज-लेबरर' (मजदूर) की तो अजीब हालत है। यह तो मारा फिरता है, कारखानेदार उसे आदमी समझते ही नहीं। उन्हें उसकी गर्ज नहीं है। यदि वे एक मजूर चाहते हैं तो दस दौड़े आते हैं। फिर गर्ज क्यों रहे? जिस प्रकार बाजार में चीजों की कीमत आपस की चढ़ाबढ़ी के कारण बहुत ज्यादा गिर जाती है, वही हालत मजदूरों की, उन की श्रमशक्ति की है। आपसी चढ़ा बढ़ी के चलते उसकी कीमत नाममात्र को ही मिलती है। इसीलिये मजदूर का उचित और असली नाम 'वेज-लेबरर' न होकर प्रोल्तारियत माना गया है। इस शब्द का अर्थ है 'सर्वहारा' - अर्थात् जिसका सब कुछ छिन गया है, हर लिया गया है। कार्लमार्क्स ने अपनी पूर्वोक्त पुस्तक में इस सर्वहारा की उपमा रेशम के कीड़े से दी है। जैसे रेशम के कीड़े को खाना इसलिये खिलाते हैं कि वह मालिक के लिये रेशम पैदा करता है। ठीक सर्वहारा को भी खाना देते हैं केवल इसलिये कि काम कर देता है। कीड़े को जिन्दा रहना है तो रेशम पैदा करे और सर्वहारा को कायम रहना है तो काम करे — "If the silkworm's object in spinning were to prolong its existence as caterpillar, it would be a perfect example of a wage-worker."

मार्क्स उसी किताब में आगे और भी लिखता है कि "इस स्वतंत्र श्रमिक (मजदूर) की तो यह हालत है कि इसे अपनी आत्मा, अपनी हस्ती को ही बेंच देना पड़ता है। सो भी एक बार नहीं, किन्तु टुकड़े-टुकड़े करके। अपने जीवन के 8,10, 12 या 15 घंटे एक दिन वह उसके हाथ नीलाम कर देता है जो सबसे ज्यादा बोली बोलता है - दाम देता है। अर्थात् जिसके पास उत्पादन के (काम करने के) साधन कच्चे माल, औजार हथियार वगैरह तथा जीवनोपयोगी अन्न वस्त्रादि होते हैं और जिसे पूंजीपति कहते हैं। यही बात फिर अगले दिन और उसके बाद बराबर होती रहती है। यह श्रमजीवी या सर्वहारा न तो किसी एक पूंजीपति के और न किसी जमीन के मातहत होता है। सिर्फ उसकी रोजाना जिन्दगी के 8, 10, 12 या 15 घंटे उस आदमी के हो जाते हैं जो उन्हें खरीदता है—"The free labourer, on the other hand, sells his very self, and that by fractions. He auctions off eight, ten, twelve, fifteen hours of his life, one day like the next, to the highest bidder, to the owner of raw materials, tools, and means of life, i.e. to the capitalist. The labourer belongs neither to an owner, nor to the soil, but eight, ten, twelve, fifteen hours of his daily life belong to whosoever buys them."

अपने विश्वविख्यात ग्रन्थ 'कैपिटल' (Capital) में मार्क्स इसी बात को संक्षेप में यों लिखता है कि "उसके पास उन साधनों में एक भी नहीं रहना चाहिये जिन पर उसकी श्रमशक्ति का प्रयोग हो सके", "ऐसे लोग जिनके पास श्रमशक्ति के अलावा और कुछ हुई नहीं"—"He must be free from everything that is essential for the realisation of his labour power." "...persons who own nothing, but their labour power." (Capital Vol. 1, Chap. III, Sec. 3).

मि. जॉन स्ट्रेची (Mr. John Strachy) ने अपनी पुस्तक (The Theory and Practice of Socialism) "समाजवाद सैद्धान्तिक तथा व्यावहारिक" में यही बात यों लिखी है कि "मजदूर वर्ग ऐसे लोगों का बना होता है जिन्हें मजबूरन अपनी जिन्दगी कायम रखने के लिये अपनी काम करने की शक्ति को कारखानेदारों या खेतवालों के हाथ काम करने के लिये बेंच देना पड़ता है— "A working class is composed of persons who are compelled to live by selling their ability to work in other men's factories or fields." (page 302).

अब हमें इसी कसौटी पर कसके देखना है कि हमारे देश के खेत-मजदूर कहे जाने वाले आया इसमें खरे उतरते हैं या नहीं, आया उनमें यह बात पाई जाती है नहीं। बेशक यहां खेतों में काम करने वाले मजदूरों के दो टुकड़े कर सकते हैं। एक दल तो उनका है जो वैज्ञानिक ढंग से की जाने वाली खेती के लिये हजारों एकड़ों के फार्मों में काम करते हैं। ऐसे मजदूर दार्जिलिंग एवं आसाम के उत्तरी जिलों के चाय बगानों में तथा नीलगिरी आदि स्थानों में कहवा या रबर के बड़े-बड़े फार्मों में पाये जाते हैं। इनके बारे में पूर्वोक्त पुस्तक में श्री पामेदत्त ने लिखा है कि "साहुकारों के गुलाम बनके जो लोग मजदूरी करते हैं, अनेक बातों में ठीक उन्हीं की सी हालत उन दस लाख से ज्यादा मजदूरों की है जो गुलामों की तरह बड़े-बड़े चाय, कहवा और रबर के बगानों में काम करते हैं। इन बगानों में 90 प्रतिशत के मालिक यूरोपियन ही हैं जो बहुत ज्यादा मुनाफा कमाते हैं"— "Akin to these in many respects is the condition of the plantation slaves, or over one million labourers on the great tea, coffee and rubber plantations, owned up to 90 percent by European companies which pay high dividends." (India Today, page 219).

प्रान्तीय सरकारों और भारत-सरकार के बड़े फार्मों में तथा कुछ गैर सरकारी फार्मों में भी इसी प्रकार के मजदूर मिल सकते हैं। मगर एक तो इनके बारे में कोई पक्की जानकारी है नहीं। दूसरे पूर्वोक्त बगानों के मजदूरों की बात निराली है। वे एक एक स्थान पर कई-कई हजार की तादाद में आज युगों से बस गये हैं। इस प्रकार वे सचमुच सर्वहारा (Proletariate) बन गये हैं। यह बात इन फार्मों में काम करने वालों में अभी तक आम तौर से है नहीं। इसीलिये बगान वालों के बारे में श्री पामेदत्त लिखते हैं कि "संगठित मजदूर आन्दोलन को चलाने की शक्ति की दृष्टि से हमें दस लाख से ज्यादा उन श्रमजीवियों को भी गिनना होगा जो बगानों में काम करते हैं। ये लोग पूर्ण रीति से वैज्ञानिक तरीके पर गुलाम बना रखने वाले चाय वगैरह के बगानों में काम करते हैं। यद्यपि वे लोग अब तक सभी प्रकार के संगठनों से वंचित रखे गये, उन्हें किसी से मिलने जुलने नहीं दिया जाता और पूर्णतया मालिकों के आधीन कर दिये गये हैं। तथापि बेचैनी और गड़बड़ी के समय उनने बहुत ऊँचे दर्जे दर्जे के संघर्षात्मक काम किये हैं "— "From the standpoint of the potential strength of the organised labour movment, we should add over one million workers employed on the plantations, who are employed in fully large scale enterprises under the most scientific slave driving conditions, and have already shown a high degree of militant activity in periods of unrest, although so far cut off from all organisation and held under conditions of complete isolation and subjection." (India Today, page 349).

अतएव ऐसे खे़त मजदूरों को मजदूर या सर्वहारा श्रेणी में दाखि़ल करने में किसी को भी आनाकानी हो नहीं सकती। वे तो उसी दल के हुई। ऐसे बगानों या फार्मों में, जो आज मौजूद हैं या आगे कायम होंगे, जो भी खेत-मजदूर होंगे वे तो दरअसल उन मजदूरों (Proletariates) से जरा भी भिन्न नहीं हो सकते जो खानों, बड़े कारखानों या ऐसे ही उद्योग-धन्दों में काम करते हैं। उन दोनों की दशा, रहन-सहन, लड़ाई और परिस्थिति प्रायः एक ही ढंग की होती है। शायद ही तफसीली या ब्योरे की बातों में कुछ अन्तर होता है। मगर असलियत एक ही होती है।

<25.7.41> खेत मजदूरों के दो दल होते हैं इस बात की पुष्टि लेनिन

के उस भाषण के एक अंश से हो जाती है जो उसने कम्युनिस्ट पार्टी की दसवीं कांग्रेस के अवसर पर सन 1921 ई. की गर्मियों में दिया था। खेत मजदूरों के जिस सर्वहारा नामक अंश का उल्लेख अभी किया गया है उसे लेनिन ने खुद उसी भाषण में स्वीकार किया है। वह अंश यों हैं "—

"In the countries of developed captalism there is a class of hired agricultural labourers which has been (sic) itself in the course of some decades. . . Where this class is sufficiently developed, the transition from capitalism to socialism is possible. We have emphasised in a whole series of writings, in all our speeches, in all our press, the fact that in Russia the situation is not like this—that in Russia we have a minority of workers in industry and an enormous majority of petty land-owners."

इसका आशय यह है :—

"जिन देशों में पूंजीवाद की काफी तरक्की हो गई है वहां कुछ मुद्दत से बनते बनते अब खेत मजदूरों का एक वर्ग तैयार हो गया है जो केवल पैसे या मिहनताने के लिये काम करता है। जिन मुल्कों में यह वर्ग काफी मजबूत और बड़ा बन गया है वहां पूंजीवाद से सीधे समाजवाद की स्थापना हो सकती है। लेकिन हमने तो अपनी लम्बी लेखमालाओं, सभी भाषणों और सभी अखबारों के द्वारा इस बात पर पूरा जोर दिया है कि रूस की परिस्थिति ऐसी नहीं है। रूस में तो अपेक्षाकृत अल्पसंख्यक ही मजदूर कल कारखानों में काम करते हैं। यहां तो अधिकांश लोग छोटे-छोटे खेतिहर हैं जो अपनी जमीनों में खेती करते हैं।"

लेनिन के इस कथन से जहां एक ओर यह बात सिद्ध होती है कि लम्बे पैमाने पर ही खेती करने पर खेतमजदूरों का सर्वहारा वर्ग तैयार होता है और उसके लिये पूंजीवाद के भरपूर विकास की जरूरत है, साथ ही उस दशा में भी इस वर्ग के तैयार होने में कुछ मुद्दत लगती है, तहां दूसरी ओर दूसरे प्रकार के खेत मजदूरों का नाम उसमें लिया ही नहीं गया है। खेत मजदूरों के सर्वहारा वर्ग के सिवाय बाकियों को लेनिन ने टुटपुजिये खेतिहर वर्ग में ही गिना है। यह तो कही नहीं सकते कि बड़े-बड़े फार्मों के सिवाय बाकी जो छोटे मोटे किसान थे उनके खेतों पर मजदूर काम करते ही न थे। रूस का इतिहास ही इस बात का साक्षी है कि ऐसे लोग थे बहुत। इतना ही नहीं। खेती सम्बंधी गुलामी प्रथा (serfdom) जब सन 1861 ई. की 19 वीं फरवरी को रूस में कानून के जरिये खत्म की गई तो हालत

यह हो गई कि कहने के लिये तो वे गुलाम आजाद किसान बन गये और उन्हें जमीनें भी मिल गईं। मगर असलियत यह थी कि इस आजादी और जमीन की प्राप्ति के लिये सरकार को हर साल उन्हें जो रकम चुकानी पड़ती थी वह उन जमीनों की पैदावार की कीमत से कहीं ज्यादा होतीं थी। यह बात प्रोफेसर वाई ई. यानसन (Professor Y.E. Yanson) ने लिखी है। यद्यपि हारकोव सरकारी वकील ने प्रोफेसर की सभी बातें अक्षरशः नहीं मानी हैं, तथापि उसने भी कबूल किया है कि बहुत से इलाकों में तो साफ ही जमीन की कमी ऐसी थी कि उसकी उपज से अपनी प्रतिदिन की सख्त जरूरतों को पूरा करना और सरकारी पावना चुकाना ये दोनों बातें किसानों के लिये असंभव थीं। श्री लान्सलाट ओयन (Launcelot A. Owen) ने सन 1906 और 1917 के बीच के किसान आन्दोलन के सम्बन्ध की अपनी किताब (The Russian Peasant Movement, 1906-1917) के छठें पृष्ठ में यह बात यों लिखी है कि "Even in 1877, the well known Professor Yanson, having statistically investigated peasant allotments and payments, showed that the total of peasant payments exceeded the return from their land. While he did not accept Professor Yanson's conclusions as being right with regard to some localities, yet it was impossible for the Procurator of the Harkov Appeal court to deny that 'in certain areas there was a manifest insufficiency of land to satisfy their very pressing needs, both to secure their mode of life and to carry out their obligations to the Government'."

इसीलिये श्री ओयन अपनी उसी किताब के 7 वें पृष्ठ में साफ ही लिखते हैं कि "इस जमीन की कमी के करते किसानों को मजबूरन या तो जमींदारों से लगान पर जमीन लेकर अपनी जरूरत को पूरा करना पड़ता था, या उन जमींदारों के खेतों में उन्हें मजदूरी करनी पड़ती थी, या गांवों से दूर जा के कहीं नौकरी चाकरी करके काम चलाना पड़ता था" —"The insufficiency of land compelled the peasants to supplement their earnings by renting land from the squires, by working on the squires' estates and by extra employment outside the confines of the village."

उसके बाद सन 1906 ई. के 9 नवम्बर की घोषणा के द्वारा जो गावों की पंचायती जमीनों को टुकड़े-टुकड़े बांटने की आजादी किसानों को जार के प्रधानमंत्री स्टालिपिन ने दी उसका भी नतीजा यही हुआ कि गांवों में दो प्रकार के किसान हो गये। एक तो वे जिन्हें पंचायत से बाहर जमीन मिलने

पर भी, जमीन की अल्पता या खेती का और सामान पास में न होने के कारण, वह जमीन मजबूरन बेंच देनी पड़ी। दूसरे थे धनी और सम्पन्न लोग, जिन्हें जमीन खरीदने की आजादी अब प्राप्त थी। सन 1907 और 1910 के भीतर कुल मिलाके प्रायः एक करोड़ एकड़ (3723000 desyatines) जमीन इस प्रकार बिक गई। यह बात श्री ओयेन की पूर्वोक्त पुस्तक के 64-65 पृष्ठों में इस तरह लिखी गई है,"—"It seemed that the separation from the land commune resulted in the exit of two village elements—the pauperised layer giving up farming and thus securing its allotments simply for sale, and the more prosperous members who were freed from communal restrictions." "Between 1907 and 1910, 3723000 desyatines of allotment land was subjected to sale, there being a consistent rise in the yearly figures."

इनके सिवाय बालटिक प्रदेश में 'बतराकी' कहे जाने वाले ऐसे लोग थे जिनकी अपनी जमीनें न होने पर भी दूसरे के खेतों पर काम करते थे। पैदावार का एक निश्चित भाग जमीन के मालिक को देने की शर्त्त पर जमीनें लेकर खेती करने वाले तो थे ही। इस प्रकार जैसे हमारे देश में हलवाहे आदि के नाम से प्रसिद्ध खेत मजदूर हैं वैसे ही रूस में भी थे। फिर भी यह सोचने की बात है कि लेनिन ने उन्हें खेत-मजदूर-Agricultural labourer न कहके टुटपुंजिये किसानों के ही नाम से पुकारा है और खेतिहरों में हीं उन्हें शामिल कर लिया है। आखिर स्टालिपिन की व्यवस्था ने ही तो रूस में कुलक नामक धनी किसानों की बृद्धि को प्रश्रय दिया था। इसीलिये उनके यहां खेतों में काम करने वालों की कमी रूस में थी नहीं। <26.7.41> यह ठीक है कि लेनिन के कथनानुसार उन्हें "जमीन वाले छोटे-छोटे किसान" भी नहीं कह सकते। लेकिन उनका पृथक उल्लेख ऐसे महत्वपूर्ण अवसर पर जो लेनिन ने नहीं किया, उससे साफ है कि जहां तक जनता की क्रांतिकारी का ताल्लुक था, किसानों से अलग उन खेती के मजदूरों की गिनती न थी। लेनिन ने उन्हें कारखानों या बड़े-बड़े फार्मों के सर्वहारा की श्रेणी के योग्य न समझ किसानों की ही श्रेणी में समझा।

लेनिन के इस कथन का और भी मतलब है। असल में क्रांतिकारी शक्तियों का विश्लेषण करते हुए ही उसने ऐसा कहा था और असली क्रांतिकारी शक्ति तो गांवों में केवल सर्वहारा श्रेणी में ही हो सकती है। क्योंकि वह दल कारखानों के सर्वहारा जैसा ही है। बाकी लोग तो उसके पीछे आते हैं। सो भी शुरू में नहीं। किन्तु आगे चल कर, जब वे देखते हैं

कि उनका मतलब सिद्ध होने वाला है। सर्वहारा श्रेणी को भी क्रांति की सफलता के लिये मजबूरन उनसे समझौता करना पड़ता है। लेनिन का तात्पर्य यही है कि केवल सर्वहारा श्रेणी को ही सर्वशक्तिमान समझ उनसे ही क्रांति की सफलता का खयाल करना भारी भूल है। वे तो देहातों में हुई नहीं हैं। देहातों में तो टुटपुजिये किसान ही अत्यधिक संख्या में पाये जाते हैं और यदि उनसे सुलह न की जायगी तो क्रांति की सफलता मिल नहीं सकती। बनी बनाई क्रांति मटियामेट हो जायगी। नई आर्थिक नीति (Nep) की जरूरत बताते हुए ही उसने यह बात कही थी और इस नीति में टुटपुजिये या साधारण किसानों के साथ काफी रिआयत करके समाजवाद के सिद्धान्त पूर्ण पालन न किया गया था। फलतः उन किसानों के साथ सर्वहारा वर्ग का एक प्रकार से समझौता हुआ था। यदि खेती के मजदूरों को सर्वहारा श्रेणी में मानते तो क्रांति की सफलता में धोखा होता। क्योंकि उनकी मनोवृत्ति किसानों जैसी ही होती है इसीलिये उस कथन के बाद ही उसी भाषण में यही बात लेनिन यों कहता है, "The other condition is an agreement between the proletariat which holds the state power and the majority of the peasant population. Only an agreement with the peasants can save the socialist revolution in Russia."

हां, तो बड़े बड़े बगानों और फार्मों में काम करने वाले दस बारह लाख मजदूर तो सर्वहारा श्रेणी में ही आते हैं जैसा कि अब तक के वर्णन से स्पष्ट हो जाता है। सर्वहारा की सब से बड़ी और असली पहचान यह है कि उनमें संगठित रूप से मिलकर लड़ने और अपना हक हासिल करने की शक्ति होती है, जिसे अंग्रेजी में collective bargaining power कहते हैं। इन फार्मों और बगानों के मजदूरों में भी यह बात पाई जाती है।

इस बात को यों देखें तो काम चले। किसी भी मिल या कारखाने को लीजिये। वहां हजारों मजदूर काम करते पाये जायंगे। एक तो वे एक ही साथ एक ही समय उठते बैठते और सोते जागते हैं। गरोह बांध के एक ही साथ काम पर जाते और वहां से लौटते हैं। समय की पाबन्दी पर पूरी नजर रखने की मजबूरी के करते उनका जीवन फौजी जवानों की तरह हो जाता है। एक प्रकार की कवायद उन्हें सीखनी ही पड़ती है आने जाने आदि के रूप में। साथ ही, बराबर सम्मिलित जीवन बिताने का भी उन पर असर पड़ता है, जैसे बैरकों के सिपाही हों। यदि वे एक राय से काम बन्द कर दें तो कारखाने वाले को अपना काम चलाना गैर मुमकिन हो जाता है। एक तो उनके कामों को आमतौर से सभी लोग कर नहीं सकते कि छोड़ देने पर

संभाल लें। दूसरे हजारों आदमियों को जमा करना आसान नहीं। तीसरे काम छोड़ने वाले मजदूर पिकेटिंग आदि के जरिये बाहरी लोगों (black-legs) को रोक भी देते हैं। चौथी बात यह होती है कि उनकी यूनियन (सभा) आसानी से उनका पथप्रदर्शन कर सकती है। क्योंकि वे लोग एक ही जगह रहते जो हैं, जिससे जब चाहें सबों से मिल जुल सकते हैं। पांचवीं बात यह होती है कि दूसरे दूसरे कारखानों के मजदूर भी उनकी सहानुभूति में काम बन्द कर देते हैं। क्योंकि यह हालत तो एक के बाद दीगरे सभी की होती है। इसलिये यदि एक कारखाने वालों ने दूसरे मिलवालों से हमदर्दी दिखाई, तो दूसरे भी मौका पड़ने पर पहले वालों से दिखाते ही हैं। सबसे बड़ी बात यह होती है कि एक स्थान पर रहने के कारण समाचार पत्रों, सामयिक किताबों , सभाओं वगैरः से फायदा आसानी से उठाया जा सकता है और मजदूरों को अपने कर्त्तव्य का पूरा ज्ञान मिल सकता है। इसके सिवाय जहां ऐसे कारखाने या बगान होते हैं वहां रेल, तार, बेतार वगैरः की आसानी रहने के कारण दुनियां की खबर वहां और वहां की दुनियां में आसानी से पहुंच जाने के कारण बाहर की जनता भी उनके साथ सहानुभूति का प्रदर्शन करती है। अतएव इन सभी बातों के फलस्वरूप उन मजदूरों को अपनी लड़ाई में आसानी होती है और सफलता भी प्रायः मिलती ही है। ये सभी बातें मिलों और फार्मों या बगानों में समान रूप से पाई जाती है। रेल तार वगैरः के बिना दोनों का ही काम नहीं चल पाता। बाकी बातें भी पाई ही जाती हैं।

इस प्रकार खेत-मजदूरों के एक भाग का विचार हो चुका। वे सोलहों आने मजदूर वर्ग में आ जाते हैं। अतएव उनकी लड़ाइयां, उनके संगठन, उनके काम ठीक वैसे ही होने चाहियें, जैसे दूसरे मजदूरों के होते हैं- उनके जो मिलों वगैरः में काम करते हैं। मगर यह याद रखना होगा कि खेत मजदूरों की जो संख्या पांच करोड़ या ज्यादा बताई गई है उसका एक महज नन्हा सा हिस्सा ऐसे मजदूरों का है। मुश्किल से दो प्रतिशत भी शायद ही हों। इसलिये अब जो 98 प्रतिशत बच गये हैं उन्हें किस श्रेणी में गिना जाय यह सवाल उठता है - अर्थात उन खेतमजदूरों के दूसरे और महत्वपूर्ण भाग का विचार भी कर लेना जरूरी है। असल में तो हमें इन 98 फीसदी से ही काम पड़ता है। 2 प्रतिशत तो कहां दूर दराज खोह और प्रदेश में पड़े हैं कौन बताये? उन तक कौन पहुंचे? जैसा कि रूस के बारे में लेनिन का वचन उद्द्त कर चुके हैं वह भारत में तो और भी अक्षरशः लागू है। यहां तो छोटे-छोटे खेत - नन्हीं-नन्हीं क्यारियों जैसे - सर्वत्र नजर आते

हैं और उनमें कहीं एक, कहीं दो, कहीं चार इसी प्रकार ख़ेत मजदूर हल चलाते या दूसरे काम करते पाये जाते हैं। कोई गांव ऐसा है जहां खुद किसान हीं अपनी खेती का काम कर लेते हैं। उन्हें हलवाहे आदि की जरूरत नहीं होती। फिर ऐसा भी गांव है जहां दो ही चार किसान हैं जिन्हें ख़ेत-मजदूरों से काम लेने की जरूरत है। जहां ज्यादा ख़ेत-मजदूर हैं ऐसे भी गांव पाये जाते हैं। कहीं गांव पास पास में हैं, तो कहीं एक से दूसरे का फासला मीलों और कोसों है। तात्पर्य यह है कि खेती के मजदूर दाने की तरह बिखरे पड़े हैं और इनका परस्पर मिलना आसान नहीं है। यदि चाहें तो भी अकसर मिल सकना प्रायः असंभव है। न तो सबों के काम के घंटे एक से निश्चित हैं और इतनी हीं देर काम करेंगे, ज्यादा देर नहीं यही तय है। फलतः काम के बाद पस्त और मुर्दे हो जाते हैं। गधे की तरह दिन रात खटना जो पड़ता है। ज्यादातर किसानों और उनके मजदूरों की-दोनों की ही- यही हालत है। फिर हिम्मत कहां कि काम के बाद मीटिंग करें ?

जातिपांति और धर्म मजहब का भेद भी इन्हें एक दूसरे से जुदा रखता है। ऊंच नीच के पुराने खयाल और संस्कार उनके दिल में यह बात आने हीं नहीं देते कि सभी ख़ेत-मजदूर हैं। फिर मिलके लड़ने की बात कैसे और क्यों कर उठ सकती है ? यदि कहीं लड़ने की हिम्मत भी इनने की तो किसान आसानी से एक की जगह दूसरे से काम ले सकता है। हर किसान को तो एक, दो, चार ही की जरूरत होती है और उतने तो आसानी से उसे मिल सकते हैं। यदि न भी मिलें तो किसान खुद भी खेती का काम कर सकता है। कल पुर्जे चलाने या मैशीन का काम तो है नहीं कि गंवार किसान चला नहीं सकता। लकड़ी के ये पुराने दकियानूसी हल तो सभी के हाथों बखूबी चल सकते हैं। असल में थोड़ा सा सम्मान की मिथ्या धारणा या धर्म का गलत खयाल ही उसे हल वगैरः चलाने से रोकता था। मगर जब भूखों मरने या झुकने की नौबत आयेगी तो ये खयाल टिक नहीं सकते। ऐसा सैकड़ों जगह हो भी चुका है। सिर्फ कयास या अन्दाज की बात नहीं है। ऐसी दशा में मिलके लड़ना या collective bargaining की गुंजाइश भी यहां कैसे हो सकती है ? और अगर कहीं कहीं खेतमजदूरों के द्वारा काम छोड़ देने (हड़ताल) की धमकी या खास हड़ताल को ही सफलता मिली है तो ज्यादा जगह विफलता भी हाथ लगी है। यह भी याद रहे कि किसानों के सजग न होने से ही यह बात हुई है। लेकिन जब यह हड़ताल संगठित रूप से चलाने की कोशिश होगी तो किसान भी सामूहिक रूप से

सजग हो जायंगे और नतीजा बुरा होगा।

मजदूरों की सम्मिलित लड़ाई की योग्यता (collective bargaining) के सम्बन्ध में पहली जितनी बातें कही गई हैं उनमें एक भी इन खेत-मजदूरों के सम्बन्ध में लागू नहीं हो सकती हैं। दूर दराज की देहातों में रेल, तार वगैरः का अभाव ही समझिये। अखबार और सामयिक साहित्य की प्राप्ति भी नहीं के बराबर ही है। मीटिगें भी शायद ही कभी कहीं हो पाती हों। उनका संगठन तो और भी कठिन है। परस्पर हमदर्दी तो शायद ही कहीं हो। उसके प्रदर्शन का मौका भी तो नहीं होता। परिणाम भी कुछ हो नहीं सकता। एक किसान का दूसरे के साथ वैसा नाता नहीं है जैसा कि एक मिल का दूसरी के साथ। अतएव इन्हें मजदूरों की श्रेणी में गिनना ठीक नहीं है। इसके लिये कोई भी कारण नहीं है। सबसे बड़ी बात तो यह है कि इन खेतमजदूरों के मकान या झोपड़े तो होते ही हैं। एकाध बकरी, गाय या सूअर वगैरः भी रहते ही हैं। और नहीं तो दो चार कट्ठे जमीन के भी होते ही हैं। ज्यादा नहीं तो मकान वाली ही जमीन इनकी होती है। यह भी बात तो है कि कल तक किसान थे। मगर जमींदार या साहुकार ने सारी जमीन नीलाम करवाली तो एकाएक आज बिना जमीन के हो गये-खेतमजदूर बन गये। मगर सर्वहारा इतनी जल्दी कैसे बन जायंगे? कही तो चुके हैं कि खेत—मजदूरों की संख्या बड़ी तेजी से बढ़ रही है। हर साल लाखों इस दल में शमिल हो रहे हैं। अतएव इन्हें किसान ही मानना ठीक है। ये उसी वर्ग में शमिल किये जा सकते हैं, किये जाने चाहियें।

लेकिन इस गोलमोल कथन से काम नहीं चल सकता। इस बात की थोड़ी और सफाई होनी चाहिये। किसान कहने से बहुत तरह के लोग आ जाते हैं। ऐसे भी लोग अपने को किसान कहते हैं, कहने की हिम्मत करते हैं जिनके पास बीसों हजार बीघा जमीन केवल रैयती है। लेकिन यदि सच पूछा जाय तो वे तो जमींदार ही हैं - भयंकर जमींदार हैं। क्योंकि किसान के नाम लोगों को आसानी से धोखा दे सकते हैं। साधारणतया किसान उसी को कहना चहिये जिसकी प्रधान जीविका खेती हो। इसका आशय यही है कि प्रधानरूप में खेती के बिना जिसकी जीविका चल न सके वह किसान कहने का दावा नहीं कर सकता। ऐसी दशा में जो लोग बहुत ज्यादा रैयती जमीनें रखते और कुछ में खेती करके बाकी को दूसरों को बन्दोबस्त कर देते हैं उनकी जीविका तो खेती के बिना भी चल ही जाती है। दूसरों लाखों रूपये या लाखों मन गल्ला लगान के रूप में लेते जो हैं। विपरीत इसके जिसके पास जरामरा अपनी जमीन हो, या न भी हो, मगर दूसरों से

ही बंटाई वगैरः के रूप में ही कुछ जमीन ले के खेती करे और मौका पाकर गैरों के खेतों पर मजदूरी भी करे, वह किसान कहा जा सकता है। लेकिन जिसके परिवार के लिये जीविका का प्रधान साधन मजदूरी ही हो वह साधारणतया किसान न समझा जाने पर भी किसान श्रेणी के बाहर तब तक माना जाना नहीं चाहिये जब तक छोटेमोटे खेतिहरों के खेतों पर काम करके ही जीविका करता है और बड़े बगानों या बड़े फार्मों में काम नहीं करता। तात्पर्य यह है कि जब तक उसे जमीन हासिल कर उसमें खेती करके गुजर करने की आशा है और जब तक इस आशा की पूर्ति की संभावना है तभी तक उसे किसान कह सकते हैं। मगर जहां आधुनिक ढंग के फार्मों में मोटर के हलों से खेती होने लगी और पूंजीवाद का खेती में भी पदार्पण हो गया वहां यह संभावना नहीं रह जाती। इसलिये वहां का खेत मजदूर जरूर ही किसान न होके मजदूर या सर्वहारा बन जाता है। फलतः जैसे जैसे ये फार्म बढ़ेंगे तैसे असली खेतमजदूर बढ़ते जायंगे।

असल में किसान तीन दलों में बांटे जा सकते हैं– (1) गरीब किसान, (2) मध्यम श्रेणी के किसान, और (3) धनी किसान। वर्त्तमान रूस के विधाता श्री स्तालिन ने 'लेनिनवाद' (Leninism) नामक सुन्दर किताब लिखी है। या यों कहिये कि स्तालिन के लेखों, भाषणों आदि का संग्रह स्वरूप ही वह पुस्तक बनी है। उसके पृष्ठ 308 में टिप्पणी इस बात पर सुन्दर प्रकाश डालती है। रूस की उस समय की दशा भारत से मिलती जुलती थी जहां तक किसानों का ताल्लुक था। इसीलिये वह टिप्पणी हमारे बड़े काम की है। वह यों है :– <27.7.41> "The Russian peasants comprise three main catagories: 1) Rich peasants or Kulaks, whose farms are large and who employ wage-labour; these form a "rural bourgeoisie." The village money-lenders and liquor sellers under the old regime were also termed 'Kulaks.' 2) Middle peasants, who work their holdings themselves with the aid of their families, but do not usually employ wage-labour. 3) Poor peasants, who have very small holdings, or none at all, being mainly agricultural labourers (for wages) and half peasants or semi proletarians, (who work in the towns at certain seasons)."

इसका अर्थ यह है कि, "रूसी किसान प्रधानतया तीन तरह के हैं। (1) धनी किसान, जिन्हें कुलक कहते हैं। इनके खे़त बड़े-बड़े होते हैं और ये लोग मजदूरी पर मजदूरों से काम करवाते हैं। ये लोग "देहाती सम्पत्ति जीवी या पूंजीपति" हैं। जारशाही के समय के गांवों के सूदखोर और शराब

बेंचने वाले भी कुलक कहे जाते थे। (2) **मध्यम किसान**, जो अपने खेतों में अपने घर वालों की ही मदद से अपने ही हाथों खुद खेती करते हैं। ये लोग साधारणतया मजदूरों से काम नहीं करवाते (3) **गरीब किसान** जिनके पास या तो बहुत ही थोड़े खेत होते हैं, या बिल्कुल ही नहीं होते। ये लोग प्रधानतया मजदूरी के लिये ही खेतों में काम करते हैं। इन्हें अर्द्ध किसान या अर्द्ध सर्वहारा कह सकते हैं। ये लोग गांवों में काम न रहने पर यानी खेती का मौसिम न होने पर शहरों में मजूरी करते हैं।"

ऊपर के इस बयान में कई महत्वपूर्ण बातें हैं। एक तो यह कि यह जो रूस के किसानों का वर्णन दिया गया है वह प्रायः भारत के किसानों की दशा से सोलहों आने मिलता जुलता ही है। जिन धनी और गरीब किसानों का उल्लेख इसमें है वे तो हमारे यहां भी ठीक-ठीक पाये जाते हैं। जरा भी अन्तर नहीं है। रूस में खेत मजदूरों को गरीब किसानों में ही गिना है। हमारे यहां भी यही बात है। हम इसे न समझें या न मानें, तो बात ही दूसरी है। मगर हालत तो दोनों जगह बराबर ही है। हां, मध्यम किसानों का जो वर्णन वहां के लिये है उसमें और यहां के मध्यम किसानों की हालत में कुछ कुछ अन्तर है। हमारे यहां धर्मवर्म का मिथ्या बखेड़ा होने के कारण मध्यम किसान बहुतेरे मजदूरों से काम करवाते हैं। ज्यादातर ब्राह्मण लोग ही ऐसा करते हैं और कुछ क्षत्रिय लोग भी। इस धर्म के बखेड़े के करते ही गरीब ब्राह्मण किसान भी खुद हल नहीं चलाते। मगर इतने से ही आर्थिक दशा में कोई अन्तर नहीं आ जाता। यहां के भी मध्यम किसान कमाते खाते ही हैं। उनकी पैदावार बेंचने के लिये शायद ही कभी होती हो। पैदावार से मेरा मतलब गल्ले से है। ऊख, मिर्च, तम्बाकू आदि किराना चीजें तो बेंची ही जाती हैं। मगर धनी बनने के लिए इनकी बिक्री वे नहीं करते, किन्तु केवल अपना खर्च चलाने के ही लिये।

दूसरी बड़ी बात इसमें यह है कि गरीब किसानों का जो तीसरा दल है वह प्रधानतया खेती के मजदूरों से ही बना है। ज्यादे से ज्यादा वे आधे किसान और आधे मजदूर हैं, यानी कुछ समय खेती का काम करते हैं और यह काम न रहने पर कुछ समय शहरों में जाकर कमाते हैं। यह बात हमारे यहां भी अक्षरशः पाई जाती है। उसमें यह भी कोष्ठक में लिखा है कि मजदूरी के लिये खेतों में काम करने वाले, जिससे प्रतीत होता है कि खेत-मजदूर उन्हें भी कहते हैं जो मजदूरी के लिये काम नहीं करते। यह बात मैंने पहले ही लिखी है विस्तार के साथ।

तीसरी बात यह है कि जिनके पास खेत बिल्कुल ही नहीं हों वे भी

गरीब किसानों में गिने जाते हैं। हम तो कही चुके हैं कि खेत पास में रहना जरूरी नहीं है। जहां तक खेत मिलने की गुंजाइश या आशा है तहां तक खेतों के मजदूरों को किसान ही कहना चाहिये। रूस में भी यही माना जाता था। हां, बड़े-बड़े फार्मों के खेतमजदूरों को खेत मिलने की कोई भी आशा न होने के कारण वही असली मजदूर हैं - वहां भी और यहां भी। बाकी तो अधिक से अधिक अर्द्धमजदूर हैं।

जिन्हें इस बात का यकीन न हो कि हमारे यहां के भी गरीब किसान एक प्रकार के मजदूर ही हैं उनके लिये आगे बहुत सी बातें लिखी जावंगी। मगर इस मौके पर बम्बई के एक सरकारी कर्मचारी अंग्रेज डाक्टर हैरोल्ड मान (Dr. Harold H. Mann) की जांच पड़ताल का नतीजा हम यहां उद्धृत कर देते है। डाक्टर मान सरकार के कृषि विभाग के डाइरेक्टर थे। उनने पूना जिले के एक गांव के किसानों की आर्थिक दशा की जांच सन 1914-15 ई. में की थी। जब जांच का नतीजा बहुत ही दर्दनाक निकला जिसके लिये वे तैयार न थे तो उन्हें विश्वास न हुआ। अतएव सन 1921 में एक और गांव की जांच उनने की। मगर जब उसका नतीजा पहले से भी भयंकर साबित हुआ तो लाचार उन्हें मानना ही पड़ा। जहां पहले गांव में कुल 103 परिवारों में सिर्फ 8 ही खेती से अच्छी तरह गुजर कर सकते थे, तहां दूसरे में पूरे 147 में केवल 10 ही ऐसे थे। एक बात और थी। पहले मौजे में कुल 103 में से 8 परिवारों को निकालने के बाद शेष 95 में 28 ऐसे थे जो खेती की आमदनी और बाहर की नौकरी की आमदनी को मिला के किसी प्रकार गुजर कर लेते थे। मगर दूसरे में तो 147 में 10 के अलग करने पर बाकियों में केवल 12 ही ऐसे थे। इस प्रकार जहां पहले गांव में पूरे 67 परिवार कुल परिवारों के 65 प्रतिशत भूखों रह जाते थे और किसी भी तरह भर पेट खा पी न सकते थे, तहां दूसरे में कुल 125 परिवार या कुल के 85 प्रतिशत की यह भयंकर दशा थी। दूसरे गांव की एक और भी दर्दनीय बात उनने लिखी है। वहां कुल 732 आदमियों में 664 प्राणी भुक्खड़ थे- यानी कुल जनसंख्या के पूरे 91 प्रतिशत। पहले गाव के पास में एक आलमोनियम (sic.) की फैक्टरी होने के कारण गांव के 30 प्रतिशत लोग उसमें कमाते थे और इस प्रकार गुजर करते थे। मगर दूसरे गांव के नजदीक ऐसी कोई चीज न होने के कारण उसकी और भी तबाही थी।

यदि पूर्व लिखे इस बयान के साथ यह भी बात जोड़ दी जाय कि डाक्टर मान ने गांव वालों की गुजर का क्या अर्थ लगाया था तो हम और भी

अचम्भे में पड़ जायंगे किसानों की गरीबी की भयंकरता को देख के। उनने किसी प्रकार कामचलाऊ पेट भरने की गई गुजरी चीज को भोजन और जैसे तैसे काम चलाने मात्र वस्त्र को कपड़े में गिना है। यही दो जरूरी चीजें हैं। यहां तक कि चिराग या लालटेन की रोशनी भी उनने निकाल दी है और सिर्फ सूर्य, चांद की रोशनी से ही काम चलाना स्वीकार किया है, जैसा कि," "This conclusion is reached on the basis of an estimate of the economic minimum for the ryots' standard of life, which touches the lowest level of scanty food and clothing with no allowance for such a luxury as an artificial light." से स्पष्ट है। चिराग को उनने व्यसन मान लिया है। ड़ाक्टर मान ने दोनों गांवों का पूरा हाल अपनी पुस्तक के दो भागों में दिया है जो 1917 और 1921 में छपी है। उसका नाम है "दक्षिण के एक गांव का जीवन और परिश्रम" "Life and labour in a Deccan Village." उन्होंने यह भी लिखा है कि "चाहे परिस्थिति हर तरह से कितनी ही अनुकूल क्यों न हो, ताहम एक मौजे में किसानों की जमीनें (holdings) ऐसी थीं कि एक में 77 फीसदी और दूसरे में 81 फीसदी जमीनें किसानों के गुजर के लायक थी ही नहीं"—"In the village where minimum economic holdings would be about 20 acres, 77 percent of the holdings were below this level." "In the first village he found that 81 percent of the holdings could not under the most favourable circumstances maintain their owners." श्री पामेदत्त की पूर्वोक्त पुस्तक के 222-223 आदि पृष्ठों में इस बात का पूरा वर्णन है।

श्री पामेदत्त ही 347 पृष्ठ में लिखते हैं कि सन 1927-28 ई० में ब्रिटेन की ट्रेड यूनियन कांग्रेस का जो प्रतिनिधि मंडल भारत में आया था उसने लिखा है कि संगठन योग्य मजदूरों की सख्या यहां ढाई करोड़ है। मगर इस ढाई करोड़ में कम से कम 2 करोड़ 15 लाख तो सिर्फ खेत मजदूर ही हैं जिनमें चाय बगानों आदि के प्रायः 10 लाख को छोड़ बाकी 2 करोड़ 5 लाख सिर्फ छोटे-छोटे खेतों में ही काम करते हैं। उन्हें काम भी बराबर नियमित रूप से नहीं मिलता। ज्यादातर वे लोग अत्यन्त भुक्खड़ किसानों के ही यहां काम करते हैं। फलतः नियमानुसार बनाई जाने वाली ट्रेड यूनियनों के जरिये उनका संगठन हो नहीं सकता। हालांकि किसान आन्दोलन में बड़ा ही महत्वपूर्ण भाग ले सकते हैं।

सन 1938 ई. में अन्तर्राष्ट्रीय मजदूर कार्यालय (I.L.O.) ने भारत के बारे में एक रिपोर्ट (Industrial Labour in India) छापी है। उसके 30 वें

पृष्ठ में लिखा है कि "The total number of agricultural labourers, which was given (sic.) 21.5 million in 1921, was shown by the Census of 1931 to be over 31.5 million, of whom 23 million were estimated by the Indian Franchise Committee in 1931 to be landless."

इसका तात्पर्य यह है कि, "खेतमजदूरों की कुल तादाद जो सन 1921 में 2 करोड़ 15 लाख बताई गई थी, 1931 में वह 3 करोड़ 15 लाख से भी ज्यादा हो गई। मगर इनमें 2 करोड़ 30 लाख के बारे में सन 1931 ई० की भारतीय मताधिकार समिति ने लिखा था कि वे बिना जमीन के हैं।" बिना जमीन कहने का अर्थ यही है कि उनकी अपनी रैयती या मालिकी कोई भी जमीन नहीं है। भले ही बंटाई या शिकमी जमीन लेकर खेती वे लोग करते हैं या न भी करते हैं। मगर मताधिकार कमिटी ने भी तो आखिर इतना कबूल ही किया है कि कम से कम 85 लाख ऐसे भी परिवार खेतमजदूरों के उस समय थे जिनकी निजी जमीनें (रैयती या मालिकी) थीं। क्यों 3 करोड़ 15 लाख में 2 करोड़ 30 लाख ही बिना जमीन के बताये गये हैं। इससे तो हमारे उसी कथन की पुष्टि होती है कि खेत-मजदूर किसान हीं हैं।

शायद कुछ लोगों को फिर भी कुछ झिझक हो कि खेतमजदूरों को किसान कैसे मानें, इसलिये जरा भीतर प्रवेश करके किसानों की हालत को देख लेना चाहिये। बम्बई सरकार के अफसर मिस्टर कीटिंज (Keatinge) का हवाला देते हुए भारतीय कृषि कमिशन की रिपोर्ट के 132 पृष्ठ में लिखा गया है कि "बम्बई हाते के किसानों की होल्डिंगें बहुत ज्यादा ऐसी हो गई हैं जिनमें सफलतापूर्वक खेती करना असंभव है। मद्रास के डाक्टर स्लेटर (Dr. Slater) इस नतीजे पर पहुंचे हैं कि वहां भी बहुत हिस्से में यही हालत है। दूसरे प्रान्तों की भी प्रायः यही दशा है"—"Mr. Keatinge has expressed the opinion that the agricultural holdings of the Bombay Presidency have to a large extent been reduced to a condition in which their effective cultivation is impossible, and Dr. Slater found that similar conditions prevailed in parts of Madras. In other provinces conditions are much the same."

इन्हीं मिस्टर कीटिंज के लेख का हवाला देते हुए पूर्वोक्त डाक्टर मान ने दक्षिण के दो गांवों की दशा जांची थी। उसके बारे में श्री पामेदत्त अपनी पूर्वोक्त किताब में लिखते हैं कि "जिस जमीन में सिचाई का प्रबन्ध नहीं है वैसी खूब अच्छी जमीन के 10 से लेकर 15 एकड़ तक की होल्डिंग को ही

आर्थिक दृष्टि से लाभकर या भारतीय किसान परिवार के गुजर योग्य (economic holding) कह सकते हैं,"—"Following Keatinge's estimate that "an economic holding of good dry land such as is [sic.] most in this village in the Western Deccan, and with an Indian ryot's standard of life," would be about 10 to 15 acres."

अब जरा पुनरपि भारतीय कृषि कमिशन की रिपोर्ट के 133 पृष्ठ को देखिये। वहां लिखा है कि "पंजाब के बारे में जो आंकड़े हासिल हैं उनसे सिद्ध है कि 22.5 फीसदी किसान सिर्फ एक एकड़ या उससे कम ही जमीन जोतते हैं, 15.4 प्रतिशत एक और ढाई एकड़ के बीच में, 17.9 प्रतिशत ढाई और पांच के बीच में , और 20.5 प्रतिशत 5 और दस के बीच में। बम्बई की भी प्रायः यही हालत है। वर्मा की शायद कुछ अच्छी हो। मगर भारत के अन्य प्रान्तों की तो और भी बुरी हालत है,"—"The Punjab figures, which are the only ones available for a province, indicate that 22.5 percent of the cultivators cultivate one acre or less, further, 15.4 percent cultivate between one and two and a half acres; 17.9 percent between two and a half and five acres, and 20.5 percent between five and ten acres. Except for Bombay which would probably show a very similar result, and Burma, which would give higher averages, all other provinces have much smaller average acres per cultivator."

इससे स्पष्ट है कि पंजाब, जो सब से सम्पन्न प्रान्त माना जाता है, के 76.3 प्रतिशत किसान ज्यादे से ज्यादा दस एक़ड़ तक ही जोतते हैं और परिवार के गुजारे के लिये, जैसा कहा गया है, दस से लेकर 15 एकड़ चाहिये। फलतः वे भूखे ही रहते हैं। यों तो सन 1921 ई० की मनुष्य गणना के अनुसार प्रान्तों के हर परिवार के जिम्मे औसतन जो जमीनें पड़ती हैं वह और भी कम हैं। उसके अनुसार तो सिर्फ बम्बई की ही औसत 10 एकड़ से ज्यादा है। बाकियों की कम ही है, जैसा कि "(1) **बम्बई** 12.2, (2) **पंजाब** 9.2, (3) **मध्यप्रान्त और बरार** 8.5, (4) **बर्मा** 5.6, (5) **मद्रास** 4.9, (6) **बंगाल** 3.1, (7) **बिहार** 3.1, (8) **आसाम** 3.0, (9) **युक्त प्रान्त** 2.5 । कृषि कमिशन के उक्त उद्धरण से भी यही स्पष्ट है कि ब्रम्बई के सिवाय अन्य सभी प्रान्तों के 76.3 प्रति से कहीं ज्यादा किसान 10 एकड़ तक ही या उससे भी कम जोतते हैं।

और जब हम इस बात पर गौर करते हैं कि जमीन के मालिक और उसे जोतने वाले किसान के बीच में दो चार से लेकर पूरे पचास तक ऐसे लोग

एक ऊपर एक (intermediaries) हैं जो लगान वसूलते और उससे मुनाफा करते हैं तब हमें पता लग जाता है कि खेती करने वाले को कितना बचता है। वह तो सचमुच ही लुट जाता है। हाल में प्रकाशित बंगाल के फ्लाउड कमिशन (Floud Commission) की रिपोर्ट में भी यह बात मानी गई है और साइमन कमिशन की रिपोर्ट के प्रथम भाग के 340 पृष्ठ में भी इन पचासों लुटेरों की बात लिखी है कि वे कुछ जिलों में पचास से ज्यादा तक पाये जाते हैं, जैसा कि :— "In some districts the sub-infeudation has grown to astonishing proportions, as many as fifty or more intermediary interests have been created between the zamindar at the top and the actual cultivator at the bottom."

जब इस प्रकार एक से दूसरा आदमी जमीन लेकर तीसरे के हाथ बन्दोबस्त करता है (sublets) और वह चौथे के साथ और जब इस प्रकार तांता बंध जाता है तो असली किसान में और मजूरी करने वाले खेत मजदूर में कुछ भी अन्तर नहीं रह जाता। इसीलिये मद्रास की बैंकिंग जांच कमेटी ने सन 1930 ई० में यों लिखा था :— "We find it difficult to draw a clear line between cultivation by farm servants and subletting. Subletting is rarely on money rental. It is commonly on a sharing system, the landlord getting 40 to 60 or even 80 percent of the yield and the tenant the rest. The tenant commonly goes on from year to year eking out a precarious living on such terms, borrowing from the landlord, being supplied by him with seed, cattle and implements. The farm servant, on the other hand, uses the landlord's seed, cattle and implements, gets advances in cash from time to time for petty requirements, and is paid from the harvest either a lump sum of grain, or proportion of the yield. The farm servant may in some cases be paid a little cash as well as a fixed amount of grain. The tenant may cultivate with his own stock and implements, but there is in practice no very clear line between the two, and when the landlord is an absentee, it is not always obvious whether the actual cultivator is a farm servant or a sub-tenant."

इसका अर्थ यों है, "खेत-मजदूर रखके उनके हाथों खेती करवाने या दर रैयत की खेती में साफ-साफ भेद करना हमारे लिये कठिन है। दर रैयत तो शायद ही नगद लगान पर जमीन पाता हो। आमतौर से उसे बंटाई पर

ही खेत मिलता है जिसमें पैदावार का 40 से लेकर 60 तक, और कभी-कभी 80 हिस्से तक भी, जमीन का मालिक लेकर बाकी किसान (दर रैयत) के लिये छोड़ता है। किसान साल ब साल इसी प्रकार किसी तरह जिन्दा रहता है। उसे जमींदार से कर्ज लेना पड़ता है। जमींदार ही उसे बीज, खेती के औजार और बैल भी देता है। विपरीत इसके हलवाहे आदि खेती के मजदूरों को मालिक समय-समय की छोटी मोटी जरूरतों के लिये नगद पैसे देता है, जमींदार के ही बीज, औजार और पशुओं से खेती करता है और फसल तैयार होने पर या तो उसे एक ही बार बंधी बधाई गल्ले की रकम मिल जाती है, या फसल का एक निश्चित भाग। कभी कभी तो ऐसा भी होता है कि हलवाहे आदि को निश्चित गल्ले के साथ ही कुछ नगद भी मिल जाता है। किसान चाहे अपने ही पशुओं और हल आदि से भले ही खेती करे। मगर व्यवहार में दोनों के बीच कोई साफ अन्तर नजर नहीं आता और अगर जमींदार खेती के मुकाम से दूर रहता हो तब तो यह पता ही नहीं चलता कि खेती करने वाला आया उसका नौकर है या दर रैयत किसान"।

अपनी पुस्तक के 220 पृष्ठ में श्री पामेदत्त ने भी लिखा है कि "लेकिन दरअसल नन्हें खेतों में खेती करने वाले अधिकांश टुटपुजिये किसानों, दर रैयतों या शिकमी किसानों की जो हालत है उसमें और खेत-मजदूरों में कोई विशेष अन्तर नहीं है और इन दोनों दलों का भेद सिर्फ बनावटी है"– "But in fact the situation of the majority of small cultivators on uneconomic holdings, of sub-let tenants and unprotected tenants is not far removed from that of the agricultural labourers, and the line of distinction between the two is an extremely shadowy one."

कृषि कमिशन की रिपोर्ट के द्वितीय भाग में जो गवाहियों का पहला हिस्सा है उसके 292 पृष्ठ में कुछ आंकड़े दिखला के कि किस प्रकार 15 एकड़ तक के जोतने वाले किसानों की ही संख्या तेजी से बढ़ रही है, एक सरकारी अफसर का बयान यों दिया है :– "केवल पांच ही वर्ष के भीतर होने वाले परिवर्त्तन के सूचक इन आंकड़ों से साफ पता लगता है कि पन्द्रह एकड़ तक जोतने वालों की वृद्धि किस खास तरह से हो रही है। चन्द ही जमीनों को छोड़ बाकी दशा में ये 15 एकड़ तक के खेत ऐसे नहीं होते कि जिनमें एक जोड़े बैलों से भी नफा के साथ खेती की जा सके।"

अब तक जो कुछ लिखा गया है उससे यह बात साफ हो जाती है कि जो असल किसान हैं, जिन्हें गरीब या मध्यम किसान कहते हैं, उनकी

हालत और 98 प्रतिशत खेत-मजदूरों की दशा में कोई भी महत्वपूर्ण अन्तर नहीं है। जहां तक इन दोनों की आर्थिक दशा और माली हालत का ताल्लुक है खेतमजदूरों और गरीब किसानों में जिनकी संख्या 80 फीसदी से कम नहीं है, कोई भेद किया जा नहीं सकता - किसी भेद की गुंजाइश नहीं है। यदि कुछ किसान भर पेट खा पी लेते हैं तो कुछ खेत मजदूर भी ऐसे जरूर हैं। ज्यादे से ज्यादा अगर कह सकते हैं तो इतना ही कि जैसे किसानों की दशा अबतर होते-होते जो उनमें सब से नीचे आ जाते हैं वही गरीब किसान हैं, ठीक वैसे ही आमतौर से उनकी दशा कुछ और गिर जाने से उन्हें खेत मजदूर कहने लगते हैं। मगर यह बताना कठिन है कि कहां से किसान कहना छूट के मजदूर कहने का श्रीगणेश होता है। ऐसी कोई सीमा (demarcation line) खींची जा सकती नहीं। इसीलिये खेत-मजदूरों को, जिनसे आमतौर से हमारा ताल्लुक है, किसान ही मानना उचित है।

मगर इस मानने का प्रयोजन केवल उनके संगठन और आन्दोलन से है। उन्हें किसान इसीलिये मानना है कि उनका आन्दोलन मजदूरों की तरह न किया जाकर किसानों की ही तरह, उनके साथ मिल कर ही, किया जाय।

3

उनकी समस्यायें

खेत-मजदूरों की तादाद वगैरः जान लेने और उन्हें किस वर्ग में शमिल किया जाय - वे किस श्रेणी के हैं - ऐसा समझने के बाद यह सवाल स्वभावतः उठता है कि आखिर इस उधेड़ बुन की जरूरत क्या है - ऐसा खोद विनोद क्यों किया जाता है? सवाल तो सही है। इसीलिये जरा अब हमें उस मतलब पर भी गौर कर लेना चाहिये जिसके लिये अब तक की सारी जांच पड़ताल की गई है। असल में हमें खेतमजदूरों की समस्याओं पर, उन्हें आये दिन जिन दिक्कतों का मुकाबिला करना पड़ता है उन पर गौर करना है। उनकी तह में पहुंच के उनकी असलियत को पहचानना है। तभी उनका ठीक-ठीक उपाय किया जा सकता है। रोग का निदान और मर्ज की तफतीश यदि बखूबी न हो सके तो इलाज कैसा होगा? ऐसी हालत में मुनासिब दवा का पता भी कैसे लग सकता है?

एक बात यह भी है कि खेत मजदूरों के नाम पर मिथ्या और गलत समस्याएं भी खड़ी की जाती हैं। इनके सवालों को बहुतेरे लोग गलत नजर से देखते हैं। इन सवालों तक पहुंचने (approach) का उनका तरीका ही गलत होता है। फलतः उन्हें सुलझाने के उपाय भी गलत ही बताये जाते हैं। यह निहायत ही खतरनाक और बुरी बात है कि इनके बारे में हमारी पहुंच ही सरासर गलत हो। तब तो हम न सिर्फ खुद धोखा खायेंगे, बल्कि औरों को भी धोखे में डालेंगे। इसीलिये जब हम खे़त - मजदूरों के प्रश्नों को खास तौर से उठाते हैं तो इसका यह भी प्रयोजन है कि उन्हें मिथ्या दृष्टिकोण और गलत नुक्ते निगाह से देखने वाले भी संभल जांय। यदि वे न भी संभलें, तो कम से कम दूसरे लोग तो आगाह हो जांय और धोखे में न पड़ें।

हमने अच्छी तरह देखा है कि लोगों ने अब तक खेत-मजदूरों के आन्दोलन को दलित जातियों के आन्दोलन के साथ मिला देने की कोशिश प्रत्यक्ष या अप्रत्यक्ष रूप से की है। वे ये समझे बैठे हैं, समझते रहे हैं कि दलितों या हरिजनों तथा खेत मजदूरों में कोई अन्तर नहीं है। यही कारण

है कि हरिजन सभाओं के लीडर ही इस आन्दोलन में अगुवा बनके अब तक आये हैं। बेशक उनके पीछे दूसरे लोग भी दीखे हैं। मगर जैसे गाय की पूंछ पकड़ के वैतरणी पार करने की बात मानी जाती है ठीक उसी प्रकार हरिजन नेताओं का पल्ला पकड़ के ही दूसरे सज्जन खेतमजदूरों के नेता बनने की हिम्मत अब तक कर सके हैं।

इसका एक बुरा नतीजा यह हुआ है कि खेत-मजदूरों की मौलिक समस्याएं और उनके बुनियादी सवाल हमारी आंखों से ओझल हो गये हैं और सिर्फ चन्द मोटे मोटे प्रश्न ही खड़े हो सके हैं। एक तो हमने इस समस्या को केवल गिनी चुनी जातियों की ही चीज मान लिया है। दूसरे इस पर धार्मिक रंग भी चढ़ जाने का अवसर मिल गया है। हमारी बदकिस्मती से मुल्क में हरिजनों के प्रश्नों को खामखाह धार्मिक रूप दे दिया गया है। और जब खेत-मजदूरों के प्रश्न भी उन्हीं के प्रश्न माने गये तो इन पर भी खामखाह धार्मिक रंग कुछ न कुछ आ ही जाता है, गो उतना तेज नहीं। मगर यह निहायत ही गलत और खतरनाक बात है। असल में तो हरिजनों का सवाल भी धार्मिक न हो के आर्थिक ही है और यह बुनियादी बात है। मगर खेत-मजदूरों के प्रश्न तो सोलहों आने आर्थिक ही हैं। इनमें तो हमारे मुल्क की सभी जातियों और धर्मो के गरीब और दुखिया लोग आ जाते हैं। यह बात हमने पहले ही सिद्ध कर दी है।

मगर खेत-मजदूरों का सवाल आर्थिक होते हुए भी उनके सम्बन्ध की असल बुनियादी बात उस प्रश्न का यह पहलू नहीं है। वास्तविक बुनियादी बात तो यह है कि यह प्रश्न किसी नियत या मुकर्रर दल (fixed class) का नहीं है। हमारी सबसे बड़ी भूल यही होगी अगर हमने यह मान लिया कि खेत-मजदूर कुछ खास जाति बिरादरी के लोगों को ही मिलाकर बने हैं और उनकी तादाद एक तरह से निश्चित सी है। तब तो इस सवाल के असली हल तक हम पहुंची न सकेंगे। खेत-मजदूरों की जमात तो रोज-रोज तेजी से बढ़ने वाली जमात है और इसमें ऐसे लोग बराबर शमिल होते रहते हैं जो कल तक सुखी सम्पन्न किसान थे। हमने ज्यों ही ऐसा मान लिया कि हम इस बड़े मर्ज की तह में जा पहुंचे। इसकी ठीक ठीक दवा भी हम उस हालत में आसानी से समझ सकेंगे, या यों कहिये कि ढूंढ़ निकालेंगे। किसानों की बड़ी जमात से बाहर इनकी जमात नहीं है, नहीं हो सकती है यह एक दूसरा मौलिक प्रश्न, बुनियादी सवाल, इनके मुताल्लिक है। क्योंकि ऐसा मान लेने पर हम उन गलतियों से बच जांयगे जो खेत-मजदूर आन्दोलन के सिलसिले में हम कर सकते हैं, यदि हमने इन्हें किसानों से जुदा मान लिया।

इस प्रश्न को धार्मिक रूप न दे के सोलहों आने आर्थिक मानना यह भी एक तीसरी बुनियादी बात हो सकती है, हालांकि यह सिर्फ इन्हीं से ताल्लुक न रख के हरिजनों के प्रश्नों से भी रखती है। मगर यदि हमने धार्मिक रूप इसे कहीं भूल से दे दिया तो इस आन्दोलन का प्राण हीं निकल जायगा। तब तो यह एक तरह से बेकार सा हो जायगा। इसीलिये हमें इन तीनों बुनियादी बातों का पूरा-पूरा खयाल रखना होगा।

<29.7.41> लेकिन यह तो दूर की बातें हैं जिनका असर खेतमजदूरों के आन्दोलन पर पड़ेगा और खतरे से बच के अच्छी तरह चलाया जा सकेगा। दूरंदेशी की ही ये बाते हैं जिन्हें मामूली खेत-मजदूर समझ नहीं सकते। उनके नेता नामधारी भी आमतौर से इन्हें समझते ही नहीं। वे इनका महत्व हृदयंगम कर नहीं सकते। फिर भी इनकी अत्यंत उपयोगिता से इनकार किया जा सकता नहीं। तो भी जिन तात्कालिक प्रश्नों के समाधान को लेकर ही ये दूर की बातें सोची जाती हैं उन्हीं को सामने लाना जरूरी है। अगर खेत-मजदूरों की आये दिन की मुसीबतें और यंत्रणायें नहीं होती तो कौन सोचने जाता कि ये किसानों की जमात में ही हैं या बाहर? कौन इस बात का खयाल भी करता कि आ या इनका दल बराबर तेजी से बढ़ रहा है, या एक प्रकर से निश्चित सा है? किसके दिमाग में यह बात समाती कि इनकी तकलीफों की वजहें आर्थिक हैं, न कि धार्मिक? तब ऐसा सोचने की आवश्यकता ही क्यों पड़ती? यह तो तब होती है जब हम चलते हैं इन्हें आफतों से बचाने और सुखी बनाने - जब हम इनके दुःख निवारण के रास्ते ढूंढ़ने बैठते हैं। तभी तो यह बात सामने आ ख़ड़ी होती है कि किस रास्ते और उपाय से इन्हें आसानी से अच्छी तरह अपना लक्ष्य मिल सकता है। इसीलिये उन्हीं तात्कालिक तथा प्रतिदिन होने वाले संकटों पर विचार करना निहायत जरूरी है कि वे कौन-कौन से हैं और कैसे हैं।

दिमाग में यह बात लाते ही सब से पहला प्रश्न पैदा होता है इनकी मजदूरी का। खेती के मजदूरों को मासिक या वार्षिक तनखाह तो दी जाती नहीं। उन्हें तो रोजाना मजदूरी मिलती है। जब काम किया तो मिली, न किया तो न मिली। मोटी तौर पर तो यह बात ठीक ही जंचती है कि काम करें तो मिहनताना पायें, न करें तो न पायें। मगर जरा भी भीतर प्रवेश करके सोचने पर इसकी असलियत का पता लग जाता है कि कितनी बुरी चीज है। इसका तो सीधा अर्थ यही होता है कि बीमारी या कमजोरी आदि की दशा में उसे सपरिवार भूखों मरना पड़ता है, यदि परिवार उसी पर

आश्रित हो। मजदूरों की जो मांगें हैं उनमें सबसे पहली तो यही है कि बीमारी, बुढ़ापे आदि के समय उनके गुजर की गारन्टी होनी चाहिये। मगर खेत-मजदूर तो असल में मजदूर श्रेणी में हैं नहीं। इसीलिये अब तक लोगों का ध्यान इस ओर नहीं जा सका है। व्यापारी या किसान का बैल जब बोझा नहीं ढोता या हल नहीं खींचता - जब उसे कोई काम नहीं रहता - तो क्या खाना नहीं पाता और भूखों मरता है? यदि नहीं, तो फिर दूसरे काम करने वाले, सो भी इन्सान, क्यों भूखों मरें यदि वे बीमार, या कमजोर हो जांय, यह बात समझ में नहीं आती। इसीलिये स्वभावतः यह कहा जा सकता है कि खेतमजदूरों के लिये भी यह गारंटी चाहिये कि अस्वस्थता, बुढ़ापा या हाथ पांव आदि खराब हो जाने की दशा में उनकी गुजर होती रहे।

मजदूरी के बारे में ही दूसरा सवाल उठता है कि वह कितनी हो। यह तो सभी स्वीकार करेंगे कि आश्रितों के सहित खेत-मजदूर का खाना, कपड़ा, दवाबीरो आदि का काम जितने से चलता रहे उतनी मजदूरी तो होनी ही चाहिये। दिक्कत इसमें यही है कि न तो सरकार ने ही और न किसी और ही सर्वमान्य संस्था ने अब तक यह बात मुकर्रर की है कि कितने से यह काम चल सकता है। देहाती लोगों के लिये कम से कम कितने रुपये या अन्नादि से गुजर बसर जरूरी है यह किसी को मालूम ही नहीं है। इसीलिये कम से कम वेतन या मजदूरी जो गुजारा करने के लिये जरूरी हो - minimum living wage - उसे तय करने में यह भारी अड़चन है। फिर भी यह प्रश्न तो अपनी जगह पर जैसा का तैसा है कि गुजर योग्य मजदूरी मिलनी हीं चाहिये। हां, इस सवाल के साथ ही, वह कितनी हो, इसकी भी पूरी जांच पड़ताल करनी होगी और यह काम उन्हीं का है जो खेत-मजदूरों के पेशवा और लीडर हैं। क्योंकि इसकी जांच न होने के कारण बे सिर पैर की बातें मांगें पेश की जाती हैं, जा सकती हैं जो कथमपि पूरी नहीं हो सकती हैं जब तक किसानों की आर्थिक दशा में भारी परिवर्त्तन नहीं हो जाता। हमें केवल आदर्शवादी न बनके व्यावहारिक बनना चाहिये। यह बात भूलनी न चाहिये कि अधिकांश गरीब और साधारण किसानों के यहां ही के खेत मजदूरों से हमारा मतलब है। अधिक संख्या उन्हीं की है और उन्हीं की मजदूरी को ठीक करना सब से जरूरी है। इसलिये हम कहीं ऐसी मांग न पेश कर दें कि घरबार और खेत बेंच कर भी उसे किसान पूरा कर न सके। फलतः सिर्फ कलह और वैमनस्य ही हमारे हाथ लगे।

मजदूरी के सिलसिले में हमें यह बात भी देखनी है कि पहले क्या हालत

थी और अब क्या है। दोनों दशाओं का मुकाबिला करने पर हीं हम मौजूदा परिस्थिति में कोई उचित दावा पेश कर सकते हैं। यों तो सर्वे सेट्लमेंन्ट की रिपोर्टों और दूसरे कागजों में अलग अलग जिलों के बारे में कुछ न कुछ बातें दी गई हैं जिनसे इस बात पर प्रकाश पड़ता है कि खेतमजदूरों की मजदूरी क्या रही है। मगर डाक्टर राधा कमल मुखर्जी ने अंग्रेजी में एक किताब लिखी है Land Problem of India - लैंड प्राबलम औफ इन्डिया - "भूमि सम्बन्धी भारत की समस्या"। उसके 222 वें पृष्ठ में, उन्होंने ढूंढ़ खोज के प्रायः सौ साल के भीतर किस प्रकार भारत में खेत-मजदूरों की मजदूरी घटी बढ़ी इस बात के आंकड़े दिये हैं। उनने सन 1842 ई॰ से शुरू किया है। घटने बढ़ने का ठीक ठीक पता लगाने के लिये मजदूरी के साथ ही उस समय चावल किस भाव से एक रुपये का मिलता था यह भी उनने लिखा है। मजदूरी रोजाना सूखे पैसे के रूप में दी गई है। उसके साथ किसी प्रकार का खाना पीना मिलने की बात नहीं है। सन 1842 में जब चावल फी रुपया 40 सेर मिलता था उनकी मजदूरी एक आना थी। दस साल बाद सन 1852 में चावल का भाव 30 सेर हो गया। मगर मजदूरी डेढ़ आने हो गई। जब 1862 में भाव 27 सेर था तो दो आने थी। फिर सन 1872 में तीन आने हुई जब चावल की दर 23 सेर थी। सन 1911 में चावल 15 सेर का मिलने पर चार आने और सन 1922 में चावल 5 सेर का रहने पर 4 से 6 आने तक रही। उनने यह भी लिखा है कि सन 1934 में युक्तप्रान्तीय सरकार ने जो पांच साला मजदूरी की रिपोर्ट प्रकाशित की उसमें प्रान्त की औसत मजदूरी तीन हीं आने लिखी है। बल्कि 326 गांवों में तो डेढ़ ही आने बताई गई है।

डाक्टर मुखर्जी ने जो कुछ लिखा है उससे यह स्पष्ट है कि जैसे-जैसे चावल या यों कहिये कि खाद्य पदार्थ की महंगी होती गई है तैसे तैसे मजदूरी बढ़ती गई है, जिससे खाना पीना चल सके और गुजर हो सके। यानी मजदूरी बढ़ाने में इस बात पर पूरा ध्यान दिया गया है। उससे यह भी पता लगता है कि खेत मजदूरों की मजदूरी में क्रमशः कुछ वृद्धि होती गई है जिससे उनका आराम थोड़ा थोड़ा बढ़ता चले। सन 1842 से लेकर सन 1911 तक यह बात बराबर देखी जाती है पूरे पचास साल तक। क्योंकि सन 1911 में जब मजदूरी चौगुनी हो गई तो चावल 15 सेर मिलता था। हालांकि इस हिसाब से दस ही सेर चाहिये। यही बात कम बेश 1852, 62 और 72 में भी पाई जाती है। यह तो ठीक ही है। मगर सन 1922 ई॰ में यह बात नहीं पाई जाती। चावल तो 40 की

जगह 5 सेर हो गया। मगर मजदूरी एक आने से बढ़के आठ आने या ज्यादा होने के बजाय ज्यादे से ज्यादा 6 आना और कहीं-कहीं तो चार ही आना रह गई। यह पहेली समझ में नहीं आती कि ऐसा क्यों हुआ, कैसे हुआ। ऐसा लगता है कि सन 1911 के बाद जो पहला साम्राज्यवादी युद्ध यूरोप में हुआ और जिसमें प्रायः दुनियां के सभी देश कूदे थे, उसने हर बात में उलट फेर कर दी। फलतः जो स्वाभाविक रीति मजदूरी बढ़ाने की थी वह भी जाती रही और आंखमूंद के लोगों ने काम करना शुरू किया। जैसे मिलों के मजदूरों के सम्बन्ध में सिद्धान्त तो यह माना जाता है कि उनके तथा उनके आश्रितों के भरणपोषण योग्य वेतन दिया जाना चाहिये, जैसा कि पहले कह चुके हैं। मगर इस सिद्धान्त का पालन अब साम्राज्यवादी युग में कतई नहीं होता। क्योंकि मजदूरों की तो अब इफरात है। इसीलिये कम से कम तनखाह दी जाती है। ठीक उसी प्रकार इधर साम्राज्यवादी युग में खेत मजदूरों के बारे में भी शायद होने लगा है। क्योंकि उनकी संख्या बेतहाशा बढ़ने के कारण एक के खोजने पर चार मिलते हैं। फिर किसी को गर्ज ही क्या होगी कि मजदूरी की कमी वेशी और भरणपोषण का विचार करे? चाहे जो भी कारण हो, मगर यह हालत शोचनीय है और किसी भयंकर बात का सूचक है। इस पर विचार करेंगे आगे चलकर।

मजदूरी से ही सम्बन्ध रखने वाली बात यह भी है कि जहां किसान लोग पैसा और अन्न दोनों को सम्मिलित रूप में मजदूरी की जगह देते हैं वहां एक तो दोनों मिलाकर भी मजदूरी काम चलाऊ शायद ही होती है। कुछ स्थानों का तो मेरा निजी अनुभव है कि हर्गिज काम चलाऊ नहीं होती। इसी के साथ दूसरी बुरी बात यह होती है कि जो अन्न दिया जाता है वह अच्छा तो होता ही नहीं। हां, बुरा कदन्न-जरूर होता है। गोया खेत-मजदूरों को हम इन्सान समझते ही नहीं। मैं मानता हूं कि निहायत गरीब किसानों की इस बात में मजबूरी होती है। वह खुद भी जो कुछ खाते पीते हैं कुछ ऐसा ही होता है। फिर भी यह एक प्रणाली सी पड़ गई है। इसीलिये देखादेखी अच्छे और खाते-पीते किसान भी वैसा ही करते हैं। वे किस अक्ल से ऐसा करते हैं ऐसा समझना गैर मुमकिन है। खेत-मजदूरों की मजबूरी से अनुचित लाभ उठाना इसे ही कहते हैं। मजदूरों के नाश्ते का सवाल भी इसी के भीतर है।

जहां फसल कटने के समय ही खेत या खलिहान में बोझों और बंडलों के ही हिसाब से मजदूरी दी जाती है, और यह बात बहुत से प्रान्तों में व्यापक रूप से पाई जाती है, वहां भी कुछ विचित्रता देखी जाती है। कहीं तो धान

या रबी की फसल के बारह बंडलों (बोझों) में एक मजदूर का हिस्सा होता है तो कहीं सोलह या बीस में और कहीं कहीं चौबीस में भी। बेशक यह चौबीस वाला हिसाब बहुत कम पाया जाता है और उससे ज्यादा बीस का मिलता है। मगर बारह और सोलह की बात तो ज्यादातर पाई जाती है। यह चीज समझ में नहीं आती। यह विषमता कब और कैसे चल पड़ी यह पता नहीं चलता। यह ठीक है कि यह एक प्रकार के ठीके की तरह की चीज है और जहां बहुत ज्यादा काटने ढोने वालों की जरूरत थी वहीं पहले पहल चालू हुई होगी। मगर अब तो व्यापक सी हो गई है। हर हालत में एक तो ठीके वाली बात ही नाजायज है। तिसपर भी उसका एक तरह का न होना और भी खटकता है।

मजदूरी के बाद दूसरा प्रश्न है कर्ज का। यह तो निहायत ही पेचीदा बात है और इसने जगह-जगह में विभिन्न रूप धारण कर लिया है। इसे कहीं हलवाही, कहीं कमिऔती और कहीं दूसरे ही दूसरे नाम भी दिये गये हैं। जाने कब से यह चल पड़ी कोई ठीक ठीक कह नहीं सकता। मगर है यह व्यापक। साथ ही, प्रचीन गुलामी प्रथा का ही रूपान्तर मालूम पड़ती है। क्योंकि इसके करते हलवाहा या खेत-मजदूर किसान का गुलाम बना रहता है। कहीं कहीं तो बनिये साहुकारों का ही गुलाम हो जाता है। सो भी बाल बच्चों के सहित पुश्त दर पुश्त के लिये। यह भी नहीं कि इस कर्ज की प्रणाली को खामखाह कानूनी रूप दिया जाता हो। बहुत जगहों में तो इसकी लिखा पढ़ी भी नहीं रहती कि कितना कर्ज उसे दिया गया है। शायद किसान के घर कहीं लिखा हो। मगर दस्तावेज या हैंड नोट वगैरः नहीं होते। केवल जबानी हीं मामला रहता है। फिर भी उन गरीबों की छाती पर भारी चट्टान की तरह बैठा रहता है, जिससे वह उठ नहीं पाते। उसके लिये यह ऐसा बंधन है कि भाग नहीं सकता जब तक चुकता न करे और चुकता करने की शक्ति उसमें होती ही नहीं। फलतः जिस किसी से रुपये लेकर चुकायेगा उसी का गुलाम बनेगा। यह ऐसा कर्ज है कि हजारों वर्ष में भी चुकता होता नहीं। किन्तु ज्यों का त्यों बना रहता है, चाहे मजदूर कर्जदार के खून को पानी बना के भी काम करता करता मर मिटे। हां, इस पर सूद नहीं चढ़ता। यह उतने का उतना ही बना रहता है, यही इसकी खूबी है। सूद वाला कर्ज तो दूसरा ही होता है और वह तो जैसा औरों का वैसा ही खेत-मजदूरों का भी होता है।

किसी जमाने में मजदूर के बापदादों ने किसी किसान से किसी ब्याह शादी वगैरः सख्त जरूरत में कुछ नगद रुपये या अन्न लेकर काम चलाया होगा।

बस, वही हमेशा बना रहता है वंश परम्परा के लिये। जिस हलवाहे ने कभी इस प्रकार कुछ भी कर्ज अपने किसान से लिया कि वह इस कीचड़ में जा फंसा। यदि कोई दूसरा किसान चाहे कि उस हलवाहे को अपने यहां रख ले तो उसे खामखाह पहले किसान का वह कर्ज चुकाना होगा। और पहला भी उस मिले हुए रुपयों को किसी और को देके अपना खेत-मजदूर बनायेगा। जिस गरीब पर कोई आफत आई और कुछ खास खर्च की जरूरत हुई कि वह इस बला में फँसा। अब तो यह बात धीरे धीरे खत्म होती जा रही है और इसका स्थान मामूली कर्ज लेने की प्रणाली ले रही है। मगर पहले तो खूब ही चालू थी और आज भी बहुत जगह है। विवाह शादी या गमी में तो भाई बन्धुओं को भोज देना और कुछ ताड़ी शराब पिलाना अन्ध परम्परा के अनुसार कुछ खास जातियों के लिये जरूरी है और वही नये सिरे से इसमें आ फंसती हैं। यही बिहार की कमिऔती या यू॰ पी॰ की हलवाही प्रथा का रहस्य है।

गुजरात वगैरः प्रान्तों में जो हाली और दुबला कहे जाते हैं वे भी खेत-मजदूर ही हैं, हालांकि पहले जमाने में वहां के असली किसान वही लोग थे। हाली का मतलब ही है हल चलाने वाला - अर्थात खेती करने वाला। सिंध्र में जिसे हारी कहते हैं वह तो पक्का किसान है। यह हारी उसी हाली का ही रूप है। गुजरात की तो हालत यह है कि साहुकार और शराब बेंचने वाले पारसी लोग इन हालियों तथा दुबला लोगों को खामखाह चढ़ाबढ़ा के विवाह आदि उनसे भोज और शराब में पैसे खर्चवाते हैं जिसे वही लोग देते हैं। इस प्रकार हालियों और दुबलों को अपने आधीन (गुलाम) बना लेते हैं। जब तक उनके पास जमीनें थीं तब तक तो रुपये दे के सस्ती जमीनें लिखवा ली और इस प्रकार हालियों को बिना खेत का कर दिया। फिर पैसे दे के उन्हें स्त्री बच्चों के साथ गुलाम बना डाला। <30.7.41> सो भी इन गरीबों की पीठ ठोंक के और 'बापदादों का नाम डूब जायगा यदि विवाह में तुमने भाइयों को शराब न पिलाई' आदि बातें बार-बार सुना के ही उन्हें फंसाया जाता है। स्वार्थी मनुष्य शैतान से भी खूंखार बन जाता है।

इस प्रकार उनसे पैसे ले के खर्चने का नतीजा यह होता है कि विवाह के बाद ही पति और पत्नी दोनों ही इन साहुकारों के क्रीतदास (bond slave) जीवन भर के लिये बन जाते हैं। कुछ रात रहते ही उसके घर आ जाते, स्नान के लिये जल गर्म करना, नहलाना, कपड़ा साफ करना, सभी कामों के लिये जल भर देना, पशुओं को खिलाना, खेती का काम कर देना आदि सभी

काम करके रात होने पर घर जाने की इन्हें फुर्सत मिलती है। यही प्रतिदिन की दिनचर्या है। यदि कभी जरा सी देर हुई तो गालियां मिलती और तमाचे लगते हैं। यदि ऊब कर भागना चाहें तो कहीं गुजर नहीं, कोई पूछने वाला नहीं। जहीं जाते वही पूछता है कि तुम किसके यहां से भागे आ रहे हो। गोया हाली और दुबला नाम पड़ते ही गुलामी की छाप लग गई। वह तो आजाद होई नहीं सकता। कहीं न कहीं किसी की गुलामी करता ही होगा, ऐसा सभी मानते हैं। इतना हीं नहीं। ये पारसी और साहुकार दो एक मुस्तंड पठान नौकर रखते हैं जो बीसियों मीलों तक ढूंढ के इन्हें फिर पकड़ लाते हैं। मारना पीटना तो मामूली सी बात है। खूबी तो यह कि जब और प्रान्तों से कमिया आदि प्रथायें स्वंय मिट रहीं हैं तब हाली प्रथा तेज हो रही है। हां, अब किसान आन्दोलन के चलते गुजरात प्रान्तीय किसान सभा ने इसकी बहुत कुछ जड़ खोद डाली है।

एक बार एक जवान दुबला ने अपनी कहानी मुझे हरिपुरा के इलाके में सुनाई। उसने कहा कि मैं एक पारसी के घर में गुलाम की तरह काम करता था। चार बजे सबेरे ही जाना पड़ता था। पानी गर्म करके गुसल खाने में पारसी को नहलाना पड़ता था। वह भी ऐसा था कि स्नान-घर में नंग धड़ंग जा बैठता और साबुन लगाके मुझे उसका शरीर मलना धोना पड़ता था। रूखड़े हाथ से देह रगड़ने में जरा सी उसे तकलीफ हुई कि चट तमाचे जड़ देता। मैं कराह के रह जाता और कुछ कर न सकता। मगर किसान सभा का उपदेश सुन के मुझे भी हिम्मत हुई और एक दिन जब पारसी ने मुझे एक तमाचा मारा, तो मैं भी उलट के उसे कई तमाचे कसके लगाये। फिर वहां से भाग निकला और अब स्वतंत्र हूं।

इन दुबला लोगों को गुलाम बनाने वालों की शरारत ऐसी है कि काम के बदले इन्हें मामूली जलपान और दिन का मोटा खाना देते हैं। रात के लिये कुछ अन्न या दो चार पैसे दे दिया करते हैं। बीमारी की हालत में दवादारू या कपड़े लत्ते कुछ नहीं देते। इन चीजों के लिये इन बेचारों को उनसे नया कर्ज लेना पड़ता है और इस तरह ऐसे फंस जाते हैं कि कभी उद्धार की आशा रही नहीं जाती, सिवाय बगावत के। बागी बन के ही तो वे लोग अब अपनी आजादी प्राप्त करने में लगे हैं।

तीसरा सवाल खेत-मजदूरों का यह है कि उन्हें बीमारी की हालत में भी, जब तक किसी प्रकार कर सकें, काम करना ही पड़ता है। नहीं तो खायेंगे क्या? इतना ही नहीं। गर्भवती स्त्रियों की भी यही हालत होती है। यहां तक कि छोटे-छोटे बच्चे भी बचने नहीं पाते। हमेशा किसान के

काम में या किसी और के ही सही, जोते जाते हैं। यदि पास में एकाध बकरी आदि पशु हुए, तब तो उन्हीं की रखवाली और खिलाने पिलाने का काम ये बच्चे करते हैं। नहीं तो चक्की के बैल की तरह किसी के यहां काम में पिसते रहते हैं। असल में उनके गुजर और खाने पीने की कोई गारंटी तो रहती नहीं। काम न करें तो भूखों मरें। फिर और क्या करेंगे सिवाय इसके कि बुखार और तकलीफ की हालत में भी काम में जुते रहें? यदि स्त्री, बच्चे, बूढ़े सभी न कमायें तो खायें पियें क्या? रहें कैसे? दिन कैसे कटे?

इसीलिये देखा जाता है कि उनके दिलों में यह चाह बराबर बनी रहती है कि किसी प्रकार उन्हें कुछ खेत मिल जाय कि उसमें फसल उपजा के गुजर बसर का पक्का उपाय कर लें। यह ठीक है कि हर हलवाहे को किसान लोग प्रायः थोड़ी बहुत जमीनें देते ही हैं। बिहार और युक्तप्रान्त में तो यह बात आमतौर से पाई जाती है। किसान के ही हल बैल से प्रायः उसमें खेती भी हो जाती है। मगर उतने से तो काम चलता नहीं। वह जमीन तो थोड़ी होती है। अलावे इसके वह तो किसान की मर्जी की बात ठहरी। यह ठीक है कि यह एक प्रकार की रूढ़ि सी हो गई है कि हलवाहों को जमीन जरूर दी जाय। फिर भी न देने पर कोई दंड तो होगा नहीं। इसीलिये कोई मजबूरी नहीं है कि खामखाह दी जाय। और अब जब खेत मजदूरों की तादाद बहुत बढ़ रही है तो जैसे मजदूरी में कोई विचार नहीं रह गया है कि कितना देना उचित है। वह तो मनमानी दी जाने लगी है। ठीक उसी प्रकार जमीन का हो सकता है और उसे देना किसान बन्द कर दे सकते हैं। इसीलिये खेत-मजदूरों की यह लालसा बराबर ही रहती है कि उन्हें काम चलने भर ऐसी जमीन मिले कि जिसे वे अपनी समझें और जो आसानी से छीनी जा न सके। मौका पाते ही ऐसी जमीन वे लोग कहीं-कहीं थोड़ी बहुत हासिल भी कर लेते हैं। मगर बड़ी फजीती के बाद। इस बात में आसानी हो यही उनका चौथा सवाल है। अपनी जमीन और उसमें अपना घर बार न होने के कारण हीं जमींदार लोग या इसी प्रकार के चलते पुर्जे आदमी उनसे बेगार करवाने या न करने पर डांटडपट की हिम्मत भी रखते हैं। क्योंकि न करें तो मकान या झोपड़ा छोड़ना पड़ जाय। इसलिये कम से कम उनके रहने के लिये तो जमीन चाहिये ही और समाज के लिये यह मजबूरी हो कि इसका प्रबन्ध खामखाह करे।

सबसे आखिरी और जरूरी बात है सलूक और बर्ताव की। खेत-मजदूरों के भीतर कुछ जातियां तो ऐसी हैं कि उन्हें समाज खामखाह तुच्छ और

नीच समझने की भारी भूल करता आया है। उन्हें अपने जैसा समझना तो इसने सीखा ही नहीं। इसीलिये आत्मसम्मान नाम की चीज उनके बारे में मानी ही नहीं जाती। यह क्या अन्धेर है कि समाज के लिये जो सबसे जरूरी हों और जिनके बिना उसका खानापीना या सारा आराम ही मिट्टी में मिल जाय, उन्हीं मनुष्यों को हम मनुष्यहीन समझें, या छोटा समझने की नादानी करें! यह तो पागलपन की पराकाष्ठा है। नतीजा यह होता है कि जो ही हलवाहा बना वही हल का बन गया। वही छोटा समझा जाने लगा। यहां तक कि हलवाहे का मतलब ही माना जाने लगा मूर्ख और निरक्षर, असभ्य और बेअक्ल। इसीलिये उनके बच्चों के पढ़ने लिखने की जरूरत कौन समझे? ऐसी दशा में उनके लिये किसके दिल में आदर सम्मान का भाव पैदा हो सकता है? वे सभ्यता की रोशनी में आयें यह कौन सोचेगा? कीड़ेमकोड़ों की तरह घुलघुल के बिना मौत मरने से उन्हें बचाने की फिक्र किसे हो सकती है? इस बला में कौन पड़े? उनकी मां बहनों की इज्जत को कौन समझ सकता है? जब कुएं में ही भांग पड़ी है तो फिर खैरियत कहां? इसीलिये तो उन्हें - स्त्री पुरूषों को - मजबूर किया जाता है कि सर पर लाद के जमींदारों के पास घी, दूध, साग तरकारी वगैरः पहुंचायें। इसी तरह की और भी छोटी मोटी बातें होती हैं जो इन्हीं पूर्वोक्त पांच बातों में ही आ जाती हैं।

इस प्रकार प्रधान रूप से पांच समस्यायें उनके तथा सभी जन-सेवकों के समक्ष मुंह बाये खड़ी हैं। जितनी ही जल्दी इनका समाधान हो जाय उतना हीं अच्छा। इसी में सब का कल्याण है।

4

उनका समाधान

तो फिर उनका समाधान कैसे हो, उनका क्या उपाय किया जाय, यह विकट प्रश्न अब आ खड़ा होता है। चाहे पुराने दकियानूसी दिमाग वाले इस का महत्व-इसकी अहमियत - समझें या न समझें। मगर जिन्हें आंखें हैं वह साफ देखते हैं, उन्हें देखना ही पड़ता है कि दुनियां में क्या हो रहा है। यह बात किसी भी दूरंदेश आदमी से छिपी नहीं है कि जालिमों और शोषकों के वे दिन लद गये जब उनकी मनमानी को पीड़ित और मज़लूम लोग - कमाने वाले - बिना जबान हिलाये ही और बगैर आह निकाले ही चुपचाप बर्दाश्त कर लेते थे। चाहे कुछ दिन और भी यह धींगामुश्ती चले। मगर यह बात नहीं हो सकती कि तूफान बरपा न हो, लोग तड़पें न, चिल्लाहट न मचायें। अन्याय के बल पर मौज करने वालों की जिन्दगी को नर्क और दोजख बना देने वाला जमाना आ गया है, यह पक्की बात है। यह शोषितों और पीड़ितों का युग है, उनके आगे बढ़ने का जमाना है। उनमें आत्म सम्मान आ गया है, आ रहा है। वे जग गये हैं, जग रहे हैं। उन्होंने हक और अधिकार समझ लिया है, वे इसे समझने में लगे हैं। ऐसी हालत में यह चोरी, यह सीना जोरी कब तक टिक सकती है। यदि समय रहते हमने इसे बन्द न किया तो वे हमारी बोलती बन्द करके ही छोड़ेंगे और इन जुल्मों के साथ ही हमें भी, जुल्म करने और चुपचाप देखने वालों को भी उठा फेकेंगे।

इसीलिये ठंडे दिमाग से हमें उनकी सभी बातों पर विचार करना और उनकी तकलीफों को समझना होगा - समझने की कोशिश करनी होगी। यदि हमें या किसानों का या उनके हमदर्दों को इस बात में झल्लाहट हो तो ठीक नहीं। न तो यहां शान की बात है और न सिर चढ़ाने की। यह भी नहीं कि जानबूझ के परेशानियां पैदा की जाती हों और उन्हीं में फंसाने की कोशिश इस रूप में की जा रही हो। आखिर असलियत को समझना ही होगा। नहीं नहीं, इतना ही नहीं। किसानों को भी समझाना होगा हिम्मत और मुस्तैदी के साथ। यदि वे पहले पहल झिझकें और सुनने को तैयार न

हों, या जली कटी भी सुना दें तो भी घबराने की कोई बात नहीं है। वे नासमझी से ही ऐसा करेंगे और जब तक उनमें नासमझी है तभी तक उन्हें हमारी जरूरत भी है। क्योंकि जब इन बातों को वे समझने लगेंगे तब तो खुद वही लीडर बन जायगे। फिर हमें क्यों पूछेंगे? इसलिये मुस्तैदी और खुले दिमाग से ये बातें हम सोचें विचारें और किसानों को भी बखूबी सोचने विचारने का मौका दें। तभी सबका कल्याण है। तभी हम खेत मजदूरों को विश्वास दिला सकेंगे कि हम जो कुछ कहते करते हैं वह ईमानदारी से उनकी और दूसरों की भलाई के खयाल से ही। हमने सहानुभूति और हमदर्दी के साथ उनकी दुखदर्द वाली दास्तानें सुननी शुरू कीं, कि हवा ही पलट गई। हम उनके दिलों तक यदि अपनी इन हरकतों से पहुंचने की कोशिश करते ही परिस्थिति पर अपनी छाप लगा देंगे। आखिर खेत-मजदूर लोग अन्धे नहीं हैं और न बिगाने। वे भी किसान ही हैं, किसानों के महत्वपूर्ण अंग ही हैं। फिर उन्हीं से घबराहट, या उन्हीं को अपना शत्रु समझ लेना? उनकी दिक्कतें किसान समझें और किसानों की वे। बस, बेड़ा पार समझिये। हमारा-किसान सभा के कार्यकर्त्ताओं और नेताओं का - यही काम होना चाहिये कि दोनों को एक दूसरे की स्थिति समझने में मदद करें और तटस्थ हो के काम करें।

अब आइये जरा उनकी समस्याओं के भीतर घुस के उन्हें समझें और उन्हें सुलझाने की कोशिश करें। कुछ समस्याएं तो ऐसी हैं जिनके बारे में विशेष कहने या सोचने की गुंजाइश ही नहीं है। उन्हें तो साफ स्वीकार कर लेने और सारी शक्ति से शीघ्र सुलझाने में ही भलाई है। दृष्टान्त के लिये कमिया लोगों के कर्ज की बात (कमिऔती) या हाली की यही बात ले सकते हैं। खुशी की बात है कि यह चीज अब खुद ही मिट रही है। समय अपना काम कर रहा है। मगर जहां कहीं यह चीज नाममात्र को भी पाई जाय, या छिपलुक के भी कोई इसे अमल में लाते पाये जांय, तो वहां फौरन हीं हमें इसका भंडाफोड़ करके ऐसे लोगों को विवश करना चाहिये कि फौरन अपनी भूल कबूल करें और इस चीज को सदा के लिये तिलांजलि दे दें। समझाने बुझाने या प्रोपैगैन्डा और प्रचार के जरिये यह बात की जाय। इसके लिये खास मीटिंगें भी जरूरत देख के की जांय। तभी तो अनुकूल वायुमंडल पैदा होगा।

मगर एक बात याद रहे कि कहीं ऐसा होने से खेत-मजदूरों को सूदखोरों के हाथ में फंस जाना न पड़े। तब तो और भी बुरा होगा। क्योंकि वे तो सूद दर सूद के जरिये पांच रुपये के पचास बात की बात में बना डालते हैं।

किसानों की कमिऔती में सूद तो नहीं लगता। इसलिये प्रबन्ध ऐसा हो कि अनिवार्य आवश्यकता के ही लिये किसान ही दो चार रुपये दे दिया करें और बिना सूद के ही असल रुपयों को धीरे धीरे दो चार पैसे या आने के रूप में वसूल करते जांय। ज्यादा रुपये तो देंगे नहीं। ताड़ी शराब के लिये तो देना हुई नहीं। केवल अनिवार्य आवश्यकताओं के ही लिये देना होगा। जब सूद का रास्ता बन्द हो जायगा तब तो सूदखोर लोग भी इन्हें न देंगे। फलतः शराब वगैरः का काम यों ही रुक जाय। तात्पर्य यह है कि उनका जरूरी काम रुके भी न और गैर जरूरी में खर्च भी न हो यही करना है। साथ ही सूदखोरी और गुलाम बनाने का खयाल लोगों के दिल से मिटा देना है। नहीं तो केवल कमिऔती बन्द करके संतोष कर लेने से इन गरीबों की हानि हो जायगी।

इसी प्रकार मनुष्यता के बर्ताव तथा सहृदयता-पूर्ण सलूक की बात को भी ले सकते हैं। इसमें बहस या विवाद की गुंजाइश ही कहां है? यदि किसानों को बर्बाद नहीं होना है, अगर वे अपने पांव में कुल्हाड़ी मारना नहीं चाहते, यदि वे नहीं चाहते कि उनके असली शत्रु उन्हीं के घर में लड़ाई लगा के उन्हें तबाह करें, तो खेतमजदूरों से समानता और भाईचारा का सलूक बिना विलम्ब करना होगा।उनसे कोई यह नहीं कहता कि उनके संग खान पान या व्याह शादी की बिरादरी बना लें। यह तो बिल्कुल ही जुदी बात है। इससे और भाईचारा या समानता के बर्ताव से कोई भी ताल्लुक नहीं। बर्ताव तो इनसानियत की चीज है। सहृदयता का व्यवहार तो पशुपक्षियों तक के साथ भी किया जाता है। कुत्ते बिल्लियों को पालने पर उनसे कितनी मुहब्बत होती है। लेकिन किसानों के हाथपांव स्वरूप ये खेतमजदूर प्रेम के पात्र न हों यह कम ताज्जुब की बात नहीं है। आखिर उनमें कमी क्या है जिससे उनसे नफरत या उनमें नीचता की भावना होती है? बाकी लोगों से वे किस बात में कम हैं? जिनके बिना न गेहूं उपजे और न बासमती और जो अपने खून को पानी बनाके फसल उपजायें, फिर भी अच्छी चीजें जिन्हें मुयस्सर न हों, ऐसे तपस्वियों और त्यागियों के साथ हृदयहीनता का व्यवहार खुद किसान करें? तब तो आसमान फट जाना चाहिये। हमने देखा है कि इन फटे दिल खेतमजदूरों को मिला लेने का मौका जमींदारों को अच्छा लगा है और उन्हें किसानों का विरोधी बना के उन्हीं के द्वारा किसानों को जमींदारों ने सर किया है, या करना चाहा है। आखिर जो आपके लिये मरें उन्हीं से पशु का सा व्यवहार आप करें तो नतीजा क्या होगा? वह भी तो आदमी हैं। उनका दिल इसी से कट जाता

है। फिर भी वे इतने भले हैं कि ज्यों ही किसान उनसे प्रेम से मिले या आर्जू मिन्नत करने लगे कि फौरन पसीज गये। इसी से कहना पड़ता है कि इन मजदूरों के साथ मनुष्यता और प्रेम का व्यवहार न करके किसान अपना ही पांव काटते हैं।

<31.7.41> खेती के लिये किसान बैल वगैरः पशुओं को पालते हैं। उनके प्रति उनकी काफी मुहब्बत होती है। जब तक पशुओं को खिलापिला न लें खुद खाते पीते तक नहीं। सवेरे उठ के अपने जलपान की पर्वा न करके पहले उन्हें खिलाते हैं। खुद भूखे रह जांय तो रह जांय, मगर उनके ये पशु भूखे रह नहीं सकते, भूखे रहने दिये जाते नहीं। यदि दैवात् पशु बीमार हो जांय या खाना छोड़ दें तो किसान की नींद हराम हो जाती है। उसकी बेकली का ठिकाना नहीं रहता। हजार उपाय करके जब तक पशुओं को नीरोग नहीं कर लेता चैन नहीं लेता। जब वे खाने पीने और जुगाली करने लगते हैं तब कहीं जा कर उसे होश होता है। तो क्या इन पशुओं जितना भी हक उसका हलवाहा या खेत-मजदूर नहीं रखता? क्या किसान के लिये डूब मरने की बात नहीं यदि खेत-मजदूरों की उतनी भी पर्वा नहीं करता जितनी पशुओं की करता है? किसान खुद अपने दिल टटोल के देखें और अपने आपसे पूछें कि मजदूरों को दर असल किस नजर से देखते हैं और अगर कुछ भी कसर पाई जाय तो न सिर्फ उसे पूरा करें, प्रत्युत आज तक की इस कसर का प्रायश्चित कर डालें। तभी खैरियत है।

असल में तो खेत-मजदूरों और उनके बाल बच्चों को जब तक किसान अपने परिवार के व्यक्ति मान कर वैसा ही सलूक न करेंगे तब तक इस पुरानी कसर, इस पुराने पाप का असली और उचित प्रायश्चित नहीं हो सकता। मजदूर, उसके बच्चे, उसकी स्त्री या बूढ़ा बाप किसान की खेती के लिये ज्यादा जरूरी हैं बनिस्बत उसके अपने बाप, बच्चे और स्त्रियों के। हल चलाने, खेत की निकाई करने, धान के बीज को उखाड़ने और रोपने में बहुत से किसानों का अपना परिवार कतई काम नहीं आता। किन्तु खेत-मजदूरों का परिवार ही वह काम करता है। और बिना धान या दूसरे गल्ले की खेती के किसान कायम कैसे रहेगा? ऐसी दशा में उनके परिवार को अपने परिवार की अपेक्षा यदि ज्यादा न मान के अपने परिवार जैसा ही माने तो इसमें किसान कोई आश्चर्य या उपकार की बात तो करता नहीं। हां, सिर्फ दूरदर्शिता और अक्लमन्दी से काम जरूर लेता है। उनकी मां बहिनों की इज्जत उतनी ही करता है जितनी अपनी मां बहनों की। यदि उनकी बेइज्जती कोई करना चाहे तो बर्दाश्त नहीं कर सकता। अगर उनमें

कोई बीमार या कष्टग्रस्त हो तो उसकी पूरी चिंता करता तथा उनके आराम न होने तक चैन नहीं लेता। बीमारी आदि की दशा में उनसे कोई काम नहीं करवाता। उन्हें भूखे देख नहीं सकता। जैसे खुद साग सत्तू खाता है तैसे उन्हें भी खिलाता है। बस, इतना करने से ही सब मामला ठीक हो जायगा - ठीक रहेगा।

इस प्रकार जहां तक सामाजिक व्यवहार या आदर सत्कार का सवाल है वहां तक तो उनकी मांगों पर नाहीं या ननुनच करने की कोई गुंजाइश रही नहीं जाती। उन्हें तो फौरन से भी पेश्तर पूरा कर देना ही उचित है। इसमें दो राय की जगह हुई नहीं। अब रहीं असली और महत्वपूर्ण समस्यायें - वे प्रश्न जिनका जमीन की चाह और मजदूरी से ताल्लुक है। यही तो असली सवाल हैं और इन्हीं को हल कर लेने से बाकी बातें आगे या पीछे खुद हल हो जांयगी। मगर इनका हल होना आसान नहीं, कठिन है। इनमें भी मजदूरी की जड़ जमीन हीं है। यदि जमीन का सवाल हल हो जाय तो मजदूरी का प्रश्न अपने आप खत्म हो जायगा। अधिक कोशिश करने की जरूरत ही न होगी। हमने जो खेत-मजदूरों को किसान श्रेणी में ही माना है वह भी इस जमीन के सवाल को देख कर ही।

इस सवाल के उठते ही हमें आंखें मूंद के चट कुछ न कह के जरा इस पर गंभीरता पूर्वक गौर करना होगा। यह पेचीदा पहेली है। सबसे पहले तो हमें यही देखना है कि इस मुल्क में कुल जमीन है कितनी और कितनी जमीन खेती के काम आ रही है। भारत सरकार ने सन 1936 ई० में इसका हिसाब लगा के बताया है कि करीब - करीब 66 करोड़ 74 लाख एकड़ जमीन कुल है। इसमें 8 करोड़ 95 लाख एकड़ तो जंगल है। 14 करोड़ 50 लाख एकड़ ऐसी मानी जाती है जो खेती के लिये मिली नहीं सकती। खेती के योग्य होने पर भी अब तक गैर आबाद 15 करोड़ 36 लाख एकड़ है। परती है 5 करोड़ 10 लाख एकड़। इस प्रकार कुल जमीन जिसमें खेती होती है सिर्फ 22 करोड़ 79 लाख एकड़ ही बच जाती है। यह भी बात है कि जमीन तो रबर की तरह फैलती नहीं। मगर जन संख्या तो बराबर बढ़ रही है। आज भारत की 40 करोड़ जनता में यदि 80 प्रतिशत भी खेतिहर मान लें तो फी आदमी पौन एकड़ भी नहीं पड़ती है। क्योंकि 32 करोड़ के लिये सिर्फ 22 करोड़ 79 लाख एकड़ में ही बंटवारा करना है। मगर इसका तो सीधा अर्थ है सभी का भूखों मरना।

सर टामस होल्डरनेस (Sir Thomas Holderness) नामक एक अंग्रेज सज्जन ने सन 1911 ई० में अंग्रेजी में एक पुस्तक "Peoples and Problems of India" लिखी थी। उसके 139 वें पृष्ठ में कुछ मजेदार बातें उनने लिखी हैं। याद रहे कि तब जनसंख्या आज की अपेक्षा बहुत कम थी। फिर उनकी बातें हृदयविद्रावक हैं। वे लिखते हैं :—

"The total population of India, including that of the protected native states, is 315 millions. Three-fourths of this vast population is supported by agriculture. The area under cultivation is not accurately known, as the returns from the native states are incomplete. But we shall not be far wrong if we assume that there is less than one acre and a quarter per head for that portion of the population which is directly supported by agriculture . . .

Not only does the land of India provide food for this great population, but a very considerable portion of it is set apart for growing produce which is exported . . . In fact it pays its bill for imports and discharges its other international debts mainly by the sale of agricultural produce. Subtracting the land thus utilized for supplying foreign markets from the total area under cultivation we shall find that what is left over does not represent more than 2/3 acre per head of the total Indian population. India therefore feeds and to some extent clothes its population from what 2/3 acre per head can produce. There is probably no country in the world where land is required to do so much."

इसका मतलब यह है कि "देशी रजवाड़ों को मिलाकर कुल भारत की जनसंख्या साढ़े एकतीस करोड़ है। इसके तीन चौथाई आदमियों की गुजर खेती से होती है। रजवाड़ों के आंकड़े ठीक-ठीक न मिलने के कारण यह ठीक कहा नहीं जा सकता कि कितनी जमीन में खेती होती है। लेकिन सीधे खेती पर निर्वाह करने वालों के सम्बन्ध में यदि हम कहें कि फी आदमी औसतन सवा एकड़ से भी कम जमीन पड़ती है, तो हम ज्यादा गलती न करेंगे।. . .

भारत की जमीन न सिर्फ इस बड़ी जनसंख्या को खाना देती है, प्रत्युत इस जमीन के एक खासे हिस्से में केवल वही चीजें पैदा की जाती हैं जो विदेशों को जाती हैं। . . . सच बात तो यह है कि बाहर से आने वाले मालों का दाम और अन्तर्राष्ट्रीय ऋणों को यह देश इसी प्रकार चुकाता है। इस प्रकार की पैदावार के लिये जो जमीनें मुकर्रर हैं उन्हें अगर खेती वाली समूची जमीनों में निकाल दें तो जितनी जमीन बचेगी सबके लिये खाना पैदा

करने को, वह समस्त जनसमूह में प्रत्येक के हिस्से दो तिहाई एकड़ से ज्यादा न होगी। इसलिये मानना पड़ेगा कि इसी दो तिहाई एकड़ की पैदावार से भारत के प्रत्येक प्राणी का खाना और बहुत अंशों में कपड़ा चलता है। संसार में शायद एक भी ऐसा देश नहीं है जहां की जमीन से इतनी ज्यादा उम्मीद की जाती हो"।

यह तो फी आदमी करीब सवा एकड़ मानकर हिसाब दिया गया है। मगर हम तो बताई चुके हैं कि असल में अब तो पौन एकड़ का भी परता शायद ही पड़ता है। इसलिये अब तो किसानों या खेती पर गुजर करने वालों की दयनीय दशा का पता और भी आसानी से लग जाता है। मगर हमें यह भूलना न चाहिये कि व्यवहार में तो यह पौन एकड़ की औसत काम नहीं करती। आखिर हर व्यक्ति इसी औसत के हिसाब से तो खाता पीता नहीं। ऐसे लोग तो लाखों हैं जो हजारों एकड़ की पैदावार खुद हजम कर जाते हैं, हड़प जाते हैं। फलतः करोड़ों के पास जमीन या उसकी पैदावार का एक अन्न भी नहीं पहुंचता। इसीलिये तो अधिकांश अत्यन्त निर्धन और गरीब हैं, तंग और तबाह हैं। फिर वे अपने खेत-मजदूरों को कहां से जमीन दें? यह तो "खुदरा फजीहत दीगरे रा नसीहत" हो जायगी। किस हिम्मत और समझ से उनसे जमीन का मुतालबा खेत-मजदूरों की ओर से किया जायगा? आखिर कोई आधार भी तो इस मुतालबे का होना चाहिये। जब खुद किसान ही मरा जा रहा है और इसीलिये न सिर्फ अपनी इंच इंच जमीन को दांतों तले पकड़े हुए है, बल्कि और जमीन की चाह और खोज में बेहाल है, तो फिर वह मजदूरों को देने की बात सुनेगा भी कैसे? यह बात उसे सुनाई भी कैसे जायगी? इसकी हिम्मत कौन पत्थर का कलेजा, संगदिल करेगा? जब उसकी पैदावार खुद किसान के लिये ही बहुत ही ना काफी है तो उसमें दूसरा साझीदार बनके और क्या करेगा। सिवाय अपनी और उसकी भूख बढ़ाने के? हां, यदि पैदावार बढ़ जाय, आबपाशी आदि का पूरा प्रबंध हो जाय और खेती के लायक जमीन बढ़ जाय तो बात दूसरी है। मगर ऐसी दशा में हमारा ध्यान सबसे पहले इन्हीं बातों की ओर जाना चाहिये, न कि जमीन के मुतालबे की ओर।

अच्छा, तो आइये जरा इस बात का भी अच्छी तरह विचार करलें कि जमीन बढ़ सकती है या नहीं। उसकी पैदावार इतनी बढ़ सकती है या नहीं कि सभी लोगों को खिला पिला सके। हमने जो पहले समूची जमीन को लिखके उसका ब्योरा देते हुए 15 करोड़ 36 लाख एकड़ खेती-योग्य

मगर अब तक गैर आबाद और 5 करोड़ 10 लाख परती लिखा है उन दोनों को मिला देने से 20 करोड़ 46 लाख एकड़ हो जाता है। यानी आज जितनी जमीन में खेती हो रही है करीब-करीब उतनी हीं जमीन और भी मिल जाती है। क्योंकि करीब साढ़े बीस करोड़ यह जमीन तो खेती के लायक हुई। सिर्फ कुछ दिक्कतें हैं और उन्हें दूर करने के लिये ज्यादा पूंजी चाहिये जो किसानों के पास नहीं है। मगर आखिर सरकार किस मर्ज की दवा है यदि यह भी नहीं करती? यदि सरकार पैसा लगा के इन जमीनों को आबाद करा दे तो बात की बात में खेती की जमीन प्रायः दूनी हो जाती है। यानी पूरे तैंतालीस करोड़ 25 लाख एकड़ हो जायगी।

लेकिन इतना ही नहीं। भारतीय कृषि कमिशन ने अपनी रिपोर्ट के 605 पृष्ठ में एक बहुत ही मार्के की बात लिखी है। पूर्व लिखे जमीन के आंकड़ों से पता लगता है कि साढ़े चौदह करोड़ एकड़ जमीन ऐसी है जो खेती के लिये मिल नहीं सकती है। यह अजीब बात है कि कुल जमीन की एक तिहाई से भी ज्यादा 22.5 प्रतिशत यों सदा के लिये खेती से बन्चित रह जाय। कमिशन का कहना है कि :—

"It is difficult to believe that the whole of the vast area now classed as "not available for cultivation," amounting, as it does, to 150 million acres or twenty-two and a half percent of the total area of British India is either not available or not suitable for cultivation."

"इस बात पर विश्वास करना कठिन है कि 15 करोड़ एकड़ जमीन का यह लम्बा भाग जो कुल जमीन का साढ़े बाईस प्रतिशत है और जिसके बारे में कहा जाता है कि या तो खेती के लिये मिली नहीं सकता, या उसमें खेती होई नहीं सकती, सचमुच ही ऐसा है।"

इसका साफ अर्थ यही है कि अब तक खेती से अछूत, मगर खेती के लायक, जो करीब साढ़े बीस करोड़ एकड़ जमीन बताई गई है और जो कुल जमीन का 35.5 प्रतिशत है, वह और भी बढ़ जायगी और जानकार लोगों का कहना है कि वह 40 प्रतिशत से कम नहीं हो सकती। यानी प्रायः तीन करोड़ एकड़ और भी मिल जायगी। इसका मतलब यों समझें कि अब जितनी जमीन है उतनी हीं नहीं, किन्तु उससे भी कुछ ज्यादा एकड़ और भी मिलेगी। इस प्रकार फी आदमी डेढ़ और दो एकड़ के बीच में पड़ेगी। करीब नौ करोड़ एकड़ जंगल की जमीन में से भी कुछ मिली सकती है यदि ठीक ठीक प्रबंध किया जाय। जंगलों के बीच में जगह-जगह खाली जमीन के बड़े-बड़े टुकड़े लाखों मिल जांयगे और अगर रुपये पैसे खूब खर्चे जांय

तथा दिमाग भी लगाया जाय तो प्रति मनुष्य दो एकड़ तक जमीन मिल जाना कोई बड़ी बात नहीं है। बड़े बड़े चौर और दलदली जमीनें खेती के योग्य बनाई जा सकती हैं। ऊसर जमीनें भी ऐसी हो सकती है। विज्ञान और पूंजी इन दोनों की मदद चाहिये जो सरकार ही कर सकती है।

और भी देखिये । श्री आर. के. दास नाम के भारतीय विज्ञ ने "भारत की उद्योग धन्दे की योग्यता" (The Industrial Efficiency of India) नामक अंग्रेजी पुस्तक सन 1930 ई० में प्रकाशित की थी। वे उसके 13 वें पृष्ठ में लिखतें हैं कि, "The net area actually sown with crops amounts to 228 million acres, or 53 percent of the total arable land. But if the areas sown more than once are taken as separate areas for each crop, the total gross area sown would amount to 262 million acres. Thanks to the climatic conditions, a considerable proportion of the arable land is adaptable to more than two crops a year; but on the other hand, a part of this area is not cultivable more than once, and some may not be available for cultivation even once for some time to come. It may, therefore, be assumed that on the average all the arable land is fit for two crops a year. The potential area of arable land would thus amount to 864 million acres, of which only 262 million acres, or about 30 percent are utilized for productive purposes; and 602 million acres or 70 percent are wasted."

"कुल असल जमीनें, जिनमें फसलें बोई जाती हैं, 22 करोड़ 80 लाख एकड़ हैं, या यूं कहिये कि खेती योग्य जमीनों की 53 प्रतिशत। लेकिन यदि दो फसला जमीनों की दूसरी फसल पैदा करने की जमीन को जुदा मान लें (अर्थात् जमीन में एक ही फसल मानें) तो सब मिलाकर 26 करोड़ 20 लाख एकड़ हो जायंगी। मुल्क में बहुत जगह की जलवायु के प्रताप से बहुत सी जमीनों में हर साल दो से ज्यादा भी फसलें होती हैं। लेकिन इसी के साथ साथ कुछ जमीनों में एक से ज्यादा भी नहीं होती और कुछ समय तक तो ऐसी जमीनें रहेंगी ही जिनमें एक भी फसल न होगी। फिर भी कुल मिलाकर इस नतीजे पर पहुंच सकते हैं कि सभी जमीनें औसतन दो फसला हैं। इस प्रकार खेती की योग्यता रखने वाली जमीनों का रकबा 86 करोड़ 40 लाख एक हो जाता है। मगर इसमें केवल 26 करोड़ 20 लाख एकड़ में ही खेती होती है, यानी सिर्फ 30 फीसदी में ही और 60 करोड़ 20 लाख एकड़ यानी पूरे 70 प्रतिशत यों ही बेकार पड़ी रह जाती है।"

यह लेख कई दृष्टियों से अत्यन्त महत्वपूर्ण है। मगर इसकी खूबियों को जानने के पहले इसका मतलब समझ लेना चाहिये। हमने जो पहले 22 करोड़ 79 लाख एकड़ लिखा है उसे ही यहां 22 करोड़ 80 लाख दिया गया है। इसी प्रकार सब जोड़ के जो हमने 43 करोड़ 25 लाख बताया है और कहा है कि इतनी जमीन खेती के लायक है उसे ही यहां दूना करके 86 करोड़ 40 लाख लिखा है। क्योंकि हर जमीन में आमतौर से औसतन दो फसल मान के दोनों की जमीनों को दो अलग अलग करार दिया है। इस प्रकार असल जमीन दूनी हो जाती है। यह बात हिसाब समझने की आसानी के लिये की गई है। किसी जमीन में तीन फसलें भी होती हैं और किसी में एक ही। कुछ दिनों तक, काफी पूंजी और विज्ञान के बल से सारी योग्य जमीनों में खेती होने नहीं लगती तब तक, कुछ जमीनें खामखाह ऐसी रहेंगी ही जिनमें खेती होई न सकेगी। फिर भी सब मिलाकर औसतन दो फसलें हर जमीन में मान लेने में कोई हर्ज नहीं है।

<1.8.41> हां, तो श्रीयुत दास ने एक तो यह दिखलाया है कि यदि सरकार पूर्णतया तत्पर हो जाय और सिंचाई वगैरः का पूरा इन्तजाम करने के साथ ही इंच इंच खेती के लायक जमीनों में उसका प्रबन्ध कर दे तो आज के मुकाबले में तीन गुने से भी ज्यादा खेती हो सकती है। सौ प्रतिशत में सिर्फ 30 ही खेती होती है और 70 फीसदी बाकी ही है। इस प्रकार यदि बीघे में पैदावार न भी बढ़े तो भी तीन मन की जगह पूरे दस मन पैदावार हो जाय, और अगर पैदावार भी फी एकड़ बढ़ाई जाय तब तो कहना ही क्या? उन्होंने ही यह बात भी सुझाई है कि भारत की हर जमीन में दो फसलें प्रतिवर्ष हो सकती हैं, और अगर शायद कोई जमीन ऐसी न हो तो उसके बजाय तीन फसलों वाली भी जमीनें बहुत हैं। उनका मतलब इस कथन से यही है कि ज्यादा से ज्यादा फसलें जितनी भी साल में हो सकती हैं पैदा की जांय। इसके लिये केवल आबपाशी और मुस्तैदी चाहिये। कहां कब कौन फसल हो सकती है इसकी छानबीन भी होनी चाहिये। आज हमारी भूमि की उत्पादन शक्ति का कितना अपव्यय हो रहा है यह बात भी उनके लेख से सिद्ध होती है। आमतौर से शायद ही कोई यह समझता हो कि इतनी जमीन बेकार सी पड़ी है जितनी उनने सिद्ध की है। हम जो निराशा के अथाह समुद्र में गोते लगा रहे थे कि जमीन तो खेती के लिये काफी हई नहीं उससे उनने बचा लिया है और आशा की सुनहली किरण झलका दी है।

यही बात श्री राधा कमल मुखर्जी ने अपनी हाल वाली किताब "चालीस

करोड़ लोगों के लिये खुराक का प्रबन्ध" (Food Planning For Four Hundred Millions) के 26 पृष्ठ में लिखी है। उसी का हवाला देते हुए श्री पामेदत्त 'इन्डिया टुडे' के 191 पृष्ठ में लिखते हैं कि "ऐसी हिसाब लगाया गया है कि खेती का मौजूदा ही तरीका रहने पर भी यदि खेती के योग्य सारी जमीनें काम में लाई जांय और सिंचाई का समुचित प्रबंध हो तो इतनी हीं जमीन से 44 करोड़ 70 लाख लोगों का काम बखूबी चल सकता है - यानी आज की अपेक्षा 7 करोड़ अधिक लोगों की खुराक मिल सकती है"—

"It has been estimated even on the existing basis of small scale technique, the available land area for cultivation in India, given necessary measures of land reclamation and irrigation could maintain a population of 447 millions, or 70 millions in excess of the existing population."

लेकिन यदि खेती के आधुनिक वैज्ञानिक तरीके काम में भरपूर लायें, वैज्ञानिक खादों का काफी इस्तेमाल हो और सिंचाई का तरीका भी आधुनिक ढंग से किया जाय - संक्षेप में खेती सोलहों आने आधुनिक ढंग से (modernize) की जाने लगें तो कहीं ज्यादा अन्नादि पैदा होंगे और सभी लोगों की जिन्दगी आनन्द से कटेगी। इतना ही नहीं। ऐसा होने पर तो एक खेत-मजदूर अनेकों का काम कर लेगा और इस प्रकार पैदावार की तरक्की के साथ ही खेती का खर्च भी अपेक्षाकृत कम होगा। यह बात और मुल्कों मे पाई जाती है। ज्यादे से ज्यादा कितनी उपज खास खास मुल्कों में एक एकड़ में होती है यह बात राष्ट्रसंघ की सालाना रिपोर्ट में सन 1932-33 (Statistical Yearbook of the League of Nations, 1932-33) में इस प्रकार दी गई है। हमें याद रखना होगा कि पैदावार पौंडों मे दी गई है और 82 पौंड का एक मन पक्का होता है। वह यों है :—

(1) भारत (धान 1357 , गेहूं 652, (2) जापान (धान 2267 , गेहूं 1508), (3) मिस्र (धान 2356 , गेहूं 1688), (4) संयुक्त राष्ट्र अमेरिका (धान 2112 , गेहूं 973 (5) ईटली (धान 4601, गेहूं 1241), (6) जर्मनी (गेहूं 1740), (7) ब्रिटेन (गेहूं 1812)।

इन आंकड़ों से यह साफ हो जाता है कि सभी प्रकार से और मुल्कों की अपेक्षा बहुत ही उपजाऊ जमीन और अत्यन्त अनुकूल जलवायु तथा मौसिम होने पर भी हमारे देश की खेती कितनी पिछड़ी है। कहां तो और देशों से हमारी पैदावार फी एकड़ बढ़ जानी चाहिये और कहां हम सबों से पीछे हैं,

सो भी बुरी तरह। जापान और मिस्र भारत की अपेक्षा एक एकड़ में करीब पौने दो गुना धान पैदा करते हैं, अमेरिका डयोढ़े से ज्यादा और इटली पूरे साढ़े तीन गुना। और जब गेहूं की हालत देखते हैं तो जहां अमेरिका प्रायः डेढ़ गुना पैदा करता है, तहां जापान सवा दो गुने से ज्यादा और मिस्र ढाई गुना। इटली भी प्रायः दो गुना, जर्मनी करीब तीन गुना और ब्रिटेन तीना उपजाते हैं। क्या हमारी जमीन ऐसा नहीं कर सकती? कर तो सकती है इससे भी ज्यादा। मगर सामान तो है नहीं। पूंजी तो हमारे किसानों के पास हुई नहीं और सरकार आँख मूंदे बैठी है। उसने कान में तेल डाल रखा है। अगर सरकार ऐसा कर दे तो करीब-करीब आज से तीन गुनी पैदावार यहां होने लगे। यहां की खास गल्ले की तो दोई फसलें हैं, गेहूं और धान। तब तो हालत यह हो जायगी कि आज जितनी पैदावार हो रही है उसकी नौ दस गुनी हो जायगी। क्योंकि जैसा कि पहले कह चुके हैं तीन गुनी से ज्यादा तो मामूली पैदावार से ही होगी। फिर उसकी तीन गुनी आधुनिक ढंग की खेती से हो जाने पर 9-10 गुनी होने में कोई भी शक नहीं।

इस विषय में हम खुद भारत सरकार के अफसर की ही राय देना उचित समझते हैं जो भारतीय बैंकिंग जांच कमिटी के सामने उसने पेश की थी और जिसे उस कमिटी की रिपोर्ट के 13 वें परिशिष्ट के 700 पृष्ठ में हम देख सकते हैं। उस अफसर का नाम है मैक्डोगल (A.P. MacDougall)। उसी सिलसिले में श्री पामे दत्त ने अपनी पूर्वोक्त पुस्तक के 198 पृष्ठ में उस वक्तव्य को उद्दृत करते हुए उसके पूर्व खुद भी एक पैराग्राफ में यह दिखाया है कि भारत में परिश्रम किस प्रकार व्यर्थ जाता है। जिस काम को और देशों में एक मजदूर कर सकता है उसे ही यहां 7-8 करते हैं। वह वक्तव्य यों है :—

"The contrast is still more marked if taken into relation with the number of workers employed on the land. In India there is one person employed in cultivation for every 2.6 acres of land, as against 17.3 acres in the United Kingdom, and 5.4 acres in Germany." (India Today-page 198).

"It has been stated that the soil of India is naturally poor. This is not correct. It has become poor. The great river valleys must at one time have been among the most fertile in the world. In Denmark and Germany the greater part of the land in its original state consisted of barren wastes of sand growing nothing but gorse and heather.

If the output per acre were raised to that of France, the wealth of the country would be increased by £ 669, 000,000. If the output were in terms of English production, it would be raised by £ 1,000,000,000 per year. Yet England is by no means highly cultivated. This does not make any allowance for part of the land in India producing two crops per year. In the other countries referred to only one can be grown. The advance should equal any loss from drought. In terms of Danish wheat production the increased wealth production would be £ 1,500,000,000 per year. It is not therefore the soil that is responsible for the poverty of rural India."

इसका अभिप्राय यह है, "अगर खेत-मजदूरों की संख्या का खयाल किया जाय, तो और मुल्कों की बनिस्बत भारत की पिछड़ी हालत और भी साफ हो जाती है। जहां भारत में एक आदमी केवल 2.6 एकड़ की ही खेती कर सकता है वहां ग्रेट ब्रिटेन में एक ही मजदूर 17.3 एकड़ की और जर्मनी में 5.4 की कर सकता है।" (श्री पामेदत्त)

"कहा जाता है कि भारत की जमीन स्वभावतः ही कम उपजाऊ है। मगर यह बात सही नहीं है। असल में यहां की जमीन कमजोर हो गई या बन गई है। बड़ी-बड़ी नदियों के कछार की जमीनें किसी समय संसार की सबसे ज्यादा पैदावार जमीनों में होंगी। डेनमार्क और जर्मनी में तो शुरू शुरू में जमीनों का अधिकांश केवल रेतीला रेगिस्तान था जिसमें झौआ जैसी झाड़ियां थीं।

यदि यहां के खेतों की पैदावार फ्रांस जैसी होने लगे तो यहां की आमदनी 66 करोड़ 90 लाख पौंड बढ़ जायगी और अगर इंगलैंड जैसी हो जाय तो एक अरब पौंड बढ़ेगी। हालांकि इंगलैंड की खेती भी अभी उतने ऊंचे दर्जे की नहीं है। आमदनी बढ़ने के इस हिसाब में हमने दो फसला जमीनों का खयाल किया ही नहीं है—(सबों की एक ही फसल मानी है)। इसलिये यदि अनावृष्टि के करते फसल मारी भी जाय तो भी कम से कम एक अरब की वृद्धि तो होगी ही। यदि यहां की पैदावार डेनमार्क जैसी हो जाय तो डेढ़ अरब पौंड की आय बढ़ जायगी। इसीलिये भारत के किसानों की गरीबी का कारण यहां की जमीन की उर्बरा-शक्ति की कमी नहीं कही जा सकती"।

यहां जों पौड लिखा है वह तेरह रुपये पांच आने चार पाई के बराबर है। अब तक मोटामोटी खेती से सारे मुल्क की आमदनी करीब बारह अरब

रुपये मानी जाती है जो एक अरब पौंड से भी कम है। मगर खेती में सुधारने से डेढ़ अरब पौंड और भी होगी - यानी आज की ढाई गुनी से भी ज्यादा होगी। मगर जैसा कि पहले कहा गया है, यदि सभी जमीनें दो फसला हो जांय और जमीन भी बढ़ के प्रायः दूनी हो जाय, तब तो आज से दस गुनी आय जरूर ही होगी। श्रीयुत आर. के. दास के वक्तव्य से भी यही बात सिद्ध की गई है। इस वक्तव्य में तो यह भी माना है कि यहां कि जमीनें दुनियां की सब से पैदाऊ जमीनों के टक्कर की हैं और अगर वे अनुर्वरा हो गई हैं तो इसीलिये किसान खाद दे सकता नहीं और सरकार को इसकी फिक्र ही नहीं है।

हमारे देश में बेकार ही ज्यादा खेतमजदूर भी लगते हैं—इंगलैंड के साढ़े सात गुने और जर्मनी के तीन गुने से अधिक। यह मानवशक्ति का नितान्त अपव्यय है। इधर पैदावार कम होती है, उधर आदमी ज्यादा लगते हैं। फलतः किसानों पर दोहरी मार पड़ती है और वे खेती से फायदा कर नहीं पाते। यदि वैज्ञानिक ढंग से खेती की जाय तो थोड़े ही खेतमजदूर ज्यादा पैदा करेंगे। लेकिन उसका यह नतीजा जरूर होगा कि जिन 7-8 आदमियों में एक ही की जरूरत खेती के लिये रह जायगी उनमें बाकी बेकार हो जायंगे। लेकिन खेती तो काफी लाभदायक हो जायगी इसमें कोई शक नहीं। रह गई इन मजदूरों की बेकारी। सोतो यों जायगी कि जब आज से तीन गुनी से भी ज्यादा जमीनें खेती की हो जायंगी तो बेकार मजदूरों में आधे तो उन जमीनों में जा लगेंगे। रह गये बेकारों के बचे बचाये आधे। सो उनके लिये नये नये कलकारखानों में जगह होगी। क्योंकि वैज्ञानिक तरीके से पूरी पूरी खेती होने का अर्थ है कि यहां आधुनिक कारखाने भरपूर खुल जायंगे। नहीं तो वैज्ञानिक खेती के सभी सामान मिलेंगे कहां? विदेशों से लाके तो करना असंभव है। किसी भी मुल्क में ऐसा नहीं होता। जब तक मुल्क में उद्योग व्यापार आधुनिक ढंग से पूरा पूरा होने लगे नहीं, तब तक आधुनिक खेती पूर्ण रूपेण हो सकती नहीं, यह मानी हुई बात है।

इस प्रकार हम देखते हैं कि जब सारे मुल्क के लिए काफी पैदावार का प्रबन्ध होगा तभी किसानों की जमीन-सम्बन्धी भूख मिटेगी और तभी खेत मजदूरों को भी जमीन मिल सकेगी। दूसरा रास्ता हई नहीं। वर्त्तमान दशा में किसानों के साथ खेत मजदूरों द्वारा की गई लड़ाई सिर्फ कफन खसोटी होगी। यही होगा कि दोनों दल भुक्खड़ों की तरह आपस में कफन के लिये, टुकड़े के लिये लड़ेगा सही। मगर नतीजा कुछ न होगा। इसीलिये हम ने इस दिक्कत की जड़ को ही पकड़ा है। इसके जरिये हमने किसानों को -

जिनमें खेत मजदूर भी आ जाते हैं - असलियत तक पहुंचा देने की कोशिश की है। हम चाहते हैं कि जड़ को पकड़े ताकि काम चले। फूल पत्तों से कुछ होने जाने का नहीं।

मगर जमीन होने पर जो यह दिक्कत है कि लाखों जमींदारों के पास जिरात और बकाश्त या खुदकाश्त के नाम पर करोड़ों एकड़ जमीनें पड़ी हैं। वे या तो खुद खेती करते नहीं, और अगर करते भी हैं तो दौलत जमा करने के ही लिये, न कि खाने के लिये। उन्हें खाने की कमी तो है नहीं। ये लोग करोड़ों की जमीनें छीन के अपने पास रखते हैं और मनमाना लगान वसूलते रहते हैं। आज जरूरत इस बात की है कि सरकार उन जमींदारों की सारी जिरात और बकाश्त की जमीनें छीन ले जो खेती से गुजर नहीं करते। जमींदार से हमारा मतलब उन लोगों से है जो अपनी जमीनें भावली या नगदी लगान (rent in kind or cash) पर गैरों को देते हैं। उनकी ऐसी जमीनें लेकर उनमें से सबसे पहले उन लोगों को दी जांय जो खेत मजदूर या इसी प्रकार के लोग हैं, जो खेती से भी गुजर करते आ रहे हैं और करना चाहते हैं। बचने पर ही वह जमीन और काम में आ सकती हैं। जिनके पास या तो जमीन है नहीं या नाममात्र को ही, ऐसे ही किसान और खेत मजदूर इन जमीनों के हकदार हैं। कुछ लोग दौलत करें जमीनों से ही और करोड़ों भूखों मरें यह नाजायज बात बन्द हो जानी चाहिये। ऐसी जमीनें जब दी जांयगी तो इन गरीब किसानों को, जिनमें खेत मजदूर भी आ जाते हैं, पंचायती खेती का अच्छा मौका मिल जायगा। सरकार और समाज का फर्ज है कि जमीनों को देने के साथ ही भरसक पंचायती खेती का भी इन्तजाम कर दे। इसी शर्त के साथ जमीनें दे।

इस प्रकार जमीन का सवाल हल हो जाने पर मजदूरी का प्रश्न खुद ब खुद हल हो जायगा। लेकिन जब तक ऐसा नहीं हो जाता तब तक तो वह सवाल उठता ही रहेगा। इसलिये उस पर भी थोड़ी रोशनी डाल देना जरूरी है। इतना ही नहीं। जमीनें मिलने पर भी वह समस्या बनी ही रहेगी। मजदूरी का प्रश्न सिर्फ पेट भरने का प्रश्न न होकर इससे कहीं बड़ा है। इसकी ठीक ठीक व्यवस्था हो जाने पर ही खेतीबारी आदि सभी काम ठीक-ठीक चल सकते हैं। नहीं तो उनमें बराबर गड़बड़ी होती ही रहेगी। मजदूर का प्रश्न हक का प्रश्न है। इसीलिये उस पर काफी ध्यान जाना चाहिये।

सबसे पहले हमें यह समझना होगा कि जो धनी किसान हैं उनके यहां तो खेत मजदूर काम करते ही हैं। मगर गरीबों के यहां भी करते हैं, जैसा

कि पहले कह चुके हैं। ऐसी हालत में अगर गरीबों को उचित मजदूरी देने में यदि दिक्कतें हों भी तो धनियों को तो होती हैं नहीं। वे तो काफी और पूरी मजदूरी देई सकते हैं। फिर भी गरीबों की देखादेखी वह भी नहीं देते। मजदूरी की दर जो बंध गई वही वह भी देते हैं। ज्यादातर तो गरीब ही होते हैं। इसलिये वह जो देते हैं वही मजदूरी की दर मान ली जाती है। मगर यह गलत है और इसके खिलाफ लड़ना पड़ेगा। उनके साथ तो जरा भी मुरब्बत नहीं हो सकती। आखिर उनकी भी तो मजबूरी है। वे खुद तो खेती अपने हाथों कर सकते नहीं। एक तो शान और दूसरे ज्यादा खेतों की खेती अकेले कैसे करेंगे। इसीलिये ज्यादा मजदूरों की उन्हें जरूरत होती है। इसी से उन्हें विवश करना होगा कि पूरी मजदूरी दें।

मगर गरीब लोग तो जरूरत होने पर खुद भी खेती का सारा काम कर ले सकते हैं। उनके सामने शान का सवाल तो वैसा होता नहीं । खेत भी ज्यादा नहीं होते। सिर्फ पुरानी प्रथा और धमवर्म के खयाल से ही नहीं करते हैं। लेकिन जब मजबूरी होगी तो खामखाह करेंगे। नतीजा यही होगा कि ज्यादा दबाव देने पर वे न मानेंगे और उनके खेत मजदूर भूखों मरने लगेंगे। इसीलिये उनके साथ रिआयत की जा सकती है। क्योंकि दोनों की मजबूरी होने से समझौता हो सकता है - होना चाहिये। खासकर जब तक जमीनों का सवाल हल हो नहीं जाता। आखिर किसी प्रकार जिन्दा तो रहना ही है। दोनों की हालत दोनों देखें और बीच का रास्ता निकालें।

<2.8.41> बात असल यह है कि जिस प्रकार ग्राह ने गज को करीब करीब ग्रस ही लिया था ठीक उसी तरह गरीब किसान जो कुछ पैदा करते हैं उसे जमींदार, साहुकार वगैरः ग्रस लेते हैं। उनके पास बचने पाता है कहां? और जो बचता भी है वह एक तो कथमपि गुजर लायक होता ही नहीं। दूसरे उस पर भी ग्राहों की दृष्टि लगी ही रहती है कि कब कैसे उसे भी हड़पें। यही कारण है कि गरीब किसान अपने मजदूरों को भरपेट खिला सकता नहीं । कारण, खुद भी तो भूखा ही रहता है। इसलिये पहला काम तो यही है कि दोनों ही मिलके इन ग्राहों के पेट से उस पैदावार को बचायें। तभी पेट भरने की आशा है। मगर जब तक दोनों बराबर लड़ेंगे और एकमत होके ग्राहों से न भिड़ेंगे कुछ होने जाने का नहीं। इसीलिये पारस्परिक समझौता होना जरूरी है। इसीलिये उसी दृष्टि से हमें उनकी मजदूरी का प्रश्न लेना होगा।

हमने खुद इसी खयाल से अनेक स्थानों में जांच की है और परस्पर मेल भी कराया है। कहीं कहीं तो ऐसा हुआ है कि सिर्फ मामूली जलपान की

ही मांग रही है और किसानों ने उसे पूरा ही कर दिया है। कहीं पाव आध सेर मजदूरी बढ़ाने की बात भी मान ली गई है। मगर समझा बुझा के ही यह काम हुआ है। इसके लिये हड़ताल जैसी भारी भूल नहीं की गई है। उससे तो किसान संगठन के मूल में ही कुठाराघात हो जाता। गरीब किसानों का, जो हमारे संगठन की रीढ़ हैं, हमसे विश्वास ही उठ जाने का उसमें खतरा जो है। इसलिये वहां तक बढ़ जाना भूल है, भारी भूल है।

कई जगह तो किसानों ने हमसे खुद प्रस्ताव किया कि नपी तुली मजदूरी की क्या बात? खेत की पैदावार की प्रायः आधा तो जमींदार ही लेता है। बचे आधे में आधा मजदूर ले लें। हम सिर्फ चौथाई मे ही गुजर करेंगे और खेती का सारा खर्च भी चलायेंगे। मगर मजदूर इस पर तैयार न हुए। यह प्रस्ताव अत्यंन्त महत्वपूर्ण है और इससे किसानों की सद्भावना और नेकनीयती पर पूरा प्रकाश पड़ता है। इसी में झगड़ा मिट जाने और सुलह का बीज छिपा हुआ है। किसानों का भविष्य उज्जवल है इसकी आशा भी हमें इसी से है। इसमें सफलता का विश्वास भी है।

5

यह हो कैसे

अब एकाएक सवाल उठता है कि खेत-मजदूरों की समस्याओं का जो समाधान बताया गया है, उनके सुलझाने की जो कुंजी सुझाई गई है वह है तो बहुत ही सुन्दर। उससे न सिर्फ खेत-मजदूरों का ही भला है, प्रत्युत किसानों का भी। मगर आखिर यह होगा कैसे? देखने में यह बात जितनी सीधी और आसान मालूम पड़ती है अमल में उतनी ही कठिन है, बीहड़ है। जमीन का प्रश्न यों देखने से तो सुन्दर जान पड़ता है। मगर उसे क्या जमींदार या सरकार पसन्द करेंगे? वे न सिर्फ नाक भौं सिकोड़ेंगे, बल्कि सारी शक्ति से उसका विरोध करेंगे। सरकार तो हजार दिक्कतें और अड़चनें पेश करेगी, और जमींदार तो जल भुनके खाक ही हो जायंगे। ऐसी हालत में उन्हें मजबूर करने का कोई रास्ता होना चाहिये। इसी प्रकार धनी किसानों को पूरी मजदूरी देने के लिये विवश करने का भी उपाय चाहिये। क्योंकि वे लोग भी आसानी से मानने वाले जीव हैं नहीं।

यह सवाल तो ठीक ही है और इसका जवाब भी मौजूद ही है। वह है लोकमत एवं प्रचंड आन्दोलन का प्रभाव। असल बात है सरकार को मनवाने की, और वह तो बिना लोकमत के दबाव के दूसरी तरह सुन सकती नहीं। इसीलिये हमें तो अपने प्रस्ताव के अनुकूल जबर्दस्त लोकमत बनाना ही होगा। इसके सिवाय चारा नहीं। इसीलिये तो हमने पहले ही कह दिया है कि किसानों और खेत-मजदूरों की संगठित तथा सम्मिलित शक्ति से ही यह काम करना होगा। यही कारण है कि दोनों के समझौते की बात हमने कही है। आखिर दोनों के स्वार्थ जब एक ही हैं तो फिर मिलके काम क्यों न किया जाय? जमींदार तो चाहेंगे ही, साहुकार भी चाहेंगे और सरकार भी, कि ये दोनों आपस में ही लड़ें और पारी पारी से दोनों के कान ऐंठें जांय। मगर इन दोनों को, और हमें भी, तो इस खतरे से सदा सजग रहना है।

अब प्रश्न हो सकता है कि आया इन दोनों के संगठन दो हों, या एक ही रहे। इस प्रश्न का उत्तर तो पहले ही दिया जा चुका है। मगर शायद

वह काफी नहीं है। एक महान् संगठन के भीतर ही दोनों का रहना निहायत जरूरी है यह बात बताई जा चुकी है। यह मौलिक सिद्धांत है। हम इससे हर्गिज विचलित हो नहीं सकते। मगर हम यह बात भी नहीं भूल सकते कि खेत-मजदूरों में प्रधानतः कुछ ऐसी जातियाँ हैं जो सदियों से दबी पड़ी हैं, जिनकी रीढ़ ही टूट चुकी है, और इसीलिये जो आसानी से उठ नहीं सकती हैं। उनमें परस्पर भी ऊंच नीच का भाव है। समाज ने उन्हें पशु से भी बदतर बना रखा है, यद्यपि धीरे-धीरे यह बात मिट रही है। वर्त्तमान समाज का निर्माण हीं ऐसा है कि शोषण एवं उत्पीड़न की भावना का मूलोच्छेद इसमें हो सकता नहीं, जब तक इसका - समाज का - आमूल परिवर्त्तन न हो जाय। जब तक इसका आधार बदल नहीं दिया जाता तब तक छोटे बड़े सबों में ही शोषण की भावना कमबेश रहेगी ही। अब तक इसका आधार रही हैं व्यक्तिगत सम्पत्ति। इसीलिये शोषण इसकी नस-नस में समाया है। इस आधार को मिटाके जब सम्मिलित सम्पत्ति को आधार बना दिया जायगा तभी यह बात मिटेगी। मगर इसमें देर है।

तब तक शोषण चलता ही रहेगा। जैसे सांप के मुंह में पड़ा मेढ़क जब तक जिन्दा है तब तक कीट पंतगों को, यदि वे पास आ जांय, खुद भी खा जाने की कोशिश करता ही है। उसकी यह मजबूरी है। ठीक उसी प्रकार जमींदार, साहुकार के चंगुल में फंसा मजलूम किसान मजबूरन खेतमजदूरों का थोड़ा बहुत शोषण करना चाहेगा ही। खूबी तो यह कि इस बात का उसे अनुभव भी न होगा कि शोषण कर रहा है। यही तो वर्त्तमान समाज में प्रविष्ट जहर की खूबी है। खेत मजदूरों में जो पिछड़ी जातियों के हैं वह भी एक दूसरे को ऊंच नीच, स्पृश्य अस्पृश्य मानते ही हैं और इसमें उन्हें कोई हिचक भी नहीं होती। क्या वे लोग अपने नाई, धोबी वगैरः को पूरी मजदूरी देते हैं? देना चाहते हैं? हर्गिज नहीं? तो क्या यह बात वे समझते हैं कि शोषण कर रहे हैं? कदापि नहीं। क्यों? इसीलिये न कि उनकी गरीबी, उनकी मजबूरी से ही ऐसा वे करते हैं? मगर समाज की मनोवृत्ति ही ऐसी है कि वे समझ पाते ही नहीं कि वे भी सचमुच शोषण करी रहे हैं। हालांकि गैरों के द्वारा होने वाले अपने शोषण के विरूद्ध वे खुद चिल्लाते हैं। यही बात दूसरे किसानों की है जो गरीब हैं। जो धनी हैं उनका तो कहना हीं नहीं।

इसीलिये जहां एक ओर हमें खेत-मजदूरों को किसानों के संगठन से, किसान सभा से हर्गिज बाहर जाने देना नहीं है और सारी शक्ति से एक ही साथ मिलाके रखना है, तहां शोषण के इस खतरे से बचने का भी उपाय

करना है ताकि इसके विपरीत मौके मौके पर वे जबर्दस्त आवाज उठा सकें। किसान सभा के भीतर से भी यह आवाज उठ सकती है। मगर शायद उतनी जबर्दस्त और प्रभावशाली न हो सके, शायद उसके ऐसी होने में अड़चनें आयें। साथ ही समय की गति के करते इस बात का खतरा है कि उनके स्वतंत्र संगठन बना के उन्हें किसानों से फोड़ने की कोशिश हो। कुछ लोग तो ना समझी से इस बात को करेंगे, ईमानदारी के साथ ही। मगर ज्यादातर स्वार्थी और स्थिर स्वार्थों के दलाल ही ऐसा कर सकते हैं। वे इस प्रकार इन मजदूरों की जागरण वाली मनोवृत्ति से अनुचित लाभ उठाना चाहेंगे। एक बात और भी होगी। जैसा कि पहले कह चुके हैं जब सरकार जिरात वगैरः जमीनें जमींदारों से ले लेगी, या अब तक बेकार पड़ी जमीनों को खेती योग्य बनायेगी तो चालाक लोग होहल्ला करके खुद ले लेंगे या लेने की कोशिश करेंगे। ऐसे मौके पर यदि खेत मजदूरों की आवाज बुलन्द न हुई और वे मुस्तैदी से न बोले तो घाटे में रह सकते हैं। उन्हें या तो जमीन कतई न मिलेगी, या बहुत ही थोड़ी। औरों और खास कर चलते पुर्जे किसानों की आवाज में उनकी आवाज विलीन हो सकती है। अभी तक डट के बोलने की न तो उनमें हिम्मत ही है और न आदत ही। इससे उन्हें घाटा हो सकता है।

तो क्या उनका अलग ही संगठन किया जाय? यह सवाल उठता है सही। मगर अलग ही संगठन का अर्थ है कि वे किसान संगठन से पृथक् हो जांय और यह सरासर गलत रास्ता होगा जैसा कि कह चुके हैं। और अगर कहा जाय कि उनका अलग भी संगठन हो तो यह बात विचारणीय है। क्योंकि किसी संगठन के भीतर रहना और स्वतंत्र संगठन में भी रहना कुछ विचित्र बात है। ये दोनों विरोधी बातें हैं। क्योंकि दोनों संगठनों की तनातनी या विरोध होने पर वह किसी एक में ही रह सकता है, जब तक एक दूसरे के आधीन न हो। मगर आधीन होने पर स्वतंत्रता कैसी? तब तो यह बात केवल हवाई ही होगी। एक बात और भी है। जो लोग किसान संगठन से बाहर या उसके विरोधी हैं वह तो जुदा संगठन करके झगड़ा लगाना चाहेंगे ही। उसका उपाय क्या होगा? वह तो हमारी मर्जी की बात है नहीं।

यहां थोड़ा रुक के हमें इधर उधर ढूंढना है। जब हम दृष्टि फैलाते हैं तो लेनिन और उसकी पार्टी की कई बातें याद आती हैं। पहली बात तो यह कि उसने और पार्टी ने "मजदूरों के एकतंत्र शासन" (Dictatorship of the Proletariat) का अर्थ बताया है "सर्वहारा और अत्यन्त गरीब किसानों के

हाथ में शासन सूत्र का आ जाना"—"The dictatorship of the proletariat is the conquest of power by the workers and poorest peasants." जैसा कि पार्टी की छठीं कांग्रेस के प्रस्ताव से जो सन 1917 ई० की जुलाई में हुई थी, स्पष्ट है। खयाल रहे कि अत्यन्त गरीब किसान poorest peasant से मतलब साफ है कि मध्यम या धनी किसान नहीं लिये जायंगे।

इसी प्रकार पेज आरनाट (R. Page Arnot) ने रूसी क्रान्ति के इतिहास में लिखा है कि" "Thus the dictatorship of the proletariat in alliance with the poorer peasantry," "and to the building up of the organisation of poor peasants." (Vol. 2, page 42, 43). इसका मतलब यही है कि "मजदूरों का एकतंत्र शासन अधिक गरीब किसानों के साथ मिल कर ही होता है", "बोलशेविक लोग देहातों में गरीब किसानों का संगठन करते थे" यहां ज्यादा गरीब (poorer) और गरीब (poor) किसानों का उल्लेख है। लेनिन के लेखों में ये तीनों शब्द - poor, poorer, poorest - सहस्त्रों बार आयें हैं। उसने अपने प्रसिद्ध "अप्रैल के मन्तव्यों" (April Theses) के 5 वें और 6 ठें मन्तव्यों में रूस में पार्लिमेन्टरी प्रणाली की जगह सर्वहारा, खेतमजदूरों और किसानों की पंचायतों (Soviets) के सम्मिलित गणतंत्र शासन—" 'a republic of Soviets of worker's, Agricultural labourer's, and Peasant's Deputies" कह के आगे लिखा है कि हमारे खेती सम्बन्धी प्रोग्राम का केन्द्रबिन्दु या प्रधान लक्ष्य होना चाहिये खेतमजदूरों की पंचायत - "The agrarian programme must be centered around the Soviets of Agricultural Labourers' Deputies." जिसका तात्पर्य है कि खेतमजदूरों को प्रधानतया लक्ष्य करके हमारा वह प्रोग्राम बनना चाहिये। मगर उसके बाद ही फिर लिखता है कि सभी जमीनों को समाज के हाथ में करके उसका प्रबन्ध खेत मजदूरों तथा किसानों की स्थानीय पंचायतों को सौंप देना चाहिये" "the disposal of such lands to be in the charge of the local Soviets of Agricultural Labourers' and Peasants' Deputies." फिर इसी के साथ यह भी कहता है कि वड़ी बड़ी जमींदारियों की जमीनों के आदर्श फार्म सौ से लेकर तीन सौ देसियातिन तक के बनाये जाकर वे खेतमजदूरों की पंचायत को ही सिपुर्द किये जांय— "The creation of model farms on each of the large estates varying from 100 to 300 desyatines. . . under the control of the Agricultural Labourers' Deputies." वहीं उसने यह भी कहा है कि गरीब किसानों की पंचायतों (सभाओं) का अलग संगठन करना होगा — "The organisation of separate Soviets of Deputies of the Poor

Peasants." खूबी तो यह है कि खेत मजदूरों की पंचायत का जिक्र किसानों की पंचायत से जुदा करके भी गरीब किसानों के ही संगठन की बात वह कहता है।

इन बातों के अलावे लेनिनिज्म में स्टालिन ने 313 पृष्ठ में यों लिखा है :— "There is distinct exploitation of wage-labour, or semi-wage-labour by the peasant proprietor (Kulak). It would, therefore, be unsuitable if we embarked upon a policy of mitigating or of moderating the fight. What we have to do is to organise the poor peasants for the struggle against the Kulaks, and ourselves to act as leaders in the fight." इसका अर्थ यह है, "धनी किसान (कुलक) खाम खाह खेतमजदूरों या अर्द्धमजदूरों का साफसाफ शोषण करते हैं। इसलिये यदि हमने उनके साथ होने वाले संघर्षो को नरम या धीमा किया तो यह अनुचित होगा। हमारा तो फर्ज यह है कि हम गरीबों किसानों को कुलक लोगों के विरूद्ध संगठित करके खुद उस लड़ाई का नेतृत्व करें"। एक बात और भी है। लेनिन ने अपने अप्रैल वाले मन्तव्यों (April Theses) में पहले में यह लिखा है कि जब तक किसानों और मजदूरों के हाथ में शासन की बागडोर नहीं आ जाती तब तक हम साम्राज्यवादी युद्ध में पड़ी नहीं सकते। यह बागडोर माने और दो और शर्तें पूरा होने पर यह लड़ाई क्रांति के रक्षार्थ मानी जायगी और हम उसमें पड़ सकते हैं। लेकिन मजदूरों और किसानों के हाथ में शासनसूत्र देने की बात कहते हुए उसने लिखा है कि किसानों से हमारा मतलब उन गरीब किसानों से है जो करीब-करीब मजदूरों जैसे हैं — " (a) that the power of Government pass to the proletariat and the poor sections of the peasantry bordering on the proletariat." इन्हीं को विदेश से लिखे गये पत्रों (Letters From Afar) में उसने semi proletariat भी लिखा है। इन बातों से स्पष्ट है कि लेनिन गरीब किसानों और खेतमजदूरों की एक ही श्रेणी — किसान श्रेणी — मानता है।

इन सब उद्धरणों को एक साथ लिख देने से कई बातें साफ हो जाती हैं। एक तो यह कि धनी और मध्य किसानों के सिवाय जो गरीब किसान हैं वह तीन तरह के हैं, (1) गरीब, (2) ज्यादा गरीब, (3) अत्यन्त गरीब। मगर व्यवहार में यह भेद नहीं मानकर गरीब किसानों के ही लिये समय समय पर तीनों शब्द बोले जाते हैं। इन उद्धरणों को गौर से पढ़ के कोई भी यह कह सकता है। दूसरी यह कि गरीब किसान हीं खेतमजदूर या अर्द्ध खेत मजदूर हैं। आखिरी उद्धरण में स्तालिन इन मजदूरों का ही शोषण लिखता

है। मगर उसे मिटाने का जो रास्ता अन्त में लड़ाई के रूप में बताता है उसके लिये संगठन करना गरीब किसानों का ही बताता है। इससे स्पष्टता और क्या चाहिये।? लेनिन के मन्तव्यों से जो उद्धरण दिये गये हैं उनसे भी यही बात स्पष्ट हो जाती है। किसान संगठन से जुदा गरीब किसानों का संगठन करने को पहले पहल उसने अप्रैल सन 1917 ई० में कहा था। किसान संगठन में तो मध्यम और धनी किसान भी आ सकते हैं, खासकर मध्यम तो जरूर ही। उस समय के रूस में किसान संगठन में तो धनी भी थे ही। बल्कि उन्हीं की और मध्यम किसानों की ही तूती उस सभा में बोलती थी। इसीलिये गरीबों की आवाज वहां सुनाई न पड़ती थी। फलतः उनका जुदा संगठन जरूरी था। मगर जहां एक ओर गरीबों का संगठन कर्त्तव्य माना गया है तहां यह भी वहीं लिखा है कि खेती या किसान सम्बन्धी प्रोग्राम प्रधानतया खेतमजदूरों की ही दृष्टि से बनना चाहिये। इस से भी स्पष्ट है कि लेनिन गरीब किसानों और खेत मजदूरों को एक ही समझता है। क्योंकि यदि दो होते तो खेत मजदूरों का संगठन न होने पर उनकी दृष्टि से प्रोग्राम क्यों कर बनता? पहले जो एक लम्बा उद्धरण दिया है। उससे भी लेनिन का यही अभिप्राय प्रकट होता है यह वहीं लिख चुके हैं। हां, यह सही है कि अकसर खेत-मजदूर कहने से बिना जमीन वाले ही किसान समझे जाते हैं। इसीलिये आदर्श फार्मों को उन्हीं की पंचायतों के हवाले करने की बात लेनिन ने लिखी है। उनके पास खेती के साधन तो होते नहीं। फलतः बड़े जमींदारों की जिरात और बकाश्त छीनकर उन्हीं के साधनों से उसी जमीन में सम्मिलित खेती खेतमजदूर करें तो ठीक हो यही लेनिन का मतलब था। इससे साम्यवाद का रास्ता साफ हो जाने को था।

फरवरी की क्रांति के बाद लेनिन ने जो पत्र विदेश से अक्टूबर वाली क्रांति के पहले उसी की तैयारी की दृष्टि से लिखे थे उनमें भी खेतमजदूरों के संगठन से जुदा, किसानों के संगठन की बात यद्यपि झलकती है। तथापि यदि गौर से पूरा प्रकरण पढ़ा जाय तो साफ हो जाता है कि वह धनी और मध्यम किसानों से गरीब किसानों को जुदा करने के ही लिये उसकी कोशिश है न कि उन किसानों को खेत-मजदूरों से जुदा करने का उसका खयाल है। वह लिखता है, "Soviets of Peasant Deputies, Soviets of Agricultural Workers - these are among our most urgent tasks. We shall thereby strive not only that the agricultural workers should establish separate soviets of their own, but also that the poorest and propertyless peasants should organise separately from the well-to-do peasants." एक लम्बे

पाराग्राफ के अन्त में यह बात लिखी है और इसका आखिरी वाक्य इस बात को स्पष्ट किये देता है कि धनियों से गरीब किसानों का जुदा संगठन हो। जो अत्यंत गरीब और सम्पत्तिहीन हैं वही तो खेतमजदूर हैं।

जब धनी किसानों के शोषण के विरुद्ध खेतमजदूरों को लड़ना ही है और उसका नेतृत्व हमें जरूर ही करना है तब तो उनका संगठन होई जायगा। लड़ाई होगी आखिर कैसे? स्तालिन भी तो यही कहता है। इस प्रकार खेत मजदूरों का संगठन इस लड़ाई के दौरान में ही हो सकता है, होना चाहिये। तभी वह पक्का और यथार्थ होगा। संघर्ष के मध्य जो संगठन शोषितों का होता है वही असली होता है। बिना संघर्ष के संगठन करने पर तो उसमें ऊलजलूल लोगों के भर जाने का खतरा रहता है। इसीलिये तो रूस में जो सोवियट बनी वह लडाई के ही दौरान में 1905 ई॰ में। उसके बाद लड़ाई खत्म हो जाने पर वह भी खत्म हुई। फिर 1917 की फरवरी वाली क्रांति के समय बनी। अतएव यों उनका जुदा संगठन हम न करेंगे। गरीब किसानों से लड़ने के लिये तो कभी भी न करेंगे यह याद रहे।

यह ठीक है कि दूसरे लोग यों भी उनका संगठन करेंगे, करते हैं। उन्हें रोकना भी असंभव है। हमारा यही काम होना चाहिये कि उसमें भी रह के उसे सीमा से बाहर न जाने देकर रास्ते पर चलने दें। ऐसा करें कि वह किसान सभा का विरोधी बनने न पाये। यदि उसमें जाने में ऐसी बाधायें हों कि जानें ही न पायें तो बाहर से ही उस पर नजर और निगरानी रखना जरूरी है। मगर यह तो हो नहीं सकता कि सच्चे किसान सेवक उनमें जाने न पायें। लेकिन हर हालत में ऐसे संगठनों पर हमारा जोर न हो कर सिर्फ उनसे जिन खतरों की संभावना है उन्हें बचाना ही हमारा ध्येय होना चाहिये। मगर यह बात भी तभी होगी जब हम धनी किसानों के विरुद्ध उनके संघर्षो को मुस्तैदी के साथ संगठित रूप से चलाते रहें। यही असली और आवश्यक काम है। इसी प्रकार उनका निजी संगठन सुन्दर रूप में खड़ा हो जायगा।। इसमें साधारण किसानों को नाक भौं सिकोड़ने का मौका भी न मिलेगा। बिना संघर्ष के यों ही खेत-मजदूरों की संस्था खड़ी कर देने पर स्वभावतः उनके कान खड़े हो सकते हैं, वे चौंक सकते हैं।

<3.8.41> किसान सभा और खेत-मजदूरों के इस प्रकार के संगठन में परस्पर विरोध भी नहीं हो सकता। क्योंकि जब किसान सभा के नेता ही यह काम करेंगे, सो भी संघर्ष के जरिये ही, तो ऐसा मौका आने ही न देंगे। संघर्ष के करते बनने वाले संगठन में बनावटी और कलह कराने वाले नेताओं की तो गुंजाइश होगी ही नहीं। वे तो इससे दूर ही रहेंगे। फिर

मतभेद करावेगा कौन? यह संगठन तो अत्यंत शोषितों का ही होगा। किसान नेताओं के लिये तो गौरव की बात होगी कि किसान संसार में जो सबसे ज्यादा दुखिया हैं और सब के नीचे दबे हैं उन्हें वे मजबूती के साथ उठायें। वही तो असल किसान हैं। फलतः एक तो हमारी नीयत का पता दुनियां को लग जायगा। दूसरे यही सभा, यही संगठन किसानों की वास्तविक चीज कुछ दिनों बाद हो जायगी। जो किसान खुद शोषित हैं और जो दूसरों का शोषण खुद करना नहीं चाहते। प्रत्युत जो शोषण और जुल्म को संसार से मिटा देना चाहते हैं वह सभी इस नये संगठन में ही धीरे-धीरे शरीक हो जायंगे। वर्त्तमान किसान सभा में जो लोग शोषण को किसी न किसी रूप में कायम करने के लिये शामिल हैं या रहेंगे वह धीरे धीरे इससे कालान्तर में खिसकेंगे। फलतः दोनों सभाएं एक ही प्रकार के लोगों की होने के कारण अन्त में एक हों जायंगी। मगर अभी यह संभव नहीं है। अभी परिस्थिति ही कुछ ऐसी है कि यह बात हो नहीं सकती।

गरीब किसानों के साथ जब कभी इन मजदूरों का झमेला मजदूरी वगैरः को लेकर होगा तो वहां भी दोनों संगठन आपस में बातें कर के आसानी से मामला तय करा देंगे। मध्यम किसानों के साथ भी निपटारा करा देंगे। क्योंकि अभी तो सभी किसान किसान सभा में शरीक हुई। फिर उसके सामने अपनी बातें कह के अन्त में उसका फैसला तो उन्हें मानना ही होगा। जो लोग ऐसा रूस के इतिहास से ही समझते हैं कि खेत मज़दूरों का किसी भी प्रकार का अलग संगठन या उसका श्रीगणेश भी अभी नहीं किया जाना चाहिये, वह परिस्थिति को समझते ही नहीं। रूस के इतिहास से हमें फायदा उठाना जरूर है। मगर उसकी सभी बातें अक्षरशः ज्यों की त्यों यहां लागू की जा सकती हैं नहीं। 20-25 वर्षों में परिस्थिति बहुत बदल चुकी है। हमें इसी के अनुसार कुछ न कुछ रद्दो बदल करना ही होगा। स्मरण रहे कि यह साम्राज्यवाद का पेचीदा युग है। इसमें यदि हम मौके पर पीछे न हटें, इधर उधर न घूमें तो मिट जायंगे। इसे ही लेनिन ने "The necessity of manoeuvering and retreating" कहा है। हर हालत में हमें तो परिस्थिति का सामना करना ही होगा।

इस प्रकार हमने जिन जिन बातों का वर्णन किया है, जो पहलू सुझायें हैं और जो रास्ते दिखाये हैं अगर उन सबों पर ठीक-ठीक गौर करके मौके मौके से उनपर अमल किया जाय, और जरूरत समझ के उनमें थोड़ी बहुत तरमीम (संशोधन) भी कर लिया जाय तो न सिर्फ खेत मजदूरों की, बल्कि समूचे किसानों की समस्याएं बखूबी हल हो जायंगी। हमें कम से कम

दिक्कतों का सामना करना पड़ेगा। इस प्रकार हम आसानी से इस बड़े देश की काया पलट का रास्ता साफ कर लेगें और जब मौका आयेगा तो उस काया पलट में पूरा भाग ले सकेंगे। संकुचित या पहले से बने बनाये खयालों को छोड़ हमें मुस्तैदी और ईमानदारी से आगे बढ़ने की जरूरत है।

Addendum

The Eastern Economist - 311 Page
Postwar Employment

Here is a proposal from Mr. D.K. Sanyal, Secretary of the appointment Board of the Calcutta University, who can undoubtedly speak with authority on the subject. According to Mr. Sanyal's estimate immediate employment must be found for nearly 3,000,000 persons. The immediate avenue of employment which he suggests are: the road transport development scheme to be completed in 10 years instead of 20 years as recommended by the Nagpur Conference, 250 million acres of land classified as cultivable waste or fallow to be brought under cultivation according to the recommendation of the Imperial Council of Agricultural Research.

Glossary

There are as many forms of transliteration from Hindi to English as there are authors engaged in the task. This glossary is no exception. The effort in what follows is not to meet particular standards of orthography or linguistic correctness but in so far as possible to follow generally accepted practice in attempting to convey the meanings Sahajanand intended when he wrote in 1941. The value of this glossary is precisely that it emerged out of the vernacular experience of the person who was arguably the most active and intimately involved peasant leader of his day, writing essentially at mid-career. Its terms and definitions were not filtered through the administrative lens of a British settlement officer, however valuable those 19th and 20th century terms and definitions may have been. It is also the case that Sahajanand was most concerned with the life experience of poor peasants and agricultural labourers on the ground, and less with the legal and judicial meanings that have emerged in much of the historical record concerned with the agrarian experience. Accordingly, many of the usages which follow will be relatively unfamiliar terms, but locally common in the perceptions of the peasants and the workers and leaders represented here through the experience and pen of Sahajanand. The local, vernacular familiarity of the terms employed in this text and in the movement and politics it reflects, is a point I wish to emphasize, despite the obvious infusion of the Sanskrit idiom by Sahajanand, emerging from his own classical background as a Dandi Sannyasi of the Dasnami order. These terms serve to reinforce the qualities of exploitation Sahajanand seeks to convey on every page of this document in making his argument. They and the graphic qualities of his language were characteristic of everything Sahajanand said and wrote in this remarkable phase of his career.

Whether we take Sahajanand's peasant activism to have begun in 1929 or the early thirties and considering that he died in 1950, the year 1941 was effectively the mid-point of his political career. The date is also important because Sahajanand, in jail at the time, was in an especially reflective frame of mind following the peak years of activism in the middle and late thirties, while at the same time involved in the continuing process of intellectual and political redefinition which marked both his career as social reformer and as peasant activist. In this case he was using the Russian experience as defined especially by Lenin to help him define more sharply the quality of the Indian experience of those on the social and economic margin of life in the countryside. But however important the Russian revolutionary experiment and the Marxist theory on which it was based, Sahajanand's roots and his experience were in the fields and villages of India and Bihar and it was that experience which informed his descriptions and understanding of rural India.

What follows then is a glossary of terms defining the condition of poor peasants and agricultural labourers as Sahajanand experienced it in the thirties and understood it in 1941. They are perceptions formed over a career of social and political reform spanning twenty-five years, sited primarily in Bihar and in the earlier period of social reform including also U.P. and from the middle and late thirties, all of India. I have attempted to define terms in the context in which they are used in the text by referring specifically to those textual usages where possible. Where numbers appear in brackets following definitions, these refer to the chapters in which the word and meaning are first or most forcefully used, although these chapter references are not meant to provide an index of terms, most of which are used frequently throughout the text. References to related terms appear in parentheses following the definitions. Please note also that Hindi terms are often defined in the text itself, especially as in Chapter II, where Sahajanand is himself concerned with the distinctions inherent in particular definitions of the term labourer. Where Sahajanand has provided such definitions or English equivalents, they appear in tthe edited translation precisely as Sahajanand gave them in the original Hindi text, either in parentheses or in inverted commas, i.e., quotation marks. If they are added for editorial clarification, they appear in brackets. These details are obvious when comparing the edited translation of Part I with the original Hindi text of Part II.

One final word of explanation on transliteration and word form in this glossary. The use of double vowels, especially at the beginnings of words will imply the long sound, single vowels the short vowel sound as in the case of Aa and a, but if meanings are not changed with such usages, the most common form, or perhaps more accurately, the one I am most comfortable with given the context, will be used. So too with the oo and u, and i and ee usages. Using the Devanagri in the glossary would have avoided this problem, but transliteration was thought to make these definitions more widely accessible, and those who read the Hindi text will benefit from Sahajanand's detailed and sometimes repetitive explanation of all terms and meanings. Persons familiar with Hindi of course will have no problem with pronunciations, or they will be appropriately critical of the amateur qualities of this effort at transliteration. But as I have indicated at the outset of these remarks, all forms of transliteration, including this one are flawed. To repeat, the effort here is to convey something of what Sahajanand was thinking and writing and what poor peasants and agricultural labourers were feeling at the time. The intention obviously is not to be exhaustive and there will certainly be those, more intimately familiar with Bihar than I, who will find omissions or who will wish to propose more sensitive definitions. The effort to access the world of peasants and agricultural labourers is clearly a continuing process.

Any glossary that purports to provide access to the social and political environment of rural Bihar cannot fail to mention the classic work of George A. Grierson, *Bihar Peasant Life Being a Discursive Catalogue of the Surroundings of the People of That Province* (Calcutta: Government of Bengal, 1885). Fortunately that remarkable document has been reissued in Delhi in a 1975 reprint by Cosmo Publications. Of almost equal value for Bihar is the earlier work of William Crooke, *Materials for a Rural and Agricultural Glossary of the North-Western Provinces and Oudh* (Allahabad: Government Press, 1879), which in fact Grierson used as a model for his own work. Crooke has also been reissued in Delhi by Oxford (1989), with editorial work by Shahid Amin, including an introduction which places Crooke and the whole glossary phenomenon in a particularly valuable context. While the early 19th century accounts and journals of Hamilton Buchanan for half a dozen Bihar districts perhaps anticipate our 20th century interests by too many years, they are nevertheless an important starting point. This material was issued sixty years ago in Patna by the Bihar and Orissa Research Society, and has at least in part been reprinted since. Finally, H.H. Wilson, *A Glossary of Judicial and Revenue Terms of British India* (Calcutta: Eastern Law House, 1940) is perhaps the best official glossary of its kind.

[Please note that no diacritical marks are used either in this glossary, or in the text itself.]

Aadhe kisan aur aadhe mazdoor: Literally, half peasant and half labourer, used by Sahajanand in developing his argument that the poor peasants and agricultural labourers are economically and qualitatively identical. Their halfness may take them either to the fields or to the towns to work for wages. Throughout this glossary and the text the terms kisan and khet mazdoor will be used interchangeably with the terms peasant and agricultural labourer. [II]

Aadhin: Subordinate, as in the case of an independent organization of agricultural labourers functioning within a wider Kisan Sabha, which essentially would be a contradiction in terms until the Kisan Sabha is reconstituted to represent the interests of the poorest kisans and agricultural labourers, which was Sahajanand's ultimate goal. [V]

Aadhunik: Modern, as in modern agriculture. Sahajanand uses the concept both in negative terms as a potential danger to agricultural labourers with the introduction of capitalism and mechanized cultivation [II], and positively as a necessary infrastructural change in developing a modern, scientific agriculture to expand productive capabilities for a growing population. [V] (See also Vaigyanik.)

Aamul parivartan: Radical social transformation, needed to overcome the economic bases and cultural attitudes of exploitation and oppression of the lowest castes, who, Sahajanand suggests, are treated worse than animals. [V]

Aanshik swatantrata: Partial freedom. In describing the social history of agriculture Sahajananad makes comparisons between slaves, serfs, and agricultural labourers and suggests that at least in outward form the latter two groups had a limited degree of freedom not enjoyed by the slaves. He makes brief comparisons over time and from country to country. [I]

Adhik se adhik: Higher of the highest, as in the highest possible rent or revenue extracted by the zamindars, in times of ecomomic stress leading to the immiseration of the peasants and their slide into the category of poor peasants and agricultural labourers. [I]

Andolan: Movement, as in peasant movement or kisan andolan, the Kisan Sabha, or on the other hand the movement of the agricultural labourers. Used throughout the text in considering the potential conflict within any combined organization of peasants and agricultural labourers and the misuse to which efforts to mobilize agricultural labourers have been put. Ultimately in Chapter V, Sahajanand explains the need for moving in the direction of such a merged organization of the poor kisans and the agricultural labourers whose organization it must then become.

Ansh, ansh matra: Section or part of society. In tracing the history of agriculture, Sahajanand refers to the emergence of various social categories, sections, sectors, groups, parts, and classes and the manner in which they were involved in agriculture. [I and II] (See also Shreni, Dal, Jamaat, Varg, Prakar, Tukare, Bhag, etc.)

Asabhya: Uncivilized, as in the manner in which the term for ploughman (*halwaha*) who is a bonded labourer is used synonymously for fool, illiterate, and uncivilized. [III] (See also Sabhya.)

Asal kisan, pakka kisan: Real kisans, real peasants defined as poor and middle kisans who are no different than the main bulk of agricultural labourers, and also the manner in which these true kisans in Gujarat have been driven into conditions of bonded labour. [II and III]

Asli kisan: Same as above.

Aswayamkrita: From the Sanskrit, meaning not done by one's self, i.e, by one's own hands, as in ploughing or doing other agricultural work, hence using agricultural labourers for that purpose. [I] (See also Swayamkrita.)

Atmasamman: Literally, self-respect, as in the case of low caste agricultural labourers, who are considered to be less than human and to have no sense of self-respect, or alternatively how the awakening among them is beginning to be expressed in a new sense of self-awareness and self-respect. [III and IV]

Attyachar: One of many terms used throughout this text to define the tyranny of the zamindars.

Attyant bhukkhar, attyant garib, attyant nirdhan: Extremely hungry, extremely poor, the poorest. Used throughout the text in referring to peasants and agricultural labourers on the social and economic margin.

Attyant shoshiton: The worst oppressed, the most exploited, in referring to the marginal kisans and agricultural labourers who will constitute the final, merged Kisan Sabha whose organization this will be. [V] (See also Dukhiya.)

Baganon: A plantation, as in the tea plantations of Darjeeling and Assam and the coffee and rubber plantations of the Nilgiris. These with other large government farms employ approximately two percent of the agricultural labourers of the country, and are categorized by Sahajanand with factory labourers as distinct from the bulk of agricultural labourers in India. [II]

Bagawat: Revolt. The means prescribed by Sahajanand for breaking the cycle of debt slavery by the *Halis* and *Dublas* of Gujarat, who will become rebels through their involvement with the Kisan Sabha. [III]

Bagi: Rebel. See Bagawat. [III]

Bahut tarah ke: Many different kinds, in this case of peasants. In defining agricultural labourers as no different from poor peasants, Sahajanand takes care to explain that the term kisan includes many different kinds of people, including those with vast holdings, who are in reality zamindars. [II]

Bakasht or khudkasht: Literally land cultivated by the landholder/ zamindar himself. In practice, in Bihar the term bakasht refers specifically to those raiyati lands resumed by the zamindar for non-payment of rent and then either cultivated by himself, kept out of cultivation, or let out on terms more attractive to the zamindar to new peasant tenants. Sahajanand here calls for the resumption by government of all bakasht and *zirat* lands from those zamindars who are not solely dependent on agriculture and their distribution to the khet mazdoors. [IV] (See zirat.)

Bandish: The conspiracy hatched by the zamindars, who in the process of exploiting the poorest peasants force them into the ranks of the khet mazdoors, then conspire even to rob them of their just wages. [I]

Barbad: Destruction. In describing the relations between kisans and khet mazdoors, Sahajanand argues that the kisans face destruction if they do not treat their agricultural labourers with sympathy, justice, and equality. They will in effect be cutting off their own arms and legs. [IV]

Bare bare farmon: Literally, very large farms, most often government farms, which like the tea plantations, employ agricultural labourers with no hope of acquiring any land or rights in land and hence are no different than factory labourers. With plantation labourers they comprise no more than two percent of agricultural labourers in India. Sahajanand also characterizes farms in America and elsewhere in these terms. [I and II]

Batai: Share cropping, the tenancy or wage settlement agreement reached between the land controller and his tenant or labourer, often on an *aadha aadhi*, or half share basis although this division is variable from place to place.

Bataidar: Sharecropper.

Beakla: Unwise, a fool, the demeaning characterization which attaches to the *halwaha*, or ploughman as bonded labourer. [III]

Beizzat, beizzati: Dishonour. With reference to those false leaders who dishonour the khet mazdoors by taking unfair advantage of them to achieve personal political gain. [Preface and V]

Bhag: Section, as in the 98 percent bulk of khet mazdoors who belong to the most significant section of agricultural labourers. [II] (See also Ansh, Shreni, etc.)

Bhai-bandhuon: Those who surround the zamindars, who with them stand in fear and panic at the intensity and strength of the Kisan Sabha. Henchmen. [Preface]

Bhaichara: Brotherhood, fraternity, i.e., the terms of justice, equity, and brotherhood which the kisans must show to their agricultural labourers. [Preface and IV]

Bhaoli: Wage payment or share payment made in kind, rather than in cash, which is *nagdi*. [IV]

Bhayankar: Dreadful, terrible, as in *bhayankar garibi*, the dreadful poverty Dr. Harold Mann found in the Poona villages he surveyed in 1914-1915 and in 1921. [II]

Bhayankar bat ka soochak: A portent or indicator of catastrophic things to come if the immiseration of the peasants and the dramatic growth in the number of agricultural labourers is not brought under control. [III]

Bhayankar zamindar: True zamindar, i.e., a dreadful zamindar, the description Sahajanand provides for those peasants who are in fact controllers of vast tracts of raiyati lands. [II]

Bhukhon marna: Literally, to starve, a consequence Sahajanand sees as the inevitable consequence of the heavy human pressure on cultivable land area, a problem which thus becomes an urgent need for the transformation of Indian agrarian society. [IV]

Bhukkhar: Starvation, starving, describing the condition of the peasants in Harold Mann's second village, 91 percent of whom were found to be almost starving. [II}

Bigha: A variable measure of land. Twenty *katthas* equal one bigha; twenty *dhurs* equal one kattha. With wide variation a bigha may equal 0.25 hectare or 0.625 acre.

Bikri ki chiz: Commodity. In his discussion of factory labour Sahajanand describes the labour power of the labourer as a commodity, whose value is affected by the market in the same way as other commodities. [II]

Bina zamin: Literally, without land, hence landless. Neither owning land [*malikana*] nor holding land in some fixed raiyati arrangement of tenancy. Landlessness in this definition may or may not include batai or *shikmi* sharecropping arrangements. [II]

Bina zamin wale kheti ke mazdoor: A landless agricultural labourer. Sahajanand describes in detail the process of immiseration whereby poor peasants are being deprived of all holdings and becoming completely landless agricultural labourers. [I]

Buri tarah piche: Backward, badly behind. In making comparisons with other world economies, Sahajanand finds Indian agriculture, despite good soil fertility and an ideal climate, lagging badly behind. [IV]

Chalwaha: A khet mazdoor who performs multiple functions of agricultural labour. [Preface]

Charwaha: Grazier, herdsman and among those Sahajanand includes in his initial definition of agricultural labourers. [Preface]

Chaur: Wetlands, which can potentially be made suitable for cultivation to increase the amount of arable land. [IV]

Chinkar: Snatching, as in zamindars snatching the lands from peasants to extend their control and amass wealth. [IV] -

Chori: Thieving, as in the kisans are awakening, hence how long can the thieving and intimidation (*seenajori*) go on? [IV]

Chote chote kisan, or chote mote kisan: Small landholding peasants. Among the many categories of peasants Sahajanand defines in this text, as in *zamin wale chote chote kisan*, literally, small landholding peasant. [II]

Crore: One hundred lakhs or ten million.

Dabi pari: Suppressed. Khet mazdoors belong chiefly to castes which have been suppressed for centuries, with a consequent set of social attitudes that results in their gross maltreatment and exploitation. [Preface and V]

Dakiyanoosi: Old orthodoxy. A frequent reference in this text to the causes for outmoded practices which prevent certain castes from engaging directly in agriculture.

Dalal: Broker, henchman of the zamindar, conspiring to organize the khet mazdoors against the kisans in what is thus a false movement. This is an issue Sahajanand begins with in the preface and pursues throughout this document.

Daldali: Marsh land, which must be reclaimed in order to expand the available area of cultivable land in India. [IV]

Daman: Oppression, repression, specifically with reference to the legal and illegal practices instituted by the zamindars against kisans and kisan activists in their effort to crush the kisan movement. [Preface]

Dar raiyat kisan: Subtenant. Sahajanand cites a number of official reports on the phenomenon of sub-infeudation and the elaboration of subtenancies and intermediaries, which by the 1930s had reached dramatic proportions. [II]

Dayniya dasha: The deplorable condition of the kisans, obliged to subsist on an average per head cultivated area of barely three quarters of an acre, the figure Sahajanand cites for the 1930s and which he defines as completely inadequate to meet basic subsistence needs. [IV]

Dhan: Paddy. The term used here specifically in the context of the high labour intensity of its cultivation, the ploughing, weeding, and transplanting process of which are done almost solely by agricultural labourers. [IV]

Dhani kisan: Rich peasant, a term used critically throughout this text, as example those rich peasants who pay the same low wages to khet mazdoors as do the poor peasants. Also as in the Russian case at the time of the revolution, "kulaks." [II, V, etc.]

Dharma: Religion. Used throughout this text to describe the orthodoxies which inhibit peasants from engaging directly in agriculture. Also to indicate that agricultural labourers come from all castes and religions, etc.

Dhur: A variable measure of land. Twenty dhurs equal one kattha.

Diwaliya kheti: The bankrupt agriculture to which peasants are forced to turn in the hope of maintaining some semblance of subsistence, all the time being driven further into poverty and into the ranks of the khet mazdoors. [I]

Doob marne ki bat: Shameful. The kisan who mistreats his agricultural labourers, showing no human sensibilities in the process must not only make amends but atone for his shameful deeds. [IV] (See also Prayashchit.)

Doorandesh: Far sightedness, visionary. Those with vision can appreciate that change is sweeping the world, a fact not understood by those with outmoded and orthodox images of our times. [IV]

Dubla: Bonded labourer, specifically in Gujarat. [III]

Dukh dard wali dastanen: The painful stories of the agricultural labourers. Only when kisan leaders listen with sympathy to these stories, will they gain the confidence of the khet mazdoors and be able then to organize them. [IV]

Dukh sukh: Realities of life. Only if kisan leaders and kisans apprehend the full realities of the life circumstances of agricultural labourers can any change in their condition be realized. [IV]

Dukhiya: The most depressed, destitute, the worst sufferers. Sahajanand uses this term frequently to describe the khet mazdoors, including the destitute and poor of all castes and religions, those at the very bottom of the kisan world. [Preface, III, and V] (See also Attyant shoshiton.)

Dusaron ke dwara kheti karwana: Literally to get the cultivation done by others, as in the case of most upper castes and many middle castes, adhering to old orthodoxies. [I]

Dushman: Enemy. Unless the kisan leaders assume the responsibility of organizing the agricultural labourers, the false leaders, the true enemies of the khet mazdoors will force the issue by taking on that role. [I]

Ek upar ek: Literally, one above the other, defining the multi-layered, multi-tiered system of intermediaries between the land controller and the actual cultivator. [II] (See also Dar raiyat kisan.)

Fate dil: Heart-rending, a description Sahajanand uses throughout to characterize the condition of the agricultural labourers, the poor, on the social and economic margin.

Gaaliyan: Abuses, as in the case of the abuses to which the *hali* and *dubla* bonded labourers of Gujarat and other khet mazdoors are regularly subjected. [III]

Galle ki kheti: Cereal crops, all of which require the work of agricultural labourers and their families in their cultivation. [IV]

Garib kisan: Poor kisan, poor peasant, whom Sahajanand characterizes with middle peasants as real kisans and no different in their condition from the vast bulk of agricultural labourers. [II]

Garibi: Poverty, as in the dreadful poverty, *bhayankar garibi* which Harold Mann found in the Poona villages he surveyed. [II]

Garoh baandh ke: The sense of community which emerges in the patterned life style of factory workers and which facilitates their ability to engage in collective strike action, a possibility, which by comparison is not likely in the more dispersed rural environment of the khet mazdoor. [II]

Ghabrahat: The fear of the kisans that khet mazdoors are their enemies, an anxiety which kisans must overcome if a resolution of their common problems is to be achieved. [IV]

Goondebazi: Goondaism, the idea that might is right, that force and the use of the big stick, the *lathi* are legitimate instruments of power. Sahajanand uses the term to characterize the indiscriminate assaults on peasants and kisan workers during the peak years of Kisan Sabha activity in the 1930s. [Preface]

Gulam, gulamon: Slave, slaves, terms which Sahajanand introduces in developing the history of classical slavery and serfdom as an element in the history of agricultural labour. [I]

Guzar karna: Subsistence, livelihood, the basic requirement Sahajanand sees in defining agricultural labourers and kisans, namely that they be dependent on agriculture to maintain subsistence. The term is also used in describing the miserable condition of those literally subsisting on the margin of existence. [Preface, II, and IV] (See also Dayniya dasha.)

Hali: Bonded labourer with specific reference to Gujarat. [III]

Halwaha: In a general sense, ploughman, specifically in the United Provinces, the halwaha is the bonded labourer of the *halwahi* system. Also used as a term of derision for the unwise, uncivilized, rustic fool, an attitude Sahajanand condemns mercilessly in this text. Used throughout, but see especially Chapter III.

Halwahi: The system of bonded labour in the United Provinces. [III]

Harap: Grabbing land, *zamin harapna*, as in the case of those zamindars who appropriate thousands of acres, thereby making the average three quarters acre per head of land for cultivation, which Sahajanand cites, a meaningless figure. [IV]

Hari: Peasant in Sindh. [III]

Hartal: Work stoppage, strike, actions which are difficult in the rural countryside. In any event, Sahajanand's plea in resolving conflict between poor kisans and khet mazdoors is for negotiation and compromise and not hartals. [IV]

Insaniyat: Humanity. Agricultural labourers are subject to gross maltreatment and abuse. In the interest of justice, equity, and decency, apart from self-interest, Sahajanand makes a consistent plea throughout this text for relations between kisans and khet mazdoors that reflect a common sense of their humanity. Especially Chapters III and IV.

Izzat: Honour, self-respect. Essentially the same issue as immediately above, involving self images of the khet mazdoors themselves, and attitudes of those above them in the social agrarian hierarchy, attitudes which Sahajanand deplores. [III and IV]

Jabani: Oral, as in the terms of indebtedness which create conditions of bonded labour, for which no written record exists, certainly between the parties involved. [III]

Jagaran, jagna, jagne: Awakening, to awaken, to become more conscious of rights and opportunities in the political climate of the 1930s, both with reference to kisans and khet mazdoors. Used throughout but see especially Preface and chapters III and IV. (See also Neend tootegi, Samajhna, Sajag.)

Jallaad: Butcher, as in blood-sucking butchers, Sahajanand's graphic description of the zamindars who exploit the peasants and khet mazdoors in all possible ways. [I] (See also Rakt peenewale.)

Jalpan: Mid-morning, mid-day meal, one of the specific demands of the khet mazdoors, that of a decent mid-day meal, which Sahajanand was able to negotiate with kisans by efforts of persuasion. [IV]

Jamaat: Class, group, etc. One of the many terms Sahajanand uses to define different social, economic, agrarian interests, in this case with specific reference to the assumption among some kisans that the Kisan Sabha is an organization of a particular class. [Preface] (See also Varg, Dal, Ansh, Shreni, etc.)

Janata: The people. [I] (See also Praja and Jansamooh.)

Janata ki krantikari: People's revolution, in this case with specific reference to the revolution in Russia and Lenin's interpretations of the roles of peasants and agricultural labourers. [II]

Jansamooh: Multitude, masses, the people at large. Sahajanand uses these terms in discussing the history of agriculture and defining the emergence of specific categories of cultivators, peasants, and agricultural labourers. [I] (See also Janata and Praja.)

Jansevak: Literally servant of the people, hence public servants, social activists, peasant activists. [I]

Jati panti: Caste, casteism, used here in describing the social divisions which divide agricultural labourers and make the mobilization of a unified movement of khet mazdoors difficult. [II]

Jhagra: Fight, conflict, used throughout this text but specifically in the conclusion of Chapter IV to describe the potential end of conflict between kisans and agricultural labourers through negotiated compromise.

Jote kore, jotna korna: To plough and work in the fields. Formerly everyone who worked in agriculture was in a general sense an agricultural labourer, whereas now the term refers specifically to those who work in the fields of others, a problem of definition Sahajanand examines and explains in some detail. [II]

Kafan: Shroud. Sahajanand comments graphically on those kisans, who, driven to poverty and wage labour are in fact victims of zamindars who will seek to rob them even of those wages, who would seek benefit even by selling the shrouds of the dead. [I]

Kamanewali janata: Literally, working people, hence workers, the masses. [Preface]

Kamiauta, kamia: Bonded labourer especially in the *kamiauti* system of bonded labour in Bihar. [III]

Kamiauti: System of bonded labour in Bihar. [III]

Karkhanon ke mazdooron: Factory workers, who along with peasants and agricultural labourers occupy a prominent place among the oppressed in society. But the latter are in fact far greater in number and hence, Sahajanand implies, deserve at least as much attention as factory workers in contemporary efforts at change and reform. [I]

Katne dhone walon: Harvesters and carriers, used by Sahajanand in considering the produce wage payment shares of these agricultural labourers. [III]

Kattha: A variable measure of land. Twenty katthas equal one bigha.

Khadon: Fertilizers, or manures as an input requirement to enhance agricultural production. [IV and V]

Khalihan: Threshing floor, threshing place.

Khan pan ya vyah shadi: The issue of commensality and marriage, which is not what justice and equity in relations between kisans and khet mazdoors requires. It is, as Sahajanand suggests, a matter of humanity. [IV]

Khet mazdoor, kheti ke mazdooron, kheti men kam karne walon: Agricultural labourers, those who work in agriculture, in the fields, etc. Used throughout this manuscript.

Kheti sambandhi gulami pratha: Serfdom, used in Sahajanand's descriptions of slavery, serfdom, and the emergence of agricultural labour as a distinct agrarian category. Also with reference to the Russian experience. [I and II]

Khetihar: Landholder, as in petty landholders, *tut pujiye khetihar*. [II]

Khooni: Cruel, as in the cruel zamindars who take as much as three fourths of the crop, leaving one fourth to the kisan. [I]

Kisan: Peasant, across the full range from poor to rich, defined throughout this tract as in conflict with the agricultural labourers they employ or at the marginal level of the poor, as potential allies.

Kisan karyakartaon: Kisan workers, peasant activists. Used throughout but see especially Preface.

Koi sima: Demarcation line, i.e., the distinction between poor peasants and agricultural labourers, a line Sahajanand suggests is essentially invisible. [II]

Krantikari shaktiyon: Revolutionary forces in Russia, to which Sahajanand refers in citing Lenin's analysis of different categories of peasant involvement. [II]

Kritdas: Bonded slave, used in Sahajanand's description of debt bondage. [III]

Kuchalne: To crush, with reference to the zamindars' efforts to crush the kisan movement of the 1930s in every possible way. [Preface]

Labhdayak: Profitable; the potential for Indian agriculture in circumstances of a full transformation in bringing more land under cultivation and making necessary infrastructural investments. [IV]

Lagan vasoolne: Rent collection, as in *zyada se zyada lagan vasoolne*, i.e,. maximum rent collection or rack-renting by the zamindars. Used throughout this text, see for example Chapter I.

Lakh: One hundred thousand.

Lambe paimane ki kheti: Large scale farming. [II]

Larai: Conflict, or alternatively, struggle for existence, used throughout in defining the realities on the ground for marginal peasants and khet mazdoors.

Lokmat: People's voice. Only with the support of an active public opinion can a powerful movement be mobilized to achieve the changes outlined in Sahajanand's proposals. [V]

Loot, looteron, lootpat: From the Hindi *lootna*, literally to loot, also looters, looting. Sahajanand makes the point that the peasants are literally being looted and hence impoverished by the infinite number of rent collecting intermediaries in the system. [II]

Lathi raj: The rule of the *lathi*, or the big stick. The idea that might is right. The references here are to the use of force, coercion, and intimidation by the dominant land controllers in the system. [Preface]

Madhyam kisan: Middle kisan, whom Sahajanand equates with poor kisans and agricultural labourers, all of whom he refers to as real kisans. He also cites at some length the work of Lenin and Stalin on poor, middle, and rich kisans. [II]

Mahajan: Moneylender, a term Sahajanand uses almost as frequently and critically as zamindar in this text, as the cause for the immiseration of the peasant. High rents and inordinate share-cropping demands by the zamindar force the peasant into the hands of the moneylender.

Maidanejang: Battle, battlefield. Sahajanand's metaphor for the arena where the struggle of the oppressed is being fought by a wide range of activists around the world. His call in this text is that the agricultural labourers now be drawn into that struggle as well. [I]

Mal: Cess, as an element of the demands of rent and revenue placed on the kisans, which was not the case at the time of the classical origins of agriculture; hence malguzari which is revenue. The term for rent is lagan. [I]

Malik, maliki: Owner, ownership, as in land under one's ownership and control. The landless agricultural labourer has no such rights or control. [I and II]

Mangen: Demands made by kisans and agricultural labourers, here used in the context of the impossible demands made by the false leaders of the agricultural labourers, which cannot be met. This is an issue Sahajanand returns to throughout this manuscript.

Manmani: Arbitrary will of the zamindars. In describing the process by which growing landlessness has occurred statistically in the twentieth century, Sahajanand refers to the immiseration of the marginal peasants who are subject to the arbitrary will of the zamindar on issues of rents and rights. [I]

Manobriti: Mentality of the peasants and the agricultural labourers in the context of the Russian revolutionary experience. [II]

Manushyata aur prem: Humanity and decency. The terms in which Sahajanand suggests kisans should and must treat agricultural labourers, in their own self interest. [IV]

Marpit, marna-pitna: Assault, to assault, to quarrel, to engage in conflict. Used here to describe the indiscriminate assaults on kisans and kisan workers in the 1930s on the one hand and the assaults and beatings administered to bonded labourers, the *halis* in Gujarat on the other. [Preface and III]

Maund: A measure of weight equal to 82.29 pounds or 37.32 kilograms. Forty seers equal one maund.

Mazboori: Helplessness, compulsion. Referring to the helpless condition of the poor kisans themselves who are hence unable to pay even minimum wages to agricultural labourers. Alternatively, precisely because of these conditions, both sides are compelled to come to terms by compromise. [III and IV]

Mazdoor: Labourer, factory worker, as distinguished throughout this manuscript from the agricultural labourer.

Mazdoori: Wages. In examining the most critical problems of agricultural labour, Sahajanand cites wages as the first. [III]

Mazdoori jo guzara karne liye zaroori ho: Minimum living wage. The most important issue in considering what wages should and must be. [III]

Mazdoori ki dar jo bandh gayi: Fixed wage as in the wages paid to agricultural labourers, or specifically that amount which the poorest kisans are able to pay, which is then taken as a standard to be paid by all kisans including those who are well-to-do. [IV]

Mazhab: Religion. Sahajanand concludes Chapter I with the assertion that the problems of agricultural labourers are not limited by caste, community or religion. They affect everyone.

Mazloom janata: The exploited, oppressed people. In conditions of the the 1930s, it appeared that in the absence of government, only the Kisan Sabha represented the interests of the oppressed peasants. [Preface]

Mehnatkash: Worker, someone who engages in actual physical labour, a distinction Sahajanand draws in elaborating his definitions of khet mazdoors. [II]

Milke larne: United and organized struggle. In contrast to factory labour, agricultural labourers live with many social and spatial constraints making mobilization and struggle difficult. [II]

Mita dena: To wipe out, as in the efforts of false leaders of agricultural labourers who seek to wipe out the movements they have inadvertently initiated in their own self interest, when the real awakening of the khet mazdoors becomes apparent. [Preface}

Moorkh: Fool, illiterate, the accepted wisdom description of the *halwaha* as khet mazdoor and bonded labourer, an attitude which Sahajanand scorns. [III]

Motor ke halon: Tractor, motorized plough. [II]

Muftkhor: Parasitic, as in parasitic, rack-renting zamindars who go on increasing in number, while peasants are driven into the ranks of the khet mazdoors. [I]

Muhabbat: The love and affection which we show to birds and animals as pets, yet deny to agricultural labourers, an attitude Sahajanand finds wrong and economically unsound. [IV]

Mukarar dal: Fixed class, the mistaken assumption that khet mazdoors belong to particular castes or communities and are fixed in number, while in fact their numbers are increasing dramatically. [III]

Museebaton aur yantranayen: With reference to the daily adversities and sufferings of the khet mazdoors. [III]

Mustand: Strongmen, utilized to control and retrieve from escape *halis* and *dublas*, the bonded labourers of Gujarat. [III]

Nafrat: Hatred and contempt, the attitude which Sahajanand finds common toward agricultural labourers, and which must be changed in the interests of kisans and khet mazdoors. It is a constant theme in this text. [IV]

Nagdi: Cash payment as opposed to *bhaoli* or rent payment in kind. [IV]

Neend tootegi: Awaken, as in the awakening of the khet mazdoors in spite of the efforts of false leaders who seek their own ends in the process. [Preface] (See also Jagaran, etc.)

Netaon: Leaders, of the Kisan Sabha, whose efforts with those of the kisan workers must be directed to achieving compromise between the kisans and the khet mazdoors. [IV]

Nihayat garib kisan: Very poor kisan, literally on the margin in a social and economic sense, effectively khet mazdoors. [III]

Nikai: Weeding the fields, along with ploughing and transplanting among the most important of the intensive activities in agriculture and carried out almost solely by the khet mazdoor and his family. [IV}

Nirakshar: See *Moorkh* above. [III]

Nirdayta: Ruthlessness, cruel, merciless. One of Sahajanand's early descriptions of the rack-renting and absentee zamindar. [I]

Padadalit: Downtrodden, as in the downtrodden and exploited masses. [I] (See also Shoshit.)

Pakka kisan: Real kisan. (See also Asal, Asli kisan.)

Panchayati kheti: Joint, co-operative, community, cultivation. Sahajanand is not specific here, but the clear implication is that he does not mean collective agriculture in the Soviet sense of the term. [IV and V]

Pichri: Backward, used here in the context of the backward condition of agriculture in India. [IV]

Pichri jatiyon: Lower castes. The reference is to the mistaken assumption that agricultural labourers are constituted only of Harijans or lower castes. [I]

Pirit, piriton: Oppressed, as in the exploited and oppressed agricultural labourers. [Preface, etc.] (See also Shoshit, Padadalit, etc.)

Prachand andolan: Intense, powerful movement. The proposals made in this text designed to benefit the khet mazdoors and kisans can be achieved only with the support of the people's voice and the influence of a powerful movement. [V]

Praja: The people.

Prakar: Type, kinds of peasants, here used in many definitions but making the point that agricultural labourers are clearly a type of poor peasant. [II] (See Ansh, Shreni, Dal, etc.)

Pran: Life, soul. Sahajanand declaims against the introduction of religion into the movement of agricultural labourers, as has unfortunately been the case in the consideration of Harijan issues. Doing so will literally destroy the soul of the movement. The issues are fundamentally economic in both cases, Sahajanand asserts. [III]

Prayashchit: Atonement, as in the case of kisans who must not only make amends but atone for their misdeeds against khet mazdoors. [IV] (See also Doob marne ki bat.)

Punjiwadi vyavastha: Capitalist system. Sahajanand uses the term in developing the idea of labourers in factory terms and their distinctions from agricultural labourers. [II]

Rakshit sena: Reserve force, used here in considering the history of agriculture and the economic roles of various castes and groups, in this case the Shudras as a service element and as a reserve force in society. [I]

Rakt peenewale zamindaron: Blood-sucking zamindars, another of Sahajanand's graphic characterizations of the dominant land controllers. [I] (See also Jallaad.)

Raiyat: A peasant tenant, a cultivator.

Sabha: Association, movement, as in Kisan Sabha, etc.

Sabhyata: Civilization. Given the maltreatment meted out to the khet mazdoors, Sahajanand wonders who will even consider educating their children or extending to them other experiences of civilization. [III]

Sacche kisan sevak: True kisan servant, worker, activist, those who work on behalf of the kisans and khet mazdoors, whatever the obstacles. [V]

Sachmuch garibon: Those who are really poor, who have their committed supporters, but are nevertheless powerfully opposed by the exploiting zamindars and the rulers. [Preface]

Sadbhavana: Generosity of the kisans, in agreeing to proposals of negotiated compromise with their agricultural labourers. [IV]

Sadharan kisan: Ordinary kisan, or petty kisan. [II] (See also Tut pujiya kisan.)

Sahukar: Banker, moneylender, person of wealth, involved in the nexus of exploitation in the rural countryside. [I]

Sajag: Awaken, in the sense of growing a consciousness and awareness. [II] (See also Neend tootegi, Jagaran, etc.)

Sakhti aur bemurawati: Extreme harshness, with reference to kisans who while participating in the activities of the Kisan Sabha nevertheless do not change their attitudes and treatment of the agricultural labourers they employ. [Preface]

Salook aur vartav: Crude and harsh treatment of the khet mazdoors, Sahajanand returns to this theme of attitudes and maltreatment throughout this text. [III]

Samajhna: Understanding, consciousness, the ongoing process of a growing awareness of their condition and rights among the oppressed kisans, moving inevitably in the direction of justice and change. [IV] (See also Sajag, Neend tootegi, Jagaran, etc.)

Samjha bujhake: Persuasion, the method used by Sahajanand with the kisans in reaching compromise agreements with their khet mazdoors. [IV]

Sammilit sampatti: Joint property, an element of the radical social transformation Sahajanand sees as essential to eradicating those qualities of exploitation and oppression in contemporary society. [V]

Sammilit larai ki yogyata: Collective bargaining, inherently difficult in the rural environment of the khet mazdoor. [II]

Samoohik roop se: Collectively, as in the collective awakening and reaction of the kisans when the khet mazdoors themselves organize. [II]

Sampann: Prosperous, in describing the economic condition of the Punjab, where nevertheless a large percentage of the kisans cultivate less than ten acres. Also with reference to the once prosperous kisans now driven into conditions of poverty. [II, III]

Sampattihin: Propertyless, i.e., the poorest, landless kisans, who are in fact agricultural labourers. [V]

Sangathan: Organization, as in kisan organization, with specific reference here to the dangers to the Kisan Sabha, whose very backbone is in fact the poor kisans, should a hartal, or strike be organized against them by the khet mazdoors. Persuasion and compromise are recommended as the desired methods in resolving conflict between the two. [IV]

Sangharsh: Struggle. The effective mobilization and organization of khet mazdoors can only emerge out of a movement of struggle. It is perhaps notable that Sahajanand's personal memoirs are titled *Mera Jivan Sangharsh*, i.e., My Life Struggle. [V]

Sanrakshit dal: Reserved group, the description for the Shudras in their early history of service to other castes. [I]

Sarmayedar: Capitalists, those who with moneylenders and zamindars depend solely on the earnings of others for their leisured wealth. [II]

Sarvahara: Proletariat. Used here in refining the definitions and distinctions between labourers and agricultural labourers. [II]

Sataye: Tortured. Khet mazdoors have historically been tortured and oppressed, and accordingly their place in the world of the exploited and organized must now also be recognized, as it will. [I]

Seenajori: Intimidation, coercion. In the new climate of awakening among the kisans and the khet mazdoors, how long can the thieving and intimidation of the zamindars continue, Sahajanand asks. [IV]

Shaitan ki antari: Intestines of the devil, a favourite metaphor of Sahajanand's, here in describing that the number of agricultural labourers goes on increasing, much like the entrails of the devil. [II]

Shan: Pride. Here the idea of false pride in the matter of engaging in direct cultivation, a pride to which many poor kisans with very small holdings are not subject. [IV]

Sharab: Fermented juice of the toddy palm and other country liquor, which with customary ritual celebrations is presumed to be a major source of indebtedness among the rural poor. [III, IV]

Shasak: Ruler. As in the anxieties and determination of exploiters and rulers about the awakening of the rural poor. [Preface]

Shatru: Enemy, the mistaken fear of kisans that the khet mazdoors are their enemies, when in fact they function as their arms and legs. [IV]

Shikmi: Variously a share cropping subtenancy or a type of cash rent tenure.

Shoshak: Exploiters, who fear the awakening of the rural poor. [Preface] (See Shasak above.)

Shoshan: Exploitation. [Preface] (See also Piriton.)

Shoshit evam pirit: Those who are exploited and oppressed. These terms appear frequently in this manuscript but here on the opening page of the preface.

Shramik: See Mehnatkash.

Shramjeevi: Labourer, worker, or proletariat in Sahajanand's definition. [I]

Shramshakti: Labour power, the only thing left to the factory labourer or free labourer. [II] (See also Swatantra shramik.)

Shreni: Category, used by Sahajanand throughout this document to distinguish various groups, sections, and classes of society. (See Ansh, Dal, Varg, Jamaat, etc.)

Soodkhoron: Moneylenders, used frequently throughout this text in the context of general indebtedness and specifically with reference to bonded indebtedness. (See also Sahukar.)

Sukhi aur sampann: Happy and prosperous, as those kisans, once happy and prosperous now driven into the ranks of the poor and landless agricultural labourers. [III] (See also Sampann.)

Sulah: Compromise, the preferred method of resolving conflict between kisans and khet mazdoors. [IV]

Swamiyon: Masters, owners, used here in the context of slave owners. [I]

Swatantra sangathan: An independent organization, of the khet mazdoors, the creation of which Sahajanand sees as a contrived effort to set kisans and khet mazdoors against one another. He subsequently develops an argument for a combined organization of all true kisans, i.e., the poor kisans and agricultural labourers. [V]

Swatantra shramik: Free labourers, namely those who have no property connections of any kind, except their labour power. [II] (See also Shramshakti.)

Swayamkrita: From the Sanskrit, i.e., done by one's own hands, as in ploughing and doing other direct agricultural work. [I]

Takleefon: Sufferings, the most extreme difficulties of the khet mazdoors and poor kisans. [Preface]

Tang aur tabah: Hardship and ruin, as experienced by the khet mazdoors. Sahajanand also accuses those who seek to lead the khet mazdoors of these very actions, hence false leaders. [Preface, IV, etc.]

Tarpen: Pain. Ultimately the poor kisans and khet mazdoors will respond to the agony and pain which they suffer and through their awakening bring these injustices to an end. [IV]

Theeke: Contract. The contract system whereby khet mazdoors are paid a share of the cut crop, in bundles, most often in a ratio of one to 12, one to 16, etc. [III]

Tukare: Parts, i.e., categories of agricultural labourers whom Sahajanand divides between that small percentage working on plantations and large farms and the vast bulk of 98 percent comprising the rest. [II] (See Ansh, Dal, etc.)

Tuksha aur neech: Base and low, mean, and hence demeaned by those castes above them, a question of attitude which Sahajanand views critically as one of the serious issues in relations between kisans and khet mazdoors. [III]

Tut pujiya kisan: Petty kisan, also used as *tut pujiya khetihar*, i.e., petty landholder. [II]

Tyagi aur tapasvi: Renouncer, ascetic. Sahajanand notes that the khet mazdoors in effect produce the fine rice and other good things of life, which they themselves are destined never to eat, yet this literal act of renunciation is not understood by those who actually employ them.

Uddhar: Liberate. No movement, once organized can be stopped, by false leaders or any others, until it fully liberates the oppressed khet mazdoors. [Preface]

Ukharana aur ropna: Literally to take out and put back in, hence to transplant, as with paddy, one of the most intensive tasks of cultivation, carried out almost exclusively by the khet mazdoors and their families. [IV]

Utpeeran: Oppression, which cannot be changed without a radical social transformation. [V]

Uzar jate hain: To be ruined in every sense, yet another of the many graphic descriptive phrases of Sahajanand's in cataloguing the condition of the khet mazdoors. [Preface]

Vaigyanik: Scientific. Apart from bringing new lands under cultivation, scientific agriculture is one of the major means by which production can and must be increased. [IV]

Varg, Varga: Class. Appears throughout this manuscript in defining the varying social and economic interests found in the rural countryside. (See also Ansh, Dal, Jamaat, etc.)

Varna, Varn: Caste, jati, used throughout this manuscript to define and distinguish social divisions in the early history of agriculture and in its modern practice as affecting kisans and khet mazdoors.

Vastavik: Real, true, as in the true organization of all kisans, those who are exploited but do not exploit others, the ideal Kisan Sabha which Sahajanand envisages in the concluding pages of this text. [V]

Vibhag: Division, as in the divisions of human society which were emerging in the early history of agriculture. [I] (See also Ansh, Dal, Shreni, etc.)

Vipada: Sorrow, as in the sorrow, suffering, dishonour, and disgrace suffered by khet mazdoors. [Preface]

Virat pradarshan: Huge demonsrations, of the Kisan Sabha in the 1930s, which were then emulated by the false organizers of the khet mazdoors. [Preface]

Zabardast awaz: The powerful voice of the khet mazdoors, which must be encouraged against exploitation by the kisans, especially in the new and unified Kisan Sabha which Sahajanand sees as the ultimate goal of the movement. [V]

Zahar: That poison which creates an atmosphere of exploitation in agrarian society, of the kisan by the zamindar, of the khet mazdoor by the kisan, and khet mazdoors, one of the other, a tragedy which must be ended. [V]

Zalimon: Tyrants, whose days in this time of awakening are numbered. [IV]

Zamindar: Literally, land holder, specifically in the 1930s the dominant land controllers, condemned by Sahajanand almost on every page of this tract as responsible for the depressed condition of the peasants and khet mazdoors.

Zamin wale chote chote kisan: Small landholding peasants. [II]

Zamin ki chah aur khoj men behal: The desperate desire/search for land which motivates both the kisan and the khet mazdoor. [IV]

Zirat: The personal land of the zamindar or malik, meant for his personal cultivation as opposed to being let out on tenancy.

Zulum: Tyranny, oppression, yet another of the terms defining the exploitation of the marginal poor in this manuscript. [Preface]

Zyada garib kisan: Very poor kisan. [V] (See also Attyant garib, Attyant nirdhan, etc.)

Zyada zamin: Vast lands, large holdings of the zamindars, which in their acquisition have increasingly driven peasants off their holdings and into the ranks of the khet mazdoors. [I]

Index

Agrarian radicalism, 68,83,109
Adhmanova, O.S., 66
All India Agricultural Labour Enquiry, 84, 85
All India anti-Compromise Conference, xiii, 29
All India Khet Mazdoor Sammelan, 3
All India Kisan Sabha (AIKS), xiii, xiv, xvii, 8, 29, 66, 88, 122
America, 24, 27, 43, 99, 121
Andhra, xviii, 8, 88, 122
Arnot, R. Page, 114, 120
Assam, 24, 47, 60
Aswayamkrita, 10,15

Backward castes, 86
Bagchi, Amiya Kumar, 33, 34
Barahiya Tal, x
Barai, 86
Bayly, C.A., 71
Bengal, 21, 22, 30, 31, 33, 34, 60, 84, 87
Bhagalpur, 29
Bhumihar Brahman Mahasabha, xv
Bhumihar Brahmans, xv, 26
Bhushan, Chandra, xvii, 64
Bihar, xiii, xiv, xv, 2, 3, 8, 29, 30, 33, 35, 38, 60, 68, 78, 79, 81, 83, 85, 86, 87, 88, 107, 109
Bihar Provincial Kisan Sabha (BPKS), xiv, 3, 85, 109
Bihar State Archives, xiv
Bihta, xiv, xvii, xviii, xix, 26, 67
Bihta Sugar Mill, 67
Blunt, E.A.H., 25, 26
Bolsheviks, 114
Bolts, William, 31
Bombay, 57, 59, 60, 61, 71
Bondage, xvi, 48, 72, 77, 78, 79, 80, 82, 87, 88, 89, 92
Bongaon, xvii
Bose, Subhas Chandra, xiii, 29
Bose, Sugata, 87
Brahmans, 12, 13, 14, 15, 56, 86
Breman, Jan, 88
Britain, xiii, xv, 17, 27, 30, 31, 32, 37, 40, 63, 99, 100
British Trade Union Congress, 58

(*Because of the brevity of Sahajanand's Khet Mazdoor, the index to the edited translation and the Editor's Notes must inevitably also be brief. Some subject references are included, but terms like kisan, peasant, khet mazdoor agricultural labourer, zamindar, etc., and Sahajanand's name itself, all of which appear with great frequency will not be indexed. Please refer also to the Glossary Ed.*)

Burma, 59, 60
Buxar, xix

Calcutta, xvii, xviii, 85
Caste, xiv, xv, xvi, 10, 12, 24, 25, 26, 33, 41, 53, 72, 73, 78, 80, 84, 112
Central Provinces and Berar, 22, 34, 60
Champaran, 29
Chandogya Upanishad, 14, 26
Chaudhuri, B., 38, 39, 42
Chaudhury, V.C.P., xix
Chayanov, A.V., 70
Class, 28, 46, 49, 54, 73, 122
Collective bargaining, 52, 54
Comolla, 66
Comintern 40
Communist Party of Great India, 40
Communist Party of India (CPI), x, 27, 29, 40, 82, 85
Communist Party of India (Marxist), CPI (M), 85
Communist Party of India (Marxist-Leninist), CPI (M-L), xix, 64, 85
Compromise, 51, 103, 104, 105, 110, 112, 118, 120, 122
Congress Party, 3, 8, 81, 83
Congress Socialist Party (CSP), x
Coolies, 24
Cultural/social attitudes, xvii, 30, 53, 68, 69, 72, 80, 89, 93, 94, 105, 112, 113

Dalits, 73, 81
Dandi Sannyasi, xv, xvii
Darbhanga, 29
Darbhanga, Maharaja of, 8
Darjeeling, 47
Das, R.K., 97, 98, 100, 107, 108
Dasnami, xv
De, Barun, 33
Deindustrialization, 28, 32, 33, 34
Dingwaney, Manjari, 87
Dutt, R. Palme, 10, 21, 22, 26, 27, 28, 36, 39, 40, 41, 42, 43, 44, 48, 58, 59, 61, 70, 98, 99
Dutt, Romesh, 31, 32

Eastern Economist, 123
Europe, 40, 43, 48, 76, 121

Farms, 23, 47, 48, 49, 51, 52, 55, 56, 65
Floud Commission, 60
Forced labour, 79
Franchise Committee, 58, 59

Gadgil, D.R., 34
Gandhi, M.K., xv, 3, 8, 66, 81
Gandhi Peace Foundation, 88
Gaya, 29, 87
George, Jose, 87
Ghazipur, xv, xviii
Gita, 82
Gita-Hriday, xvii, xix, 82
Gopal, Surendra, xviii
Gould, Harold, 68
Goyal, S.K., xi
Grass, Gunter, 30
Guha, Ranajit,71
Guha, Sumit, x, 33, 34, 84
Gujarat, 8, 78, 88
Gujarat Provincial Kisan Sabha, 78
Gupta, Amit Kumar, 67
Gupta, Ranjan Kumar, 33

Habib, Irfan, 33, 34
Hagen, James R., xviii, 29, 30, 69, 107
Hamilton, C.J., 32
Harijans, 24, 73, 81, 82
Haripura, 3, 78
Harnetty, Peter, 34
Hartal, 54, 103
Haryana, 30, 107
Hauser, Walter, xvii, xix, 26, 29, 68, 109
Haynes, Edward S., 29, 107
Hazaribagh Central Jail, xiii, 5, 7, 26, 29, 40, 64, 65, 69, 82
Heston, Alan, 35, 36
Hindi Pracharak Sansthan, xviii
Holderness, Sir Thomas, 95, 106, 107
Hossain, Hameeda, 33

Imperial Council of Agricultural Research, 123
Imperialism, 76, 115, 119
Indebtedness, xvi, 72, 77, 78, 79, 80, 82, 87, 88, 89, 92
Indian Historical Review, xvii, xix, 26
Indian People's Front (IPF), 68, 85, 109
Indupur, x
Industrial development, 101, 105, 108, 109
Institute for Studies in Industrial Development (ISID), xi
International Labour Office (ILO), 58, 70
Irrigation, 96, 98, 107, 108

Jategaon Budruk, 69
Jha, Hetukar, xviii
Jha, K.C., xi, xviii
Jha, Shashi Kant, x, 66, 121
Josh, Bhagwan, 40, 67
Joshi, Shashi, 40
Joshi, V.C., xviii

Kayastha, xv, 86
Keatinge, Gerald Francis, 59, 71
Kerala, 84
Kirdee, 70
Kisan Sabha, x, xiv, xv, xvii, xviii, 2, 3, 4, 5, 8, 9, 67, 68, 79, 81, 92, 103, 110, 113, 114, 117, 118, 120, 121
Klein, Martin, 88
Koeris, xv
Kotovski, G.G., 70
Kranti Aur Samyukta Morcha, xvii, xix, 64
Krishnamurty, J., 37, 38, 42, 43
Kshatriya, 14, 56
Kulak, 51, 55, 115
Kumar, Dharma, x, 32, 33, 35, 36, 37, 41, 42, 84, 88
Kumar, Ravinder, x
Kurian, George Thomas, 108
Kurmis, xv

Land hunger, xvi, 72, 79, 80, 89, 90, 94, 101, 107
League of Nations, 98
Lenin, V.I., 27, 40, 41, 44, 48, 49, 50, 51, 53, 55, 66, 69, 114, 115, 116, 119, 120, 121
Limaye, Madhu, 40
Linlithgow Commission, 71
Lower castes, 10, 24

MacDougall, A.P., 99
Madhubani, xi, 68, 86
Madras, 22, 33, 41, 42, 59, 60, 84
Mahabharata, 12, 13, 30
Maithil Brahman, 68
Mann, Harold H., 57, 58, 59, 69, 70, 71
Manu, 13, 15, 45, 64
Marla, Sarma, 88
Marx, Karl, 8, 10, 16, 27, 28, 32, 40, 47, 70, 82, 121
Mehta, Dinkar, 88
Mera Jivan Sangharsh, xvii, xix
Mishra, Madhusudan, x, 25
Modernized agriculture, 17, 23, 47, 55, 90, 98, 99, 100, 101, 105,
Monghyr, x, 29
Morris, Morris David, 32
Motihari, 3
Mukerjee, Radhakamal, 75, 98, 108
Mukherji, Bankim, xvii
Mundle, Sudipto, 87
Munro, Sir Thomas, 21, 42
Muzaffarpur, 29

Nagpur, 123
Narayan, Jayaprakash, 81
National Archives of India, xiv, 67
Nehru Memorial Museum and Library, x, xvii, xviii, 27, 30, 66, 67, 69, 81, 88
Nellore, 84
New Economic Policy (NEP), 51
Nilgiris, 48

Owen, Launcelot A., 49, 50, 65

Palamau, 86, 87
Palasa, xiii, 29
Panchayati cultivation, 102, 109, 121
Parsi, 78, 79
Patel, Surendra J., 28, 37, 38, 41, 42
Patel, Vallabhbhai, 3, 4, 8, 81
Pathan, 78
Patna, xiv, xix, 3, 29, 30, 69, 81
Patna University, xviii
Patnaik, Utsa, 87, 122
People's War, 29, 82
Pimpla Saudagar, 69
Plantations, 48, 52, 55, 58
Poona, 57, 58, 69
Prakash, Gyan, 87
Prasad, Jadunandan, xi, xviii
Prasad, Rajendra, 8, 81
Proletariat, 46, 47, 48, 49, 51, 52, 54, 55, 56, 66, 114, 115
Punjab, 22, 30, 59, 60, 107
Purnea, 29

Rajput, xv
Ram, Jagjivan, 81
Ramachandran, V.K., 84
Ramamurti, B., 84
Ramgarh. xiii, 29
Ranga, N.G., 8, 88
Rao, K.S. Chalapati, xi
Rao, V.K.R.V., 85
Raychaudhuri, Tapan, 32
Rebels, 79
Reddy, M. Atchi, 84
Religion, 10, 24, 53, 56, 72, 73
Revolt, 79
Richards, John F., 29, 107
Royal Commission of Agriculture, 61, 70, 71, 79, 96, 97, 107, 123,

Russia, 8, 27, 29, 40, 44, 49, 50, 51, 53, 55, 56, 63, 65, 66, 70, 109, 111, 114, 116, 117, 118, 120, 121

Sahajanand Shodh Sansthan, xix, 64
Saharsa, 29
Sahay, Dayanand, 83
Sanyal, D.K., 123
Saran, 29
Sen Gupta, Dabjani, 84
Serfs, 15, 16, 49
Shahabad, 29, 81
Shankardass, Rani Dhavan, 87
Sharma, K.P., xi, xviii
Sharma, Panchanand, x
Shri Sitaram Ashram, x, xiv, xix
Shri Swami Sahajanand Smarak Nyas, xix
Shudras, 14
Simon Commission, 60
Sindh, 78
Singh, K. Suresh, xviii
Sinha, Arun, xix
Sinha, N.K., 34
Slater, Gilbert, 59
Slaves, 15, 16, 19, 24, 46, 48, 77, 78, 79, 88, 92
Socialism, 27, 40, 47, 49, 51, 121
Specker, Konrad, 33
Stalin, Joseph, 55, 56, 69, 115, 116, 117, 121
Steinbeck, John, 43
Stolypin, 50, 51
Strachey, John, 47, 65
Strike, 52, 54, 103
Sundarayya, P., 122
Swayamkrita, 10, 15

Tamilnadu, 84
Thapar, Romila, x, 25, 64
Tharoor, Shashi, 30
Thorner, Alice, 32
Thorner, Daniel, 32, 70
Trotsky, Leon, 66

United Provinces, xiv, xv, 22, 25, 26, 35, 60, 75, 78, 79, 83, 85, 86
Untouchables, xv, 10, 72, 81, 82, 86

Vaishya, 12, 13, 14
Varanasi, xviii, xix, 64
Varna, 12, 13, 14, 15, 17, 25, 27
Vedas, 12, 13
Vicziany, Marika, 33
Vimalanand Saraswati, Swami, xvii, xix

Wages, xvi, 16, 20, 24, 27, 45, 46, 47; 55, 56, 64, 72, 74, 75, 76, 80, 82, 83, 84, 86, 89, 90, 94, 102, 103, 105, 109, 110, 111, 115, 118, 122
Weavers, 17, 18, 30, 31, 32, 33, 34
Weiner, Myron, xi, xvii
West Bengal, xiv, xvii
White, David, x, 25, 26

Yadavas, xv, 86
Yagnik, Indulal, 8, 88
Yanson, Y.E., 49

Zamindari abolition, 109